FLASHMAPS WASHINGTON DC

Editor
Robert Blake

Creative Director
Fabrizio La Rocca

Cartographer
David Lindroth

Designer
Tigist Getachew

Editorial Contributors
Steven Amsterdam
Kristen Goldman
Allison Pritchard

Cartographic Contributors
Edward Faherty
Sheila Levin
Page Lindroth
Vicki Robinson
Eric Rudolph

Contents

Special Sales

Fodor's Travel Publications are available at special discounts for bulk purchases for sales promotions or premiums. Special editions, including personalized covers, excerpts of existing guides, and corporate imprints, can be created in large quantities for special needs. For more information, contact your local bookseller or write to Special Markets, Fodor's Travel Publications, 201 East 50th St., New York, NY 10022. Inquiries from Canada should be directed to your local Canadian bookseller or sent to Random House of Canada, Ltd., Marketing Dept., 1265 Aerowood Dr., Mississauga, Ontario L4W 1B9. Inquiries from the United Kingdom should be sent to Fodor's Travel Publications, 20 Vauxhall Bridge Rd., London, England SW1V 2SA. **ISBN 0-679-03020-4**

MANUFACTURED IN THE UNITED STATES OF AMERICA 10 9 8 7 6 5 4 3 2 1

Area Codes: DC (202); Maryland (301), (410); Virginia (703). All (202) unless otherwise noted.

EMERGENCIES

Ambulance, Fire, Police ☎ 911

AAA Emergency Road Service ☎ 703/222-5000

Adult Protective Services ☎ 727-2345

AMEX Lost Travelers Checks ☎ 800/221-7282

Animal Bites ☎ 576-6665

Animal Clinic ☎ 363-7300

Battered Women ☎ 347-2777

Children's Protection ☎ 727-0995

Deaf Emergency ☎ 727-9334

Dentist/Doctor Referral ☎ 362-8677

Drug/Alcohol Hotline ☎ 800/821-4357

FBI ☎ 324-3000

Hazardous Wastes ☎ 673-3212

Poison Control ☎ 625-3333

Psychiatric Response ☎ 727-0739

Rape & Assault ☎ 333-7273

Suicide Prevention ☎ 751-0123

US Coast Guard/Rescue ☎ 267-2100

US Park Police ☎ 619-7300

SERVICES

AAA ☎ 703/222-6000

AARP Travel Services ☎ 434-3660

AIDS Hotline ☎ 332-2437

Alcoholics Anonymous ☎ 966-9115

American Red Cross ☎ 728-6400

Better Business Bureau ☎ 393-8000

Chamber of Commerce ☎ 347-7201

Civil Defense ☎ 727-6161

Crime Solvers ☎ 393-2222

DC Government ☎ 727-1000

Dept. of Aging ☎ 619-0724

Federal Information ☎ 647-4000

Food Stamps ☎ 727-0858

Foreign Exchange Rates ☎ 408-1200

Human Services ☎ 619-0257

Immigration & Naturalization ☎ 307-1501

Legal Aid Society ☎ 628-1161

Mayor's Office ☎ 727-2980

Medicaid ☎ 724-5173

Medicare ☎ 800/233-1124

Motor Vehicle Information ☎ 727-6680

Passport Office Information ☎ 647-0518

Planned Parenthood ☎ 347-8500

Salvation Army ☎ 783-4050

Sanitation ☎ 576-7387

Social Security ☎ 800/772-1213

Special Olympics ☎ 544-7770

Supreme Court ☎ 479-3000

Time of Day ☎ 703/844-2525

Transportation for Handicapped ☎ 462-8658

US Capitol ☎ 224-3121

US Coast Guard Information ☎ 267-2229

US Customs Services ☎ 410/962-2620

US Postal Service ☎ 682-9595

US Secret Service ☎ 435-5100

Virginia Travel Center ☎ 659-5523

Washington Convention & Visitors Association ☎ 789-7000

Washington DC Accommodations ☎ 289-2220; 800/554-2220

Weather ☎ 703/936-1212

YMCA ☎ 232-6700

YWCA ☎ 626-0700

Visitors Information ☎ 347-2873

Zoo Information ☎ 673-4800

TRANSPORTATION

Airport Connection ☎ 301/441-2345

Amtrak ☎ 484-7540

Amtrak Metroliner Service ☎ 800/872-7245

Amtrak Package Express Service ☎ 906-3125

Andrews Air Force Base ☎ 301/981-1110

Baltimore-Washington International Airport ☎ 301/261-1000

Brunswick Line Commuter ☎ 800/325-7245

Capitol Cab ☎ 546-2400

Diamond Cab ☎ 387-6200

Dulles International Airport ☎ 703/661-2700

Area Codes: DC (202); Maryland (301), (410); Virginia (703). All (202) unless otherwise noted.

Greyhound Bus Information ☎ 800/231-2222; 800/752-4841

Marc-Camden Line Commuter ☎ 800/325-7245

Marc-Penn Line Commuter ☎ 800/325-7245

Metrobus & Metrorail Transit Information ☎ 637-7000; 638-3780

Union Station Information ☎ 289-1908

Washington Flyer ☎ 703/685-1400

Washington National Airport ☎ 703/417-8000

Yellow Cab ☎ 544-1212

TOURS

Black History National Recreation Trail ☎ 208-4747

C&O Barge Trips ☎ 301/299-2026

Construction Watch and Site Seeing ☎ 272-2448

Dandy Cruises ☎ 703/683-6076

Goodwill Embassy Tours ☎ 636-4225

Gray Line Tours ☎ 301/386-8300

National Cathedral ☎ 537-6200

Old Town Trolley Tours ☎ 301/985-3021

Potomac Party Cruises ☎ 703/683-6090

Scandal Tours ☎ 783-7212

Smithsonian Resident Associate Program ☎ 357-3030

Spirit of Mount Vernon ☎ 554-8000

Spirit of Washington ☎ 554-8000

Tourmobile ☎ 554-7950

Washington Post ☎ 334-7969

White House Tours ☎ 456-7041

PARKS AND RECREATION

Arlington National Cemetery ☎ 703/697-2131

Canoe Cruisers Hotline ☎ 301/656-2586

Cherry Blossom Festival ☎ 728-1137

C&O Canal Park Service ☎ 301/299-2026

Cycling ☎ 872-9830

DC Armory ☎ 546-3337

DC Parks & Recreation ☎ 673-7660

Dial-A-Museum ☎ 357-2020

Dial-A-Park ☎ 619-7275

Dial-An-Event ☎ 673-7671

East Potomac Park ☎ 485-9880

Great Falls Visitor Center ☎ 703/285-2966

Laurel Race Course ☎ 301/725-0400

National Aquarium ☎ 482-2825

National Arboretum ☎ 245-2726

National Park Service ☎ 619-7222

National Zoo ☎ 673-4800

Oriole Park at Camden Yards ☎ 410/685-9800

Patriot Center ☎ 703/933-3000

Road Runners Club ☎ 703/836-0558

Robert F. Kennedy Stadium ☎ 546-3337

Rock Creek Park ☎ 282-1063

Rosecroft Raceway ☎ 301/567-4000

Tennis Information ☎ 673-7646

US Air Arena ☎ 301/350-3400

Washington Bullets ☎ 301/622-3865

Washington Capitals ☎ 301/386-7000

Washington Redskins ☎ 547-9077

Wolf Trap Farm Park ☎ 703/255-1800

ENTERTAINMENT

Barnes of Wolf Trap ☎ 703/938-2404

Choral Arts Society ☎ 244-3669

Dial-A-Museum ☎ 357-2020

Ford's Theatre ☎ 426-6924

Kennedy Center ☎ 467-4600

Lincoln Theater ☎ 328-6000

Lisner Auditorium ☎ 994-6800

Metro Center Ticket Place ☎ TICKETS

Nat'l Symphony Orchestra ☎ 416-8100

National Theatre ☎ 783-3372

Nissan Pavillon ☎ 703/754-6400

Smithsonian Information Center ☎ 357-2700

Ticketmaster ☎ 432-7328

Warner Theater ☎ 783-4000

Washington Ballet ☎ 362-3606

Washington Opera ☎ 800/87-OPERA

Wolf Trap ☎ 703/255-1800

SALES TAX

Washington, D.C.: 5.75%

Maryland: 5%

Virginia: 4.5%

PENNSYLVANIA
76
81
Appalachian Trail
Gettysburg
Battlefield
Park
70
Antietam
Battlefield
Park
MARY
Frederick
Martinsburg
50
Romney
Augusta
522
Harper's
Ferry
270
Winchester
Berryville
WEST
VIRGINIA
Strausburg
Rockville
50
495
81
Woodstock
Front
Royal
66
Manassas
Battlefield
Park
Arlington
Edinburg
Alexandria
Mt. Jackson
Shenandoah
Nat'l Park
29
Luray
Woodbridge
Stanley
Dale City
Indian
Head
33
Harrisonburg
Culpeper
Elkton
Spotsylvania
Nat'l Military Park
Falmouth
Fredericksburg
301
Staunton
Gordonsville
17
Waynesboro
Charlottesville
95
Bowling
Green
64
33
81
VIRGINIA
64
29
Buena Vista
Appalachian Trail
Gum
Spring
Ashland
Aylett
Colleen
60
64
295
360
Amherst
Richmond
Dillwyn
Bon Air
60
Lynchburg
Appomattox
Courthouse
Nat'l Hist. Park
95
Sherwood
Forest
460
Appomattox
Hopewell
Farmville
Colonial Heights
Petersburg
Nat'l
Battlefield
360
Burkeville
460
Petersburg
Brookneal
Waverly
Blackstone
Victoria
85
Wakefield
Kenbridge
Chatham
Lawrenceville
South Boston
29
58
58
Emporia
Danville
58
360
Kerr
Reservoir
Lake
Gaston
95
Roanoke
Rapids
Oxford
Henderson
NORTH
85

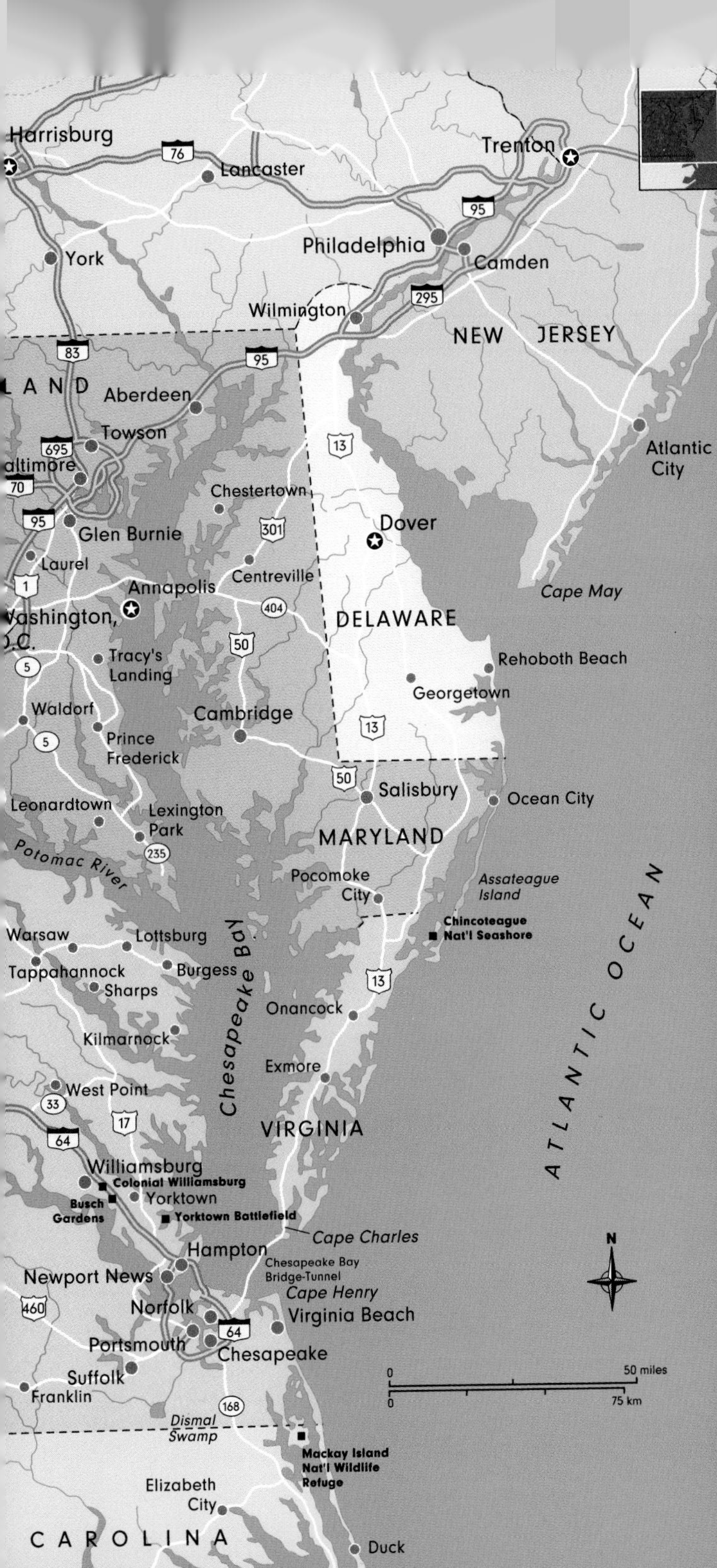

Harrisburg
76
Lancaster
Trenton
95
York
Philadelphia
Camden
295
Wilmington
NEW JERSEY
83
95
LAND
Aberdeen
Towson
695
altimore
70
13
Atlantic City
Chestertown
95
Glen Burnie
301
Dover
Laurel
Centreville
Cape May
1
Annapolis
404
Washington, D.C.
DELAWARE
50
5
Tracy's Landing
Rehoboth Beach
Georgetown
Waldorf
Cambridge
5
Prince Frederick
13
50
Salisbury
Ocean City
Leonardtown
Lexington Park
MARYLAND
235
Potomac River
Pocomoke City
Assateague Island
Chincoteague Nat'l Seashore
Warsaw
Lottsburg
Tappahannock
Burgess
Sharps
Chesapeake Bay
13
Onancock
Kilmarnock
Exmore
West Point
33
17
VIRGINIA
ATLANTIC OCEAN
64
Williamsburg
Colonial Williamsburg
Busch Gardens
Yorktown
Yorktown Battlefield
Cape Charles
Hampton
Chesapeake Bay Bridge-Tunnel
N
Newport News
Cape Henry
460
Norfolk
Virginia Beach
64
Portsmouth
Chesapeake
0
50 miles
Suffolk
0
75 km
Franklin
168
Dismal Swamp
Mackay Island Nat'l Wildlife Refuge
Elizabeth City
CAROLINA
Duck

2 Washington DC/Baltimore Corridor

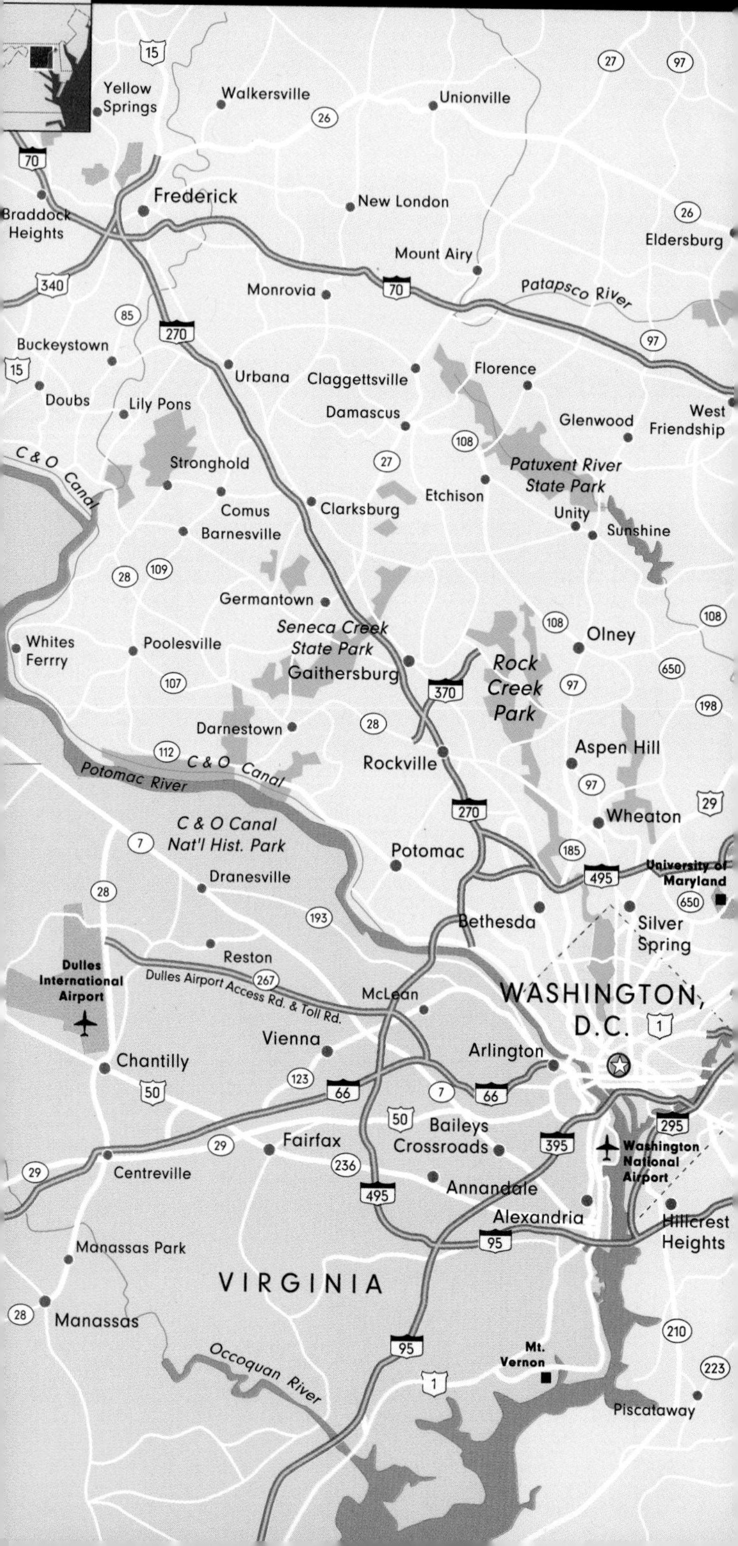

Yellow Springs
Walkersville
Unionville
Frederick
New London
Braddock Heights
Eldersburg
Mount Airy
Monrovia
Patapsco River
Buckeystown
Urbana
Claggettsville
Florence
Doubs
Lily Pons
Damascus
Glenwood
West Friendship
C & O Canal
Stronghold
Patuxent River State Park
Etchison
Comus
Clarksburg
Unity
Barnesville
Sunshine
Germantown
Seneca Creek State Park
Olney
Whites Ferrry
Poolesville
Gaithersburg
Rock Creek Park
Darnestown
Aspen Hill
C & O Canal
Rockville
Potomac River
Wheaton
C & O Canal Nat'l Hist. Park
Potomac
Dranesville
University of Maryland
Bethesda
Silver Spring
Reston
Dulles International Airport
Dulles Airport Access Rd. & Toll Rd.
McLean
WASHINGTON, D.C.
Vienna
Arlington
Chantilly
Fairfax
Baileys Crossroads
Washington National Airport
Centreville
Annandale
Alexandria
Hillcrest Heights
Manassas Park
VIRGINIA
Manassas
Mt. Vernon
Occoquan River
Piscataway

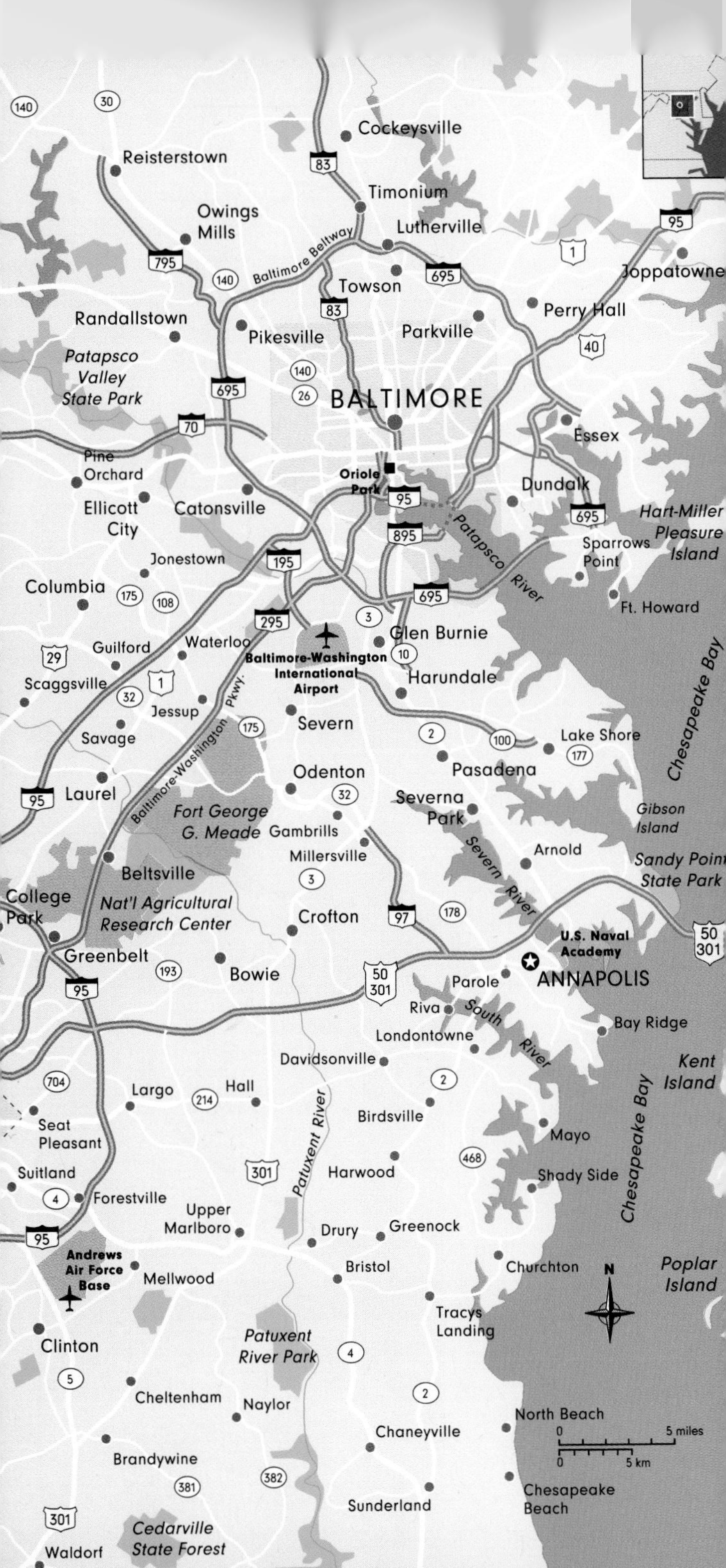

Cockeysville
Reisterstown
Timonium
Owings Mills
Lutherville
Baltimore Beltway
Towson
Joppatowne
Perry Hall
Randallstown
Pikesville
Parkville
Patapsco Valley State Park
BALTIMORE
Essex
Pine Orchard
Oriole Park
Dundalk
Ellicott City
Catonsville
Hart-Miller Pleasure Island
Sparrows Point
Jonestown
Patapsco River
Columbia
Ft. Howard
Glen Burnie
Guilford
Waterloo
Baltimore-Washington International Airport
Harundale
Scaggsville
Jessup
Severn
Lake Shore
Savage
Baltimore-Washington Pkwy.
Pasadena
Chesapeake Bay
Odenton
Laurel
Severna Park
Gibson Island
Fort George G. Meade
Gambrills
Arnold
Millersville
Sandy Point State Park
Beltsville
Severn River
College Park
Nat'l Agricultural Research Center
Crofton
U.S. Naval Academy
Greenbelt
Bowie
ANNAPOLIS
Parole
Riva
South River
Bay Ridge
Londontowne
Davidsonville
Kent Island
Largo
Hall
Birdsville
Seat Pleasant
Mayo
Patuxent River
Harwood
Suitland
Shady Side
Forestville
Upper Marlboro
Drury
Greenock
Andrews Air Force Base
Mellwood
Bristol
Churchton
Poplar Island
Tracys Landing
Clinton
Patuxent River Park
Cheltenham
Naylor
North Beach
Chaneyville
Brandywine
5 miles
5 km
Chesapeake Beach
Sunderland
Cedarville State Forest
Waldorf

MARYLAND
DISTRICT OF COLUMBIA
VIRGINIA
Kensington
Bethesda
Glen Echo
Somerset
Chevy Chase
Langley
McLean
Dulles
Tysons Corner
Falls Church
Arlington
Arlington National Cemetery
Annandale
Alexandria
Rock Creek Park
National Zoological Park
Roosevelt Island
Potomac River
C&O Canal
Cabin John Br.
University Blvd.
Georgia Ave.
River Rd.
Falls Rd.
Persimmon Tree Rd.
Bradley Blvd.
Wilson La.
Wisconsin Ave.
Connecticut Ave.
Bradley La.
MacArthur Blvd.
Goldsboro Rd.
Beach Dr.
Oregon Ave.
Utah Ave.
Military Rd.
Georgetown Pike
George Washington Memorial Pkwy.
Massachusetts Ave.
Dolley Madison Blvd.
Old Dominion Dr.
Westmoreland St.
Kirby Rd.
N. Glebe Rd.
Military Rd.
Canal Rd.
Calvert St.
New Hampshire Ave.
Maple Ave.
Dulles Airport Access Rd.
Williamsburg Blvd.
Glebe Rd.
Lee Hwy.
Washington Blvd.
Wilson Blvd.
Curtis Memorial Pkwy.
Gallows Rd.
Leesburg Pike
Arlington Blvd.
George Mason Dr.
Columbia Pike
Jefferson Davis Hwy.
Capital Beltway
Annandale Rd.
Sleepy Hollow Rd.
Carlin Springs Rd.
Henry G. Shirley Memorial Hwy.
Hummer Rd.
King St.
Seminary Rd.
Quaker Ln.
Mt. Vernon Ave.
Little River Tnpk.
Backlick Rd.
Van Dorn St.
Duke St.
Braddock Rd.
Old Keene Mill Rd.
Franconia Rd.
Beulah St.
Telegraph Rd.
South Kings Hwy.
Richmond Hwy.
Fort Hunt Rd.
Hooes Rd.
NW
SW

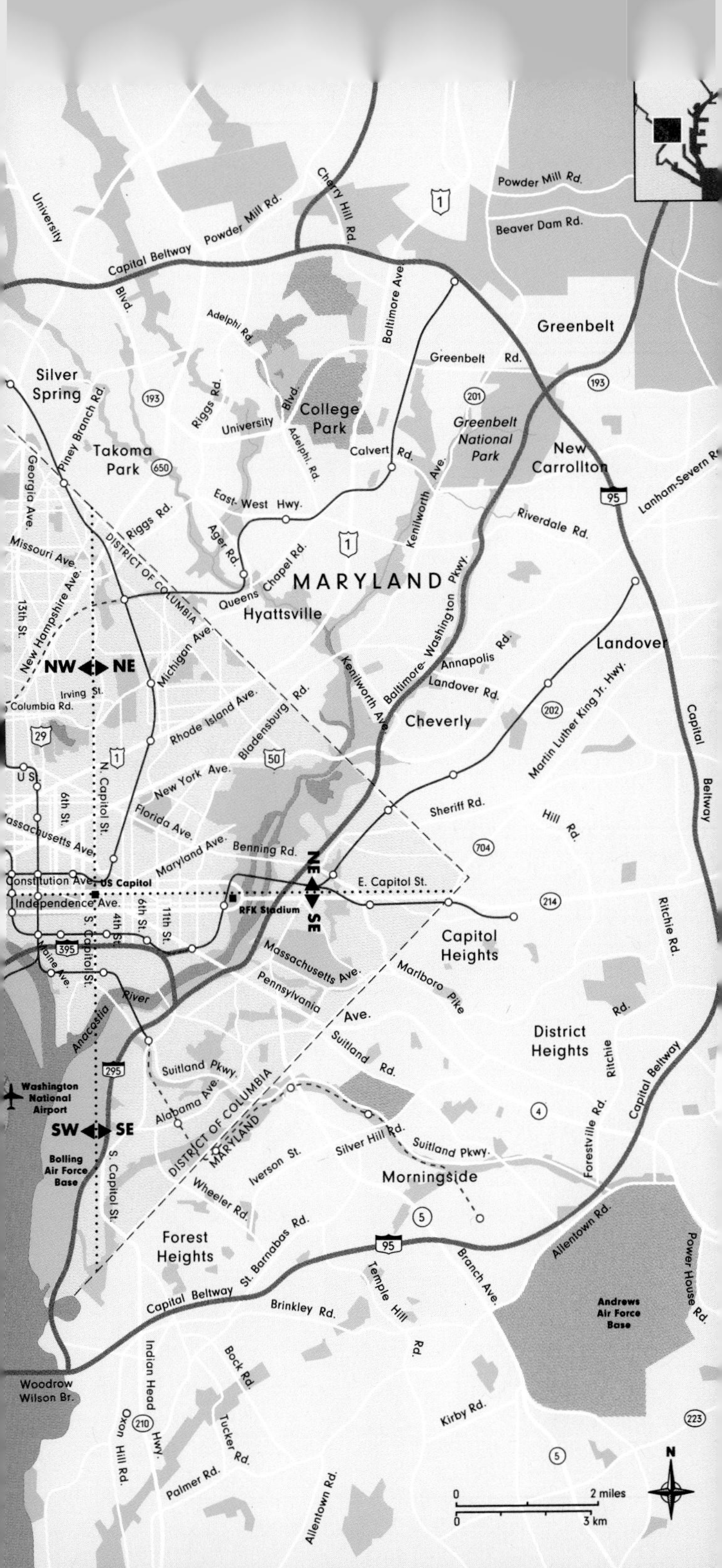

Powder Mill Rd.
Beaver Dam Rd.
Cherry Hill Rd.
University
Powder Mill Rd.
Capital Beltway
Blvd.
Adelphi Rd.
Baltimore Ave.
Greenbelt
Greenbelt Rd.
Silver Spring
Piney Branch Rd.
Riggs Rd.
College Park
University Blvd.
Adelphi Rd.
Greenbelt National Park
New Carrollton
Takoma Park
Calvert Rd.
Lanham-Severn Rd.
Georgia Ave.
East-West Hwy.
Kenilworth Ave.
Riverdale Rd.
Riggs Rd.
Missouri Ave.
DISTRICT OF COLUMBIA
Ager Rd.
Queens Chapel Rd.
MARYLAND
Hyattsville
Baltimore-Washington Pkwy.
13th St.
New Hampshire Ave.
Michigan Ave.
Landover
NW
NE
Annapolis Rd.
Irving St.
Columbia Rd.
Kenilworth Ave.
Landover Rd.
Martin Luther King Jr. Hwy.
Capital Beltway
Rhode Island Ave.
Bladensburg Rd.
Cheverly
U St.
N. Capitol St.
New York Ave.
6th St.
Florida Ave.
Sheriff Rd.
Hill Rd.
Massachusetts Ave.
Maryland Ave.
Benning Rd.
Constitution Ave.
US Capitol
E. Capitol St.
Independence Ave.
RFK Stadium
Ritchie Rd.
6th St.
4th St.
11th St.
S. Capitol St.
Capitol Heights
Maine Ave.
Massachusetts Ave.
Marlboro Pike
Pennsylvania Ave.
River
Anacostia
Suitland Rd.
District Heights
Rd.
Ritchie
Suitland Pkwy.
Washington National Airport
Alabama Ave.
DISTRICT OF COLUMBIA
MARYLAND
Capital Beltway
SW
SE
Silver Hill Rd.
Suitland Pkwy.
Forestville Rd.
Bolling Air Force Base
S. Capitol St.
Iverson St.
Morningside
Wheeler Rd.
Allentown Rd.
Forest Heights
St. Barnabas Rd.
Branch Ave.
Power House Rd.
Temple Hill Rd.
Capital Beltway
Brinkley Rd.
Andrews Air Force Base
Woodrow Wilson Br.
Indian Head Hwy.
Bock Rd.
Oxon Hill Rd.
Tucker Rd.
Kirby Rd.
Palmer Rd.
Allentown Rd.
0
2 miles
3 km
N

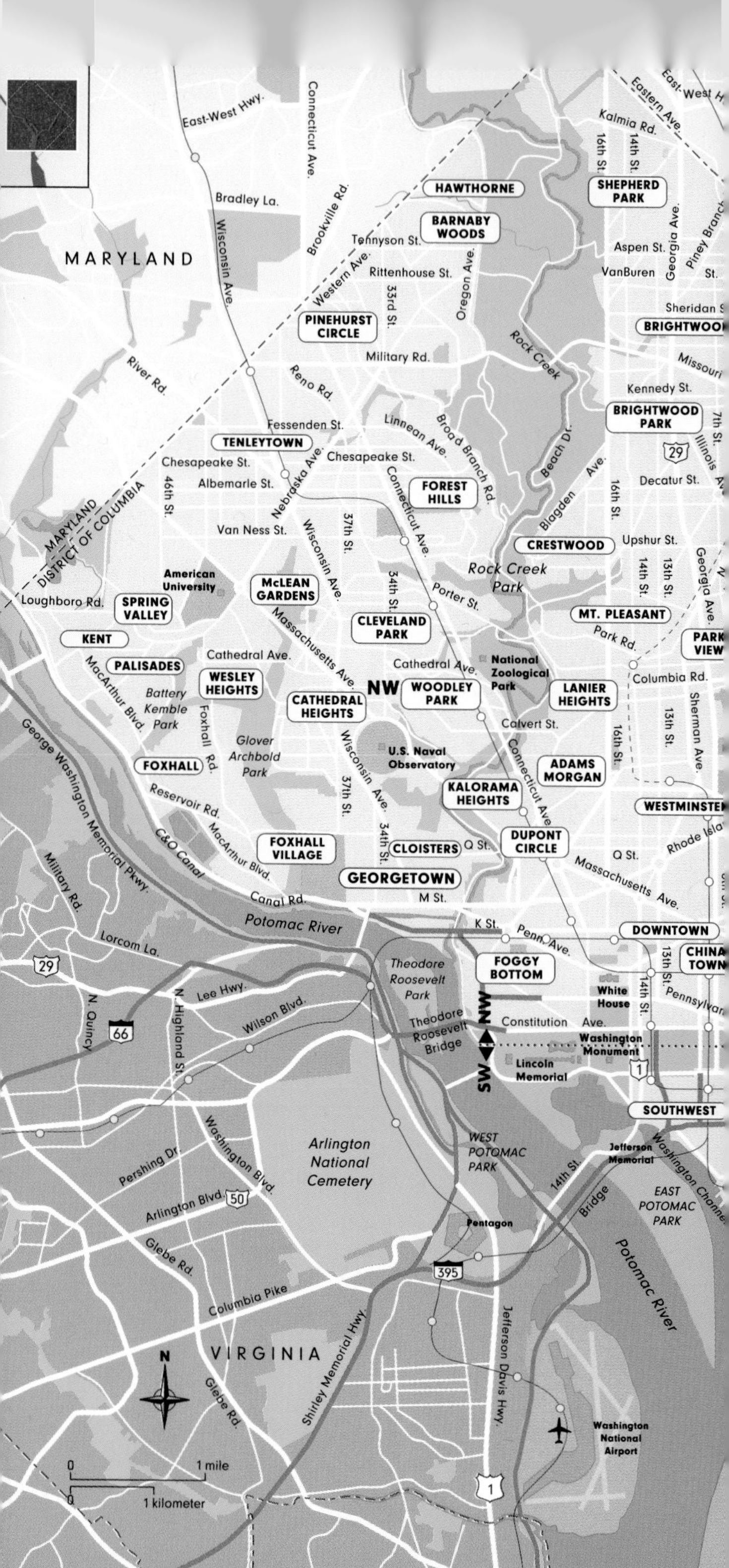

MARYLAND
DISTRICT OF COLUMBIA
VIRGINIA
HAWTHORNE
SHEPHERD PARK
BARNABY WOODS
PINEHURST CIRCLE
BRIGHTWOOD
BRIGHTWOOD PARK
TENLEYTOWN
FOREST HILLS
CRESTWOOD
Rock Creek Park
American University
SPRING VALLEY
McLEAN GARDENS
CLEVELAND PARK
MT. PLEASANT
PARK VIEW
KENT
PALISADES
WESLEY HEIGHTS
Battery Kemble Park
CATHEDRAL HEIGHTS
NW
WOODLEY PARK
National Zoological Park
LANIER HEIGHTS
U.S. Naval Observatory
Glover Archbold Park
FOXHALL
ADAMS MORGAN
KALORAMA HEIGHTS
WESTMINSTER
FOXHALL VILLAGE
CLOISTERS
DUPONT CIRCLE
GEORGETOWN
DOWNTOWN
CHINATOWN
FOGGY BOTTOM
Theodore Roosevelt Park
Theodore Roosevelt Bridge
White House
Washington Monument
Lincoln Memorial
SW
SOUTHWEST
Jefferson Memorial
WEST POTOMAC PARK
EAST POTOMAC PARK
Arlington National Cemetery
Pentagon
Washington National Airport
Potomac River
C&O Canal
N
0 1 mile
0 1 kilometer

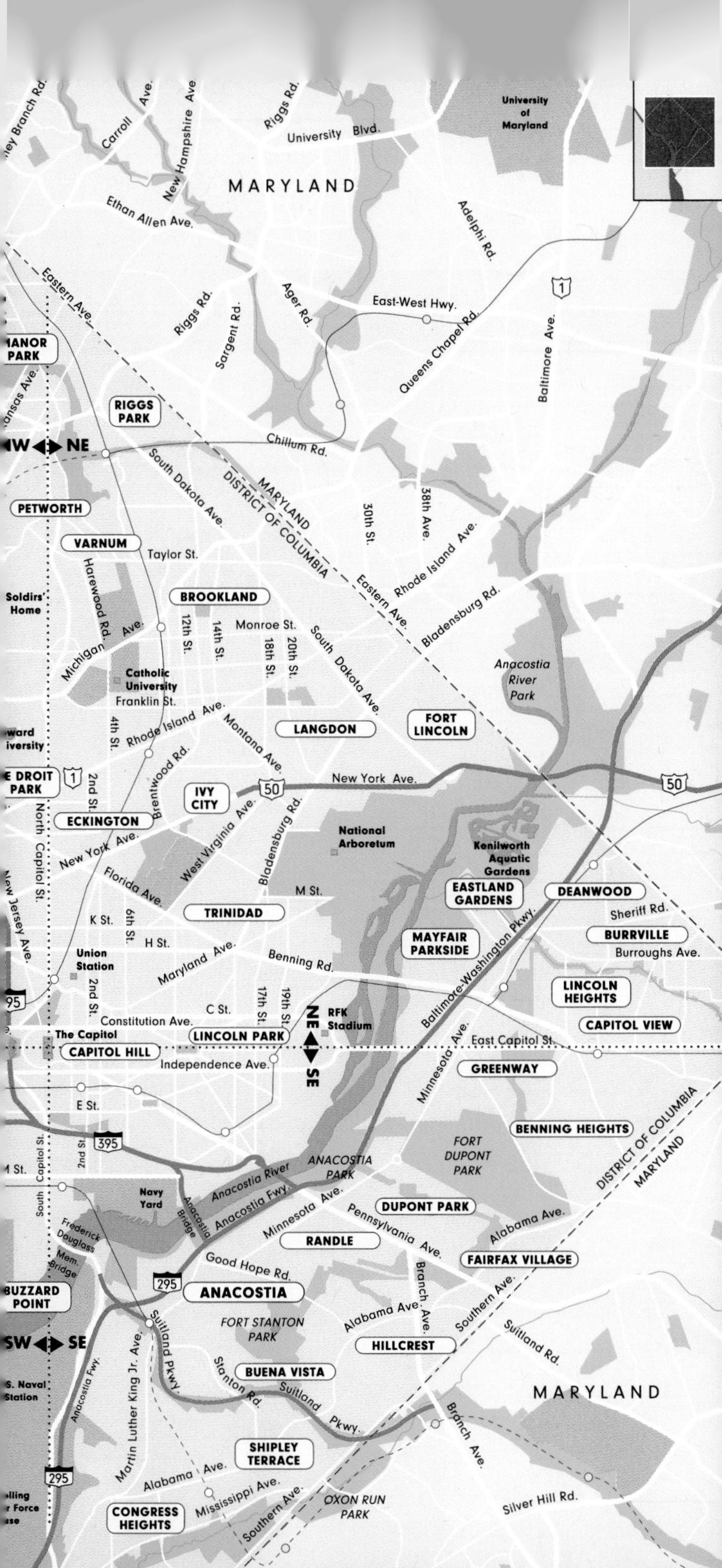

MARYLAND
University of Maryland
University Blvd.
Riggs Rd.
Carroll Ave.
New Hampshire Ave.
Ethan Allen Ave.
Adelphi Rd.
East-West Hwy.
Ager Rd.
Sargent Rd.
Riggs Rd.
Eastern Ave.
Queens Chapel Rd.
Baltimore Ave.
1
RIGGS PARK
Chillum Rd.
NE
South Dakota Ave.
MARYLAND
DISTRICT OF COLUMBIA
PETWORTH
VARNUM
Taylor St.
30th St.
38th Ave.
Rhode Island Ave.
Eastern Ave.
Bladensburg Rd.
Soldirs' Home
Harewood Rd.
BROOKLAND
Michigan Ave.
12th St.
14th St.
Monroe St.
18th St.
20th St.
South Dakota Ave.
Catholic University
Franklin St.
Anacostia River Park
4th St.
Rhode Island Ave.
Montana Ave.
LANGDON
FORT LINCOLN
2nd St.
Brentwood Rd.
IVY CITY
50
New York Ave.
ECKINGTON
North Capitol St.
New York Ave.
West Virginia Ave.
Bladensburg Rd.
National Arboretum
Kenilworth Aquatic Gardens
Florida Ave.
M St.
EASTLAND GARDENS
DEANWOOD
Sheriff Rd.
K St.
6th St.
TRINIDAD
MAYFAIR PARKSIDE
BURRVILLE
H St.
Burroughs Ave.
Union Station
Maryland Ave.
Benning Rd.
Baltimore-Washington Pkwy.
2nd St.
LINCOLN HEIGHTS
C St.
17th St.
19th St.
RFK Stadium
Constitution Ave.
CAPITOL VIEW
The Capitol
LINCOLN PARK
NE
SE
East Capitol St.
CAPITOL HILL
Independence Ave.
Minnesota Ave.
GREENWAY
E St.
BENNING HEIGHTS
FORT DUPONT PARK
395
2nd St.
South Capitol St.
ANACOSTIA PARK
DISTRICT OF COLUMBIA
MARYLAND
Anacostia River
Navy Yard
Anacostia Bridge
Anacostia Fwy.
Minnesota Ave.
DUPONT PARK
Pennsylvania Ave.
Frederick Douglass Mem. Bridge
RANDLE
Alabama Ave.
FAIRFAX VILLAGE
Good Hope Rd.
BUZZARD POINT
295
ANACOSTIA
Branch Ave.
Southern Ave.
FORT STANTON PARK
Alabama Ave.
SW
SE
Suitland Pkwy.
HILLCREST
Suitland Rd.
Martin Luther King Jr. Ave.
BUENA VISTA
Stanton Rd.
Suitland Pkwy.
MARYLAND
Anacostia Fwy.
Branch Ave.
SHIPLEY TERRACE
295
Alabama Ave.
Mississippi Ave.
Southern Ave.
OXON RUN PARK
Silver Hill Rd.
CONGRESS HEIGHTS

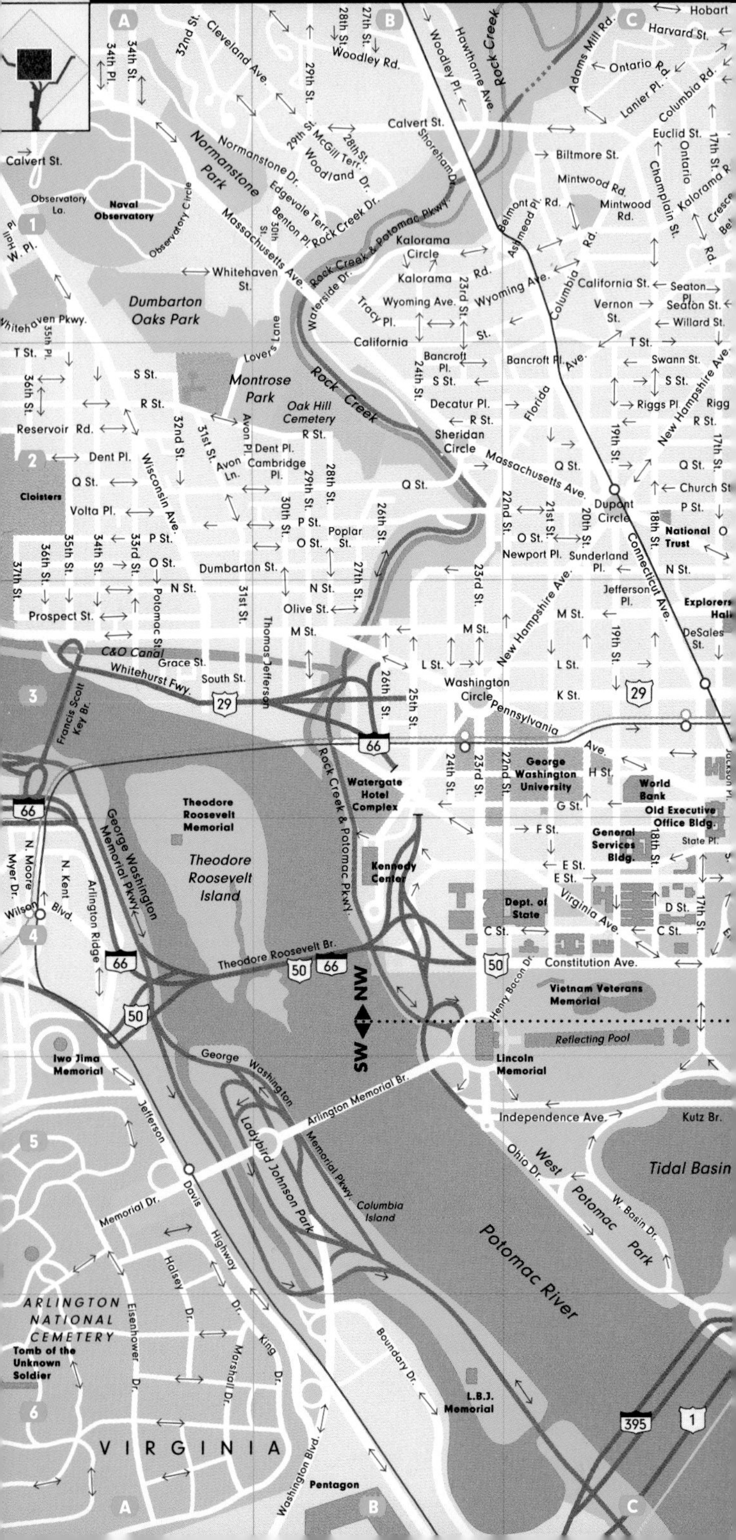

Street Finder/Central Washington DC

A
B
C
1
2
3
4
5
6

Hobart
Harvard St.
Adams Mill Rd.
Ontario Rd.
Lanier Pl.
Columbia Rd.
Euclid St.
17th St.
Ontario
Kalorama Rd.
Champlain St.
Rock Creek
Woodley Pl.
Hawthorne Ave.
27th St.
28th St.
Woodley Rd.
32nd St.
Cleveland Ave.
29th St.
34th St.
34th Pl.
Calvert St.
Biltmore St.
Mintwood Rd.
Mintwood Rd.
Shoreham Dr.
Normanstone Park
Normanstone Dr.
29th St.
McGill Terr.
28th St.
Woodland Dr.
Edgevale Terr.
Benton Pl.
30th St.
Rock Creek Dr.
Rock Creek & Potomac Pkwy.
Massachusetts Ave.
Observatory La.
Naval Observatory
Observatory Circle
Belmont Rd.
Ashmead Pl.
Kalorama Circle
Kalorama Rd.
Columbia Rd.
California St.
Seaton Pl.
Seaton St.
Willard St.
W. Pl.
Whitehaven St.
Waterside Dr.
Wyoming Ave.
Wyoming Ave.
Tracy Pl.
23rd St.
Vernon St.
T St.
Dumbarton Oaks Park
Whitehaven Pkwy.
35th Pl.
T St.
Lovers Lane
California St.
Bancroft Pl.
Bancroft Pl.
Florida Ave.
Swann St.
S St.
New Hampshire Ave.
36th St.
S St.
24th St.
S St.
R St.
Montrose Park
Oak Hill Cemetery
Rock Creek
Decatur Pl.
R St.
Riggs Pl.
Riggs
R St.
Reservoir Rd.
32nd St.
31st St.
Avon Pl.
Dent Pl.
R St.
Sheridan Circle
Dent Pl.
Avon Ln.
Cambridge Pl.
Massachusetts Ave.
Q St.
19th St.
Q St.
17th St.
Q St.
29th St.
28th St.
Q St.
Wisconsin Ave.
Cloisters
Church St.
Volta Pl.
30th St.
P St.
Poplar St.
26th St.
22nd St.
21st St.
20th St.
Dupont Circle
P St.
18th St.
National Trust
P St.
O St.
O St.
Newport Pl.
Sunderland Pl.
Connecticut Ave.
37th St.
36th St.
35th St.
34th St.
33rd St.
O St.
Dumbarton St.
27th St.
N St.
N St.
N St.
Potomac St.
31st St.
N St.
23rd St.
Jefferson Pl.
Prospect St.
Olive St.
M St.
Explorers Hall
Thomas Jefferson
M St.
M St.
DeSales St.
C&O Canal
Grace St.
Whitehurst Fwy.
South St.
L St.
19th St.
L St.
29
Washington Circle
K St.
29
26th St.
25th St.
Pennsylvania Ave.
Francis Scott Key Br.
66
Rock Creek & Potomac Pkwy.
24th St.
23rd St.
22nd St.
George Washington University
H St.
World Bank
Jackson Pl.
66
Theodore Roosevelt Memorial
Watergate Hotel Complex
G St.
Old Executive Office Bldg.
George Washington Memorial Pkwy.
F St.
General Services Bldg.
State Pl.
Theodore Roosevelt Island
E St.
E St.
18th St.
N. Moore
N. Kent
Myer Dr.
Wilson
Blvd.
Arlington Ridge
Kennedy Center
Dept. of State
Virginia Ave.
D St.
17th St.
C St.
C St.
66
Theodore Roosevelt Br.
50
66
50
Henry Bacon Dr.
Constitution Ave.
Vietnam Veterans Memorial
50
NW
SW
Reflecting Pool
Iwo Jima Memorial
George Washington
Lincoln Memorial
Arlington Memorial Br.
Jefferson
Independence Ave.
Kutz Br.
Ladybird Johnson Park
Memorial Pkwy.
Ohio Dr.
West Potomac Park
Tidal Basin
W. Basin Dr.
Memorial Dr.
Davis Highway
Columbia Island
Potomac River
Halsey Dr.
King Dr.
ARLINGTON NATIONAL CEMETERY
Eisenhower Dr.
Marshall Dr.
Boundary Dr.
Tomb of the Unknown Soldier
L.B.J. Memorial
395
1
VIRGINIA
Washington Blvd.
Pentagon

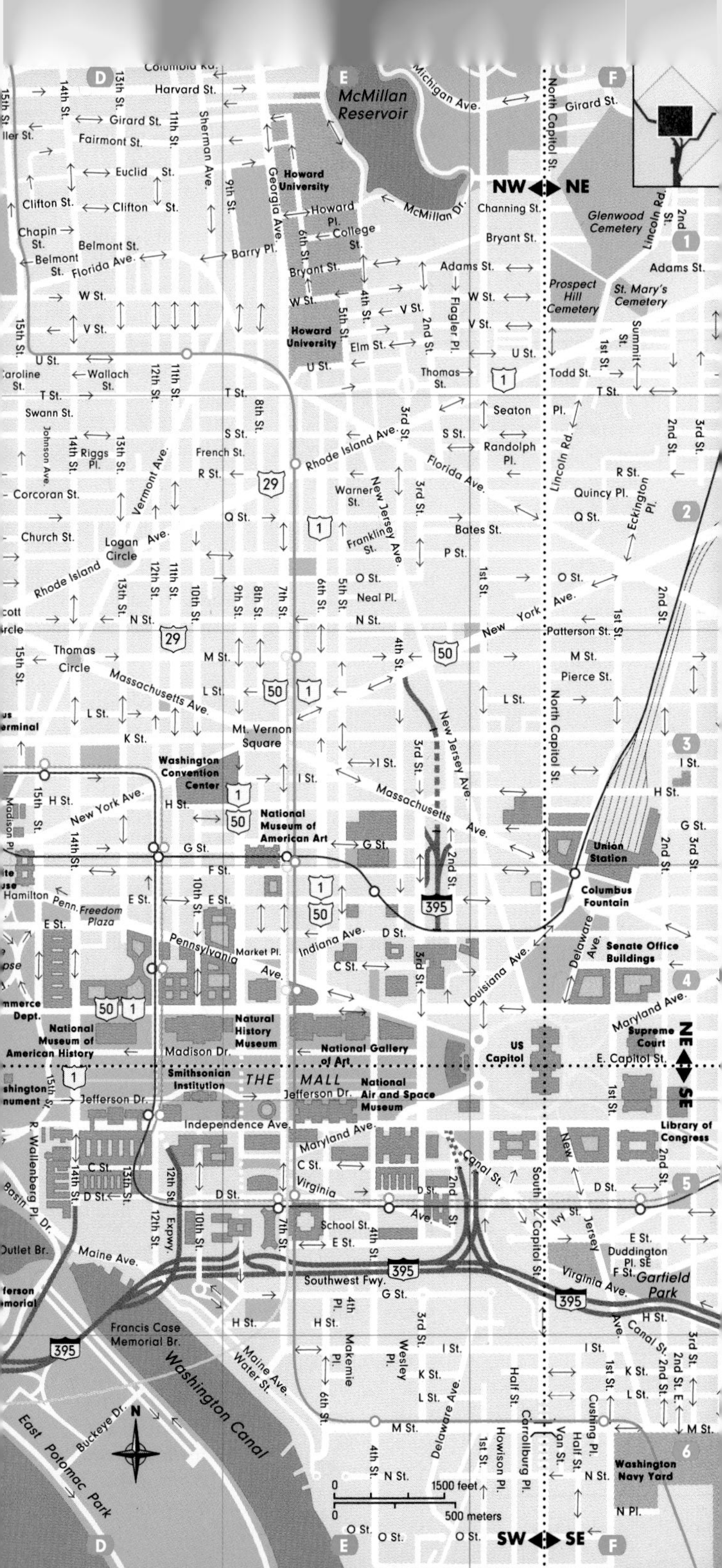

D
E
F
1
2
3
4
5
6
McMillan Reservoir
Howard University
NW
NE
SW
SE
Glenwood Cemetery
Prospect Hill Cemetery
St. Mary's Cemetery
Logan Circle
Thomas Circle
Mt. Vernon Square
Washington Convention Center
National Museum of American Art
Union Station
Columbus Fountain
Freedom Plaza
Senate Office Buildings
Supreme Court
US Capitol
Library of Congress
Natural History Museum
National Museum of American History
National Gallery of Art
Smithsonian Institution
THE MALL
National Air and Space Museum
Garfield Park
Washington Navy Yard
Francis Case Memorial Br.
Washington Canal
East Potomac Park
N
0
1500 feet
500 meters

Street Finder/Central Washington DC

Numbers refer to grid locations on map

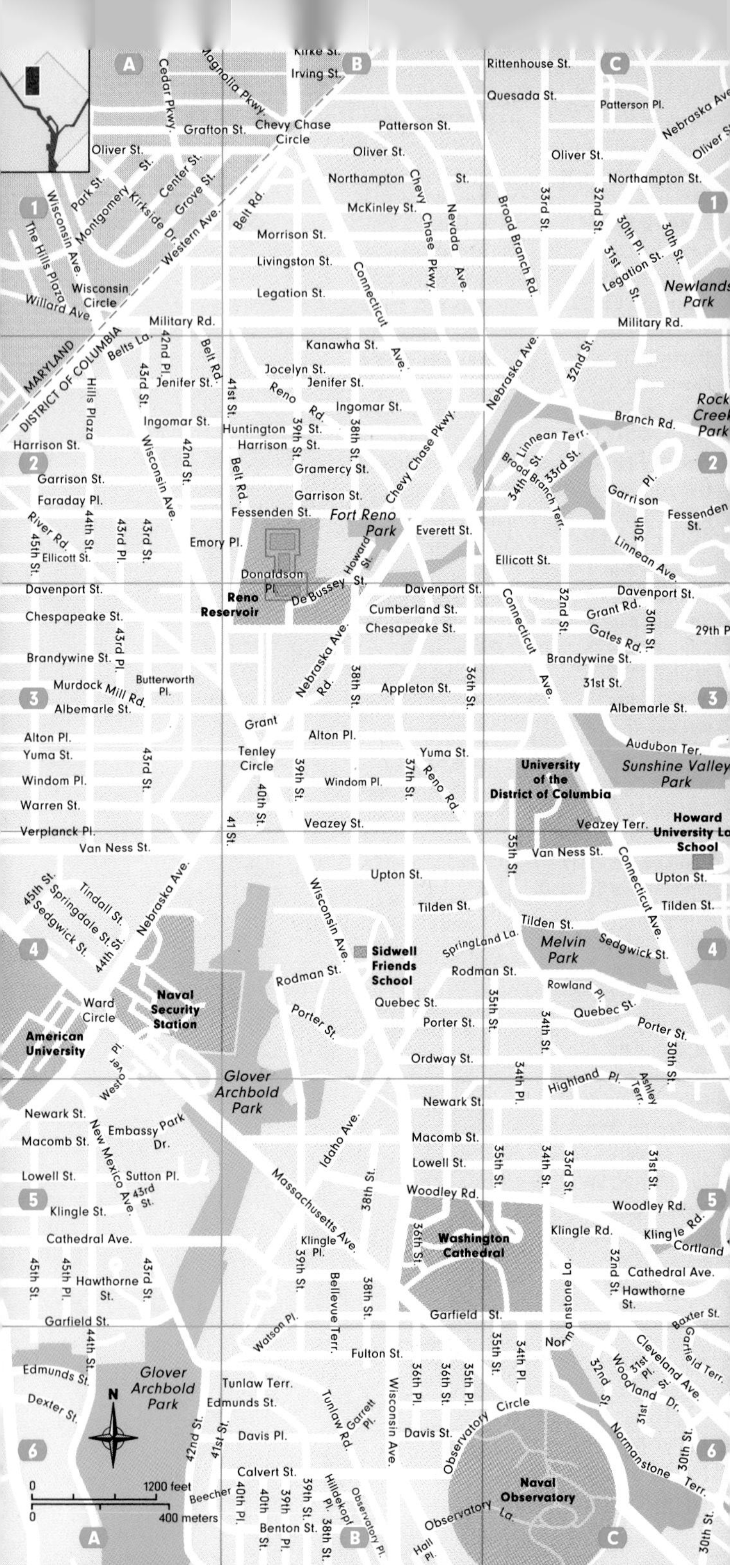
A
B
C
1
2
3
4
5
6
Kirke St.
Irving St.
Rittenhouse St.
Quesada St.
Patterson Pl.
Nebraska Ave.
Oliver St.
Cedar Pkwy.
Magnolia Pkwy.
Grafton St.
Chevy Chase Circle
Patterson St.
Oliver St.
Oliver St.
Oliver St.
Center St.
Northampton St.
Northampton St.
Park St.
Montgomery St.
Kirkside Dr.
Grove St.
Belt Rd.
McKinley St.
Chevy Chase Pkwy.
Nevada Ave.
Broad Branch Rd.
33rd St.
32nd St.
30th Pl.
30th St.
Wisconsin Ave.
The Hills Plaza
Western Ave.
Morrison St.
Livingston St.
Legation St.
Legation St.
31st St.
Newlands Park
Wisconsin Circle
Willard Ave.
Connecticut Ave.
Military Rd.
Military Rd.
MARYLAND
DISTRICT OF COLUMBIA
Belts La.
42nd Pl.
Belt Rd.
Kanawha St.
Nebraska Ave.
32nd St.
Jocelyn St.
Jenifer St.
Jenifer St.
Reno Rd.
Rock Creek Park
43rd St.
Hills Plaza
41st St.
Ingomar St.
Ingomar St.
Branch Rd.
Huntington St.
Harrison St.
Harrison St.
39th St.
38th St.
Chevy Chase Pkwy.
Linnean Terr.
Broad Branch Terr.
34th St.
33rd St.
Wisconsin Ave.
42nd St.
Gramercy St.
Garrison St.
Garrison St.
Garrison
Faraday Pl.
Belt Rd.
Fessenden St.
Fessenden St.
Fort Reno Park
30th Pl.
River Rd.
44th St.
43rd Pl.
43rd St.
Emory Pl.
Howard St.
Everett St.
Ellicott St.
Ellicott St.
Linnean Ave.
45th St.
Donaldson Pl.
De Bussey St.
Davenport St.
Davenport St.
Davenport St.
Reno Reservoir
Cumberland St.
Connecticut Ave.
32nd St.
Grant Rd.
30th St.
Chespapeake St.
Chesapeake St.
Gates Rd.
29th Pl.
43rd Pl.
Nebraska Ave.
Brandywine St.
Brandywine St.
Butterworth Pl.
38th St.
Appleton St.
36th St.
31st St.
Murdock Mill Rd.
Albemarle St.
Albemarle St.
Rd.
Grant
Alton Pl.
Alton Pl.
Tenley Circle
Audubon Ter.
Yuma St.
Yuma St.
Sunshine Valley Park
University of the District of Columbia
Windom Pl.
Windom Pl.
39th St.
37th St.
Reno Rd.
Warren St.
40th St.
Veazey St.
Veazey Terr.
Howard University Law School
Verplanck Pl.
41 St.
Van Ness St.
Van Ness St.
35th St.
Connecticut Ave.
Upton St.
Upton St.
45th St.
Springdale St.
Tindall St.
Nebraska Ave.
Tilden St.
Tilden St.
Tilden St.
Sedgwick St.
Sedgwick St.
44th St.
Wisconsin Ave.
Sidwell Friends School
SpringLand La.
Melvin Park
Rodman St.
Rodman St.
Rowland Pl.
Ward Circle
Naval Security Station
Quebec St.
Quebec St.
35th St.
34th St.
Porter St.
Porter St.
Porter St.
American University
Weston Pl.
Ordway St.
30th St.
Glover Archbold Park
34th Pl.
Highland Pl.
Ashley Terr.
Newark St.
Newark St.
Embassy Park Dr.
Macomb St.
Macomb St.
Idaho Ave.
New Mexico Ave.
Lowell St.
Lowell St.
Sutton Pl.
35th St.
34th St.
33rd St.
31st St.
43rd St.
Massachusetts Ave.
38th St.
Woodley Rd.
Woodley Rd.
Klingle St.
Klingle Rd.
Klingle Rd.
Cathedral Ave.
Klingle Pl.
36th St.
Washington Cathedral
Cortland
45th St.
45th Pl.
Hawthorne St.
43rd St.
39th St.
Bellevue Terr.
38th St.
Normanstone La.
32nd St.
Cathedral Ave.
Hawthorne St.
Garfield St.
Garfield St.
Baxter St.
44th St.
Watson Pl.
Garfield Terr.
Fulton St.
35th St.
34th Pl.
Nor
Cleveland Ave.
Edmunds St.
Glover Archbold Park
36th Pl.
36th St.
35th Pl.
31st Pl.
32nd St.
Woodland Dr.
Tunlaw Terr.
31st St.
Dexter St.
N
Edmunds St.
Tunlaw Rd.
Garrett Pl.
Circle
Wisconsin Ave.
42nd St.
41st St.
Davis Pl.
Davis St.
Observatory Circle
Normanstone Terr.
30th St.
Calvert St.
0
1200 feet
Beecher
40th Pl.
40th St.
39th Pl.
39th St.
Hildekopf Pl.
Observatory Pl.
Naval Observatory
Observatory La.
0
400 meters
Benton St.
38th St.
Hall Pl.
30th St.

Numbers refer to grid locations on map

Albemarle Rd. A3, C3
Alton Pl. A3, C3
Appleton St. B3, C3
Ashley Ter. C4
Audubon Ter. C3
Baxter St. C5
Belt Rd. A2, B3
Benton St. B6
Branch Rd. C2
Brandywine St. A3, C3
Broad Branch Rd. B1, C2
Broad Branch Ter. C2
Calvert St. B6
Cathedral Ave. A5, C5
Cedar Pkwy. A1
Center St. A1
Chesapeake St. A3, C3
Chevy Chase Circle B2
Chevy Chase Pkwy. B1, B2
Cleveland Ave. C5, C6
Connecticut Ave. B1, C5
Cortland Pl. C5
Davenport St. A3, C3
Davis Pl. B6
Davis St. B6
DeBussey St. B3
Dexter St. A6
Edmunds St. A6, C6
Ellicott St. A2, C2
Embassy Park Dr. A5
Emory Pl. A2
Faraday Pl. A2
Fessenden St. A2, C2
Foxhall Rd. A5, A6
Fulton St. A6, C6
Garfield St. A5, C5
Garfield Ter. C6
Garrison St. A2, C2
Gates Rd. C3
Grafton St. A1, B1
Gramercy St. B2
Grant Rd. B3
Grove St. A1
Hall Pl. B6
Harrison St. A2, B2
Hawthorne St. A5, C5
Hesketh St. A1, B1
Highland Pl. C5
Hildekoper Pl. B6
Huntington St. B2
Idaho Ave. B4, B5
Ingomar St. A2, B2
Jenifer St. A2, C2
Jocelyn St. B2, C2
Kanawha St. B2
Kirke St. A1, B1
Kirkside Dr. A1
Klingle Rd. C5
Klingle St. A5
Legation St. A1, C1
Linnean Ave. C2
Linnean Ter. C2
Livingston St. A1, C1
Lowell St. A5, C5
Macomb St. A5, C5
Magnolia Pkwy. A1, B1
Massachusetts Ave. A4, C6
McKinley St. B1, C1
Military Rd. A1, C1
Montgomery St. A1
Morrison St. A1, C1
Murdock Mill Rd. A3
Nebraska Ave. A5, C1
Nevada Ave. B1
New Mexico Ave. A5, A6
Newark St. A5, C5
Normanstone Pl. C5, C6
Normanstone Ter. C6
Northampton St. B1, C1
Observatory Circle B6, C6
Observatory La. B6, C6
Observatory Pl. B6
Oliver St. A1, C1
Ordway St. B4, C4
Park Ave. A1
Park St. A1
Patterson Pl. C1
Patterson St. B1, C1
Porter St. B4, C4
Quebec Pl. C4
Quebec St. B4, C4
Reno Rd. B2, B4
Rittenhouse St. B1, C1
River Rd. A2, A3
Rodman St. B4, C4
Rowland Pl. C4
Sedgwick St. A4, C4
Springdale St. A4
Tenley Circle B3
Tilden St. B4, C4
Tindall St. A4
Tunlaw Rd. B6
Tunlaw Ter. B6
Upton St. B4, C4
Van Ness St. A4, C4
Veazey St. B3, B4
Veazey Ter. C3, C4
Verplanck Pl. A3, A4
Ward Circle A4
Warren St. A3, C3
Watson Pl. B6
Western Ave. A2, B1
Willard Ave. A1
Windom Pl. A3, B3
Wisconsin Ave. A1, B6
Woodland Dr. C6
Woodley Rd. B5, C5
Yuma St. A3, C3
29th Pl. C6
29th St. C3
30th Pl. C1, C2
30th St. C1, C6
31st Pl. C6
31st St. C1, C4
32nd St. C1, C6
33rd St. C1, C5
34th Pl. C2, C6
34th St. C2, C6
35th Pl. B6
35th St. C3, C6
36th Pl. B2, B6
36th St. B2, B6
37th St. B3, B4
38th St. B1, B5
39th Pl. B6
39th St. B1, B6
40th Pl. B6
40th St. B6
41st St. B1, A6
42nd St. A1, A6
43rd Pl. A2, A3
43rd St. A2, A5
44th St. A2, A6
45th Pl. A2, A5
45th St. A2, A5

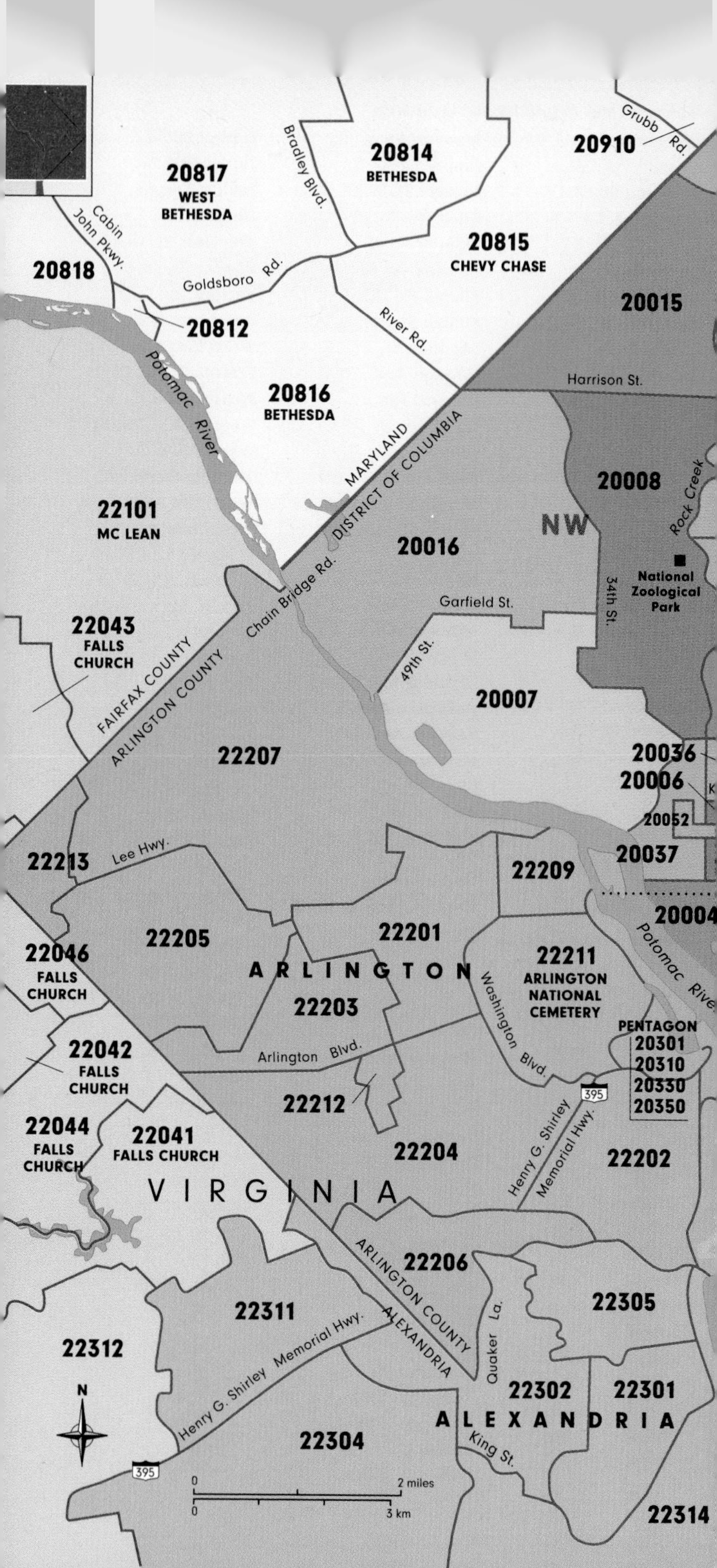

20817
WEST BETHESDA
20814
BETHESDA
20910
Grubb Rd.
Bradley Blvd.
Cabin John Pkwy.
20818
Goldsboro Rd.
20815
CHEVY CHASE
20812
River Rd.
20015
Potomac River
20816
BETHESDA
Harrison St.
MARYLAND
DISTRICT OF COLUMBIA
20008
Rock Creek
22101
MC LEAN
NW
20016
National Zoological Park
Chain Bridge Rd.
Garfield St.
34th St.
22043
FALLS CHURCH
49th St.
FAIRFAX COUNTY
ARLINGTON COUNTY
20007
22207
20036
20006
20052
22213
Lee Hwy.
20037
22209
20004
22205
22201
22211
ARLINGTON NATIONAL CEMETERY
22046
FALLS CHURCH
ARLINGTON
Washington Blvd.
Potomac River
22203
PENTAGON
20301
20310
20330
20350
22042
FALLS CHURCH
Arlington Blvd.
395
22212
22044
FALLS CHURCH
22041
FALLS CHURCH
22204
Henry G. Shirley Memorial Hwy.
22202
VIRGINIA
22206
ARLINGTON COUNTY
ALEXANDRIA
22305
22311
Quaker La.
22312
Henry G. Shirley Memorial Hwy.
22302
22301
N
ALEXANDRIA
22304
King St.
395
0
2 miles
0
3 km
22314

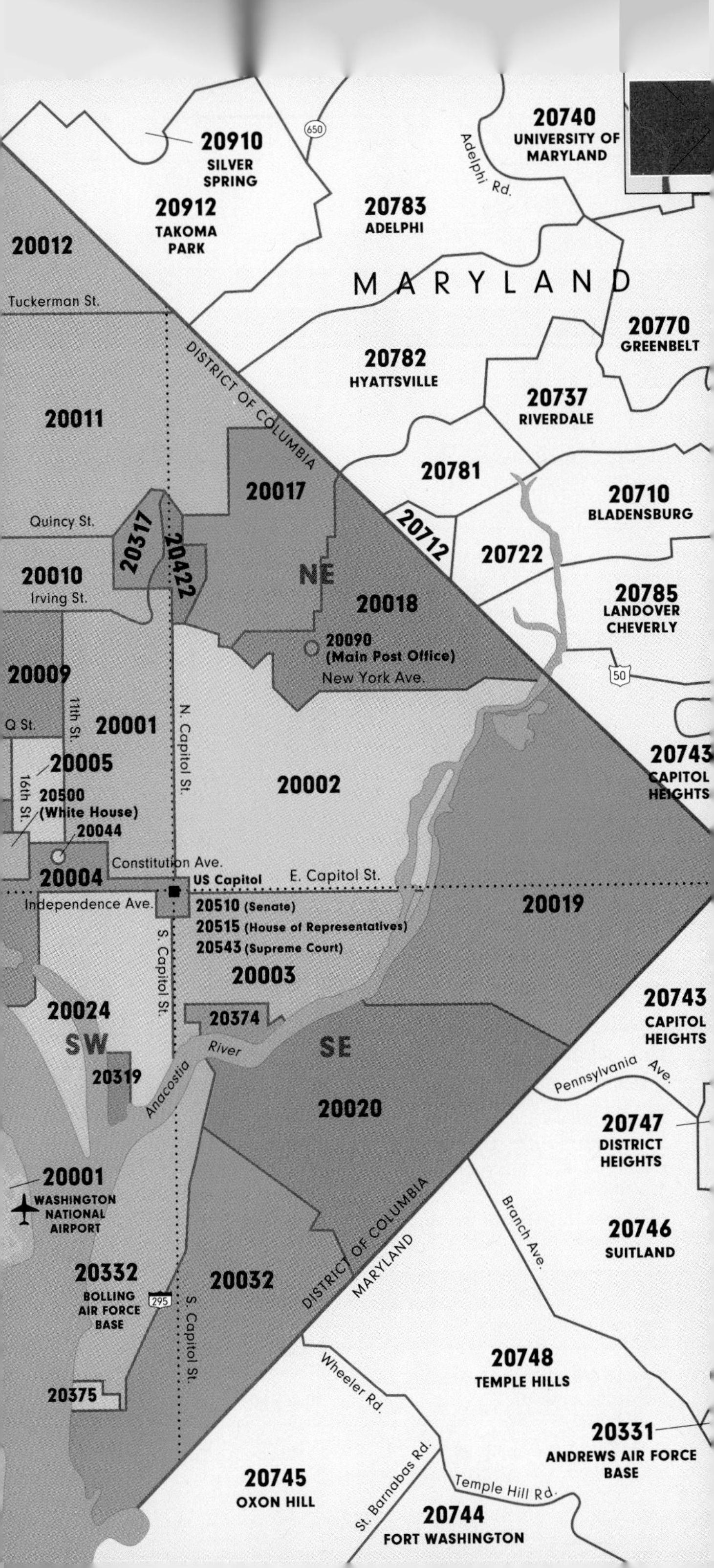

20910
SILVER SPRING
20912
TAKOMA PARK
20012
20783
ADELPHI
20740
UNIVERSITY OF MARYLAND
Adelphi Rd.
MARYLAND
Tuckerman St.
20770
GREENBELT
20782
HYATTSVILLE
20737
RIVERDALE
DISTRICT OF COLUMBIA
20011
20017
20781
20710
BLADENSBURG
Quincy St.
20317
20422
20712
20722
20010
Irving St.
NE
20018
20785
LANDOVER CHEVERLY
20090
(Main Post Office)
New York Ave.
50
20009
11th St.
20001
Q St.
N. Capitol St.
20743
CAPITOL HEIGHTS
20005
16th St.
20500
(White House)
20002
20044
Constitution Ave.
20004
US Capitol
E. Capitol St.
Independence Ave.
20510 (Senate)
20515 (House of Representatives)
20543 (Supreme Court)
20019
S. Capitol St.
20003
20743
CAPITOL HEIGHTS
20024
SW
20374
River
SE
Anacostia
Pennsylvania Ave.
20319
20020
20747
DISTRICT HEIGHTS
20001
WASHINGTON NATIONAL AIRPORT
Branch Ave.
DISTRICT OF COLUMBIA
MARYLAND
20746
SUITLAND
20332
BOLLING AIR FORCE BASE
295
20032
S. Capitol St.
20748
TEMPLE HILLS
Wheeler Rd.
20375
20331
ANDREWS AIR FORCE BASE
St. Barnabas Rd.
Temple Hill Rd.
20745
OXON HILL
20744
FORT WASHINGTON

MAP 8 Hospitals & Late-Night Pharmacies

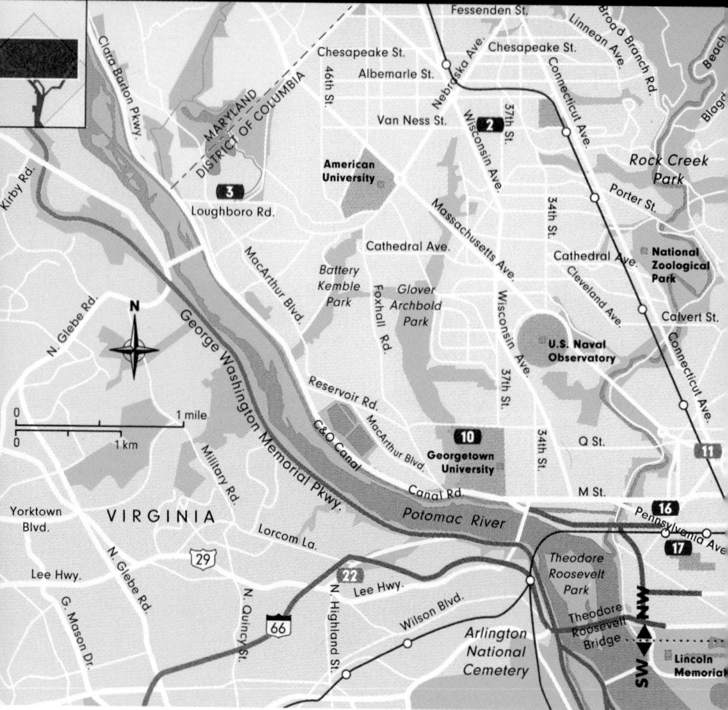

Listed by Site Number

1 Walter Reed Army Medical Center
2 Psychiatric Institute of DC
3 Sibley Memorial
4 Providence
5 Hospital for Sick Children
6 Veterans Administration Medical Center
7 National Rehabilitation
8 Children's
9 Washington Hospital Center
10 Georgetown University
11 CVS Drug Stores
12 DC General
13 CVS Drug Stores
14 Howard University
15 Giant Food

Listed Alphabetically

HOSPITALS

Capitol Hill, 18. 700 Constitution Ave NE ☎ 675–0500

Children's, 8. 111 Michigan Ave NW ☎ 745–5000

Columbia Hospital for Women, 16. 2425 L St NW ☎ 293–6500

DC General, 12. 1900 Massachusetts Ave SE ☎ 675–5000

Georgetown University, 10. 3800 Reservoir Rd NW ☎ 687–5055

George Washington University Medical Center, 17. 901 23rd St NW ☎ 994–1000

Greater SE Community, 20. 1310 Southern Ave SE ☎ 574–6000

Hadley Memorial, 21. 4601 Martin Luther King Jr Ave SW ☎ 574–5700

Hospital for Sick Children, 5. 1731 Bunker Hill Rd NE ☎ 832–4400

Howard University, 14. 2041 Georgia Ave NW ☎ 865–6100

National Rehabilitation, 7. 102 Irving St NW ☎ 877–1000

Providence, 4. 1150 Varnum St NE ☎ 269–7000

Psychiatric Institute of DC, 2. 4228 Wisconsin Ave NW ☎ 965–8200

Sibley Memorial, 3. 5255 Loughboro Rd NW ☎ 537–4000

St Elizabeth's Campus, 19. 2700 Martin Luther King Jr Ave SE ☎ 562–4000

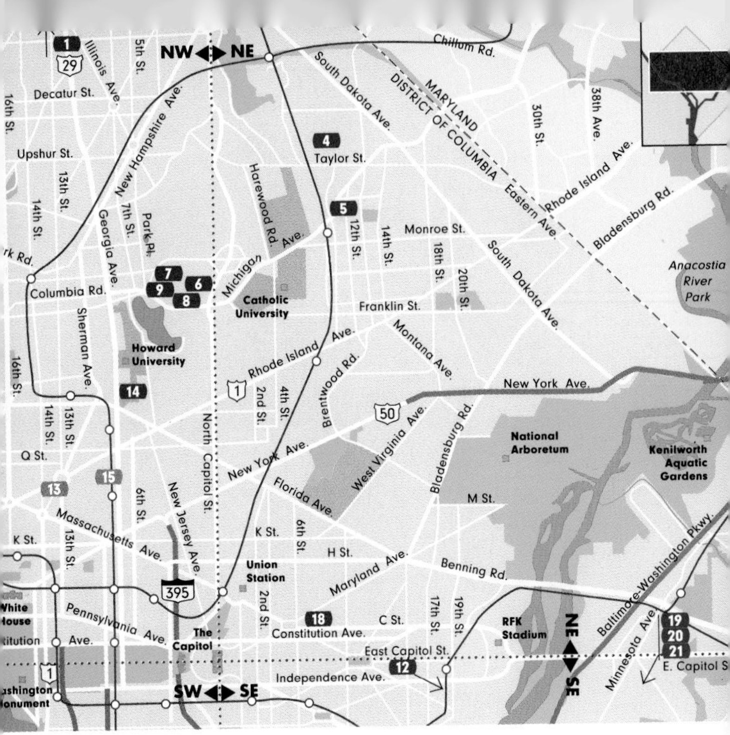

Listed by Site Number (cont.)

16 Columbia Hospital for Women

17 George Washington University Medical Center

18 Capitol Hill

19 St Elizabeth's Campus

20 Greater SE Community

21 Hadley Memorial

22 CVS

Listed Alphabeticallyr (cont.)

Veterans Administration Medical Center, 6. 50 Irving St NW ☎745-8000

Walter Reed Army Medical Center, 1. 6900 Georgia Ave NW ☎782-3501

Washington Hospital Center, 9. First & Irving Sts NW ☎877-6267

Giant Food, 15. 1414 8th St NW ☎628-0577

LATE-NIGHT/24-HOUR PHARMACIES

CVS Drug Stores, 13. 1211 Vermont Ave NW ☎628-0720

CVS Drug Stores, 11. 6-7 Dupont Circle NW ☎785-1466

CVS, 22. 3133 Lee Hwy Arlington, VA ☎703/522-0260

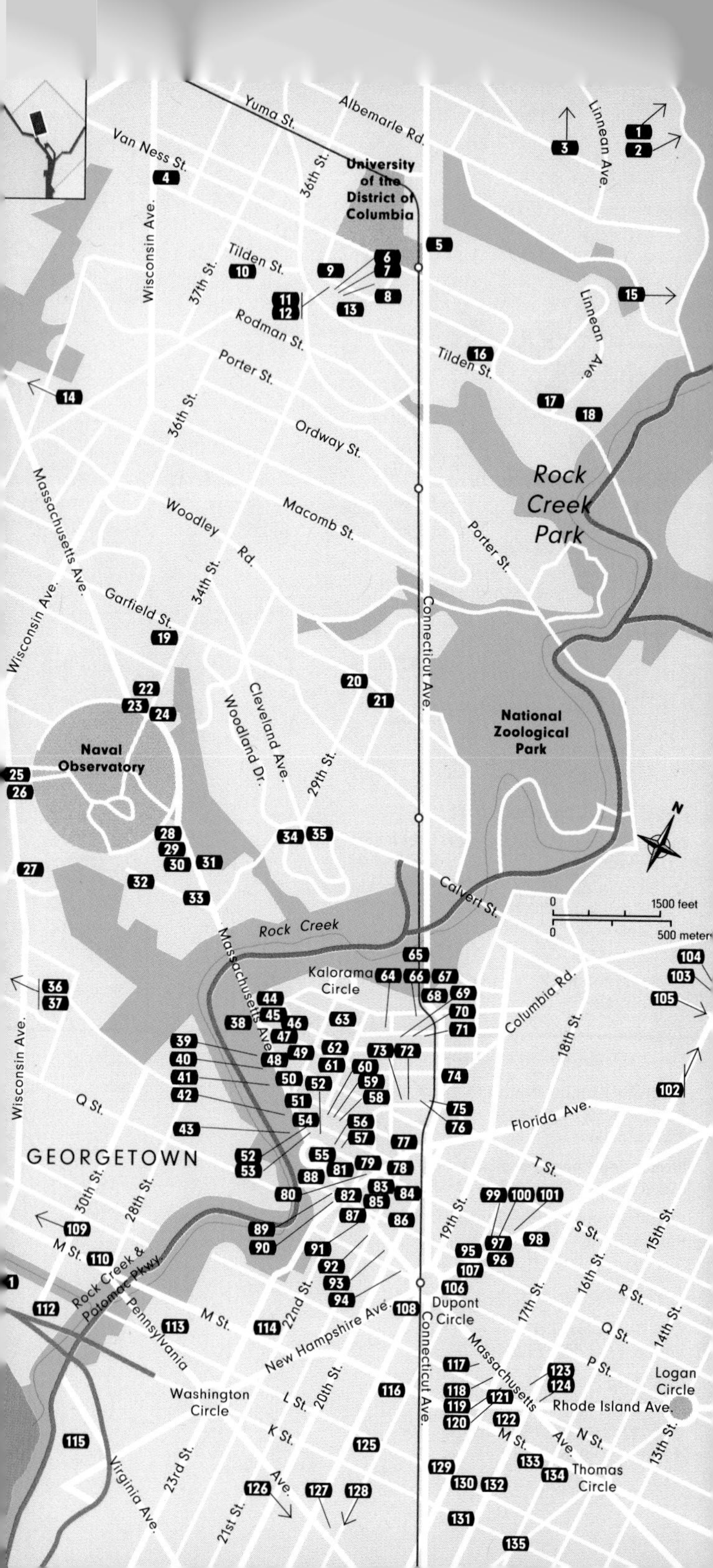

Yuma St.
Albemarle Rd.
Van Ness St.
University of the District of Columbia
Linnean Ave.
Wisconsin Ave.
36th St.
37th St.
Tilden St.
Rodman St.
Porter St.
Ordway St.
Macomb St.
Woodley Rd.
34th St.
Massachusetts Ave.
Garfield St.
Rock Creek Park
Porter St.
Connecticut Ave.
National Zoological Park
Naval Observatory
Cleveland Ave.
Woodland Dr.
29th St.
Calvert St.
Rock Creek
Kalorama Circle
Columbia Rd.
18th St.
Florida Ave.
Q St.
GEORGETOWN
30th St.
28th St.
T St.
19th St.
S St.
15th St.
16th St.
R St.
17th St.
14th St.
Q St.
M St.
Rock Creek & Potomac Pkwy.
Pennsylvania
22nd St.
New Hampshire Ave.
Dupont Circle
Massachusetts Ave.
P St.
Logan Circle
Rhode Island Ave.
Washington Circle
L St.
20th St.
N St.
M St.
K St.
23rd St.
Virginia Ave.
21st St.
Thomas Circle
13th St.
0
1500 feet
500 meters

Listed Alphabetically

Afghanistan, 63. 2341 Wyoming Ave NW ☎ 234-3770

Algeria, 67. 2118 Kalorama Rd NW ☎ 265-2800

Argentina, 95. 1600 New Hampshire Ave NW ☎ 939-6400

Armenia, 130. 1660 L St NW ☎ 296-9076

Australia, 123. 1601 Massachusetts Ave NW ☎ 797-3000

Austria, 9. 3524 International Ct NW ☎ 895-6700

Bahamas, 89. 2220 Massachusetts Ave NW ☎ 319-2660

Bahrain, 11. 3502 International Dr NW ☎ 342-0741

Bangladesh, 26. 2201 Wisconsin Ave NW ☎ 342-8372

Barbados, 70. 2144 Wyoming Ave NW ☎ 939-9200

Belarus, 97. 1619 New Hampshire Ave NW ☎ 986-1604

Belgium, 19. 3330 Garfield St NW ☎ 333-6900

Benin, 21. 2737 Catherine Ave NW ☎ 232-6656

Bolivia, 30. 3014 Massachusetts Ave NW ☎ 483-4410

Bosnia/Herzegovina, 129. 1707 L St NW ☎ 833-3612

Botswana, 10. 3007 Tilden St NW ☎ 244-4990

Brazil, 33. 3006 Massachusetts Ave NW ☎ 745-2700

Bulgaria, 80. 1621 22nd St NW ☎ 387-7969

Burkina Faso, 43. 2340 Massachusetts Ave NW ☎ 332-5577

Burundi, 26. 2233 Wisconsin Ave NW ☎ 342-2574

Cameroon, 51. 2349 Massachusetts Ave NW ☎ 265-8790

Canada, 126. 501 Pennsylvania Ave NW ☎ 682-1740

Cape Verde, 23. 3415 Massachusetts Ave NW ☎ 965-6820

Central African Republic, 82. 1618 22nd St NW ☎ 483-7800

Chad, 84. 2002 R St NW ☎ 462-4009

Chile, 117. 1732 Massachusetts Ave NW ☎ 785-1746

China (People's Republic of), 65. 2300 Connecticut Ave NW ☎ 328-2500

Colombia, 76. 2118 Leroy Pl NW ☎ 387-8338

Costa Rica, 58. 2114 S St NW ☎ 234-2945

Croatia, 48. 2343 Massachusetts Ave NW ☎ 588-5899

Cyprus, 57. 2211 R St NW ☎ 462-5772

Czech Republic, 17. 3900 Linnean Ave NW ☎ 274-9100

Denmark, 32. 3200 Whitehaven St NW ☎ 234-4300

Dominican Republic, 79. 1715 22nd St NW ☎ 332-6280

Ecuador, 102. 2535 15th St NW ☎ 234-7200

Egypt, 8. 3521 International Ct NW ☎ 895-5400

El Salvador, 61. 2308 California St NW ☎ 265-9671

Estonia, 87. 2131 Massachusetts Ave NW ☎ 588-0101

Ethiopia, 66. 2134 Kalorama Rd NW ☎ 234-2281

Fiji, 25. 2233 Wisconsin Ave NW ☎ 337-8320

Finland, 14. 3216 New Mexico Ave NW ☎ 363-2430

France, 37. 4101 Reservoir Rd NW ☎ 944-6000

Gabon, 86. 2034 20th St NW ☎ 797-1000

Gambia, 134. 1155 15th St NW ☎ 785-1399

Georgia (Republic), 135. 1511 K St NW ☎ 393-5959

Germany, 36. 4645 Reservoir Rd NW ☎ 298-4000

Ghana, 6. 3512 International Dr NW ☎ 686-4520

Great Britain, 29. 3100 Massachusetts Ave NW ☎ 462-1340

Greece, 81. 2221 Massachusetts Ave NW ☎ 939-5800

Grenada, 101. 1701 New Hampshire Ave NW ☎ 265-2561

Guatemala, 55. 2220 R St NW ☎ 745-4952

Guinea, 75. 2112 Leroy Pl NW ☎ 483-9420

Listed Alphabetically (cont.)

Guyana, 46. 2490 Tracy Pl NW ☎ 265-6900

Haiti, 53. 2311 Massachusetts Ave NW ☎ 332-4090

Honduras, 131. 1612 K St NW ☎ 223-0185

Hungary, 18. 3910 Shoemaker St NW ☎ 362-6730

Iceland, 133. 1156 15th St NW ☎ 265-6653

India, 45. 2531 Massachusetts Ave NW ☎ 939-7000

Indonesia, 94. 2020 Massachusetts Ave NW ☎ 775-5200

Iraq, 106. 1801 P St NW ☎ 483-7500

Ireland, 88. 2234 Massachusetts Ave NW ☎ 462-3939

Israel, 7. 3514 International Dr NW ☎ 364-5500

Italy, 105. 1601 Fuller St NW ☎ 328-5500

Ivory Coast, 39. 2424 Massachusetts Ave NW ☎ 483-2400

Jamaica, 107. 1520 New Hampshire Ave NW ☎ 452-0660

Japan, 44. 2520 Massachusetts Ave NW ☎ 939-6700

Jordan, 12. 3504 International Dr NW ☎ 966-2664

Kenya, 56. 2249 R St NW ☎ 387-6101

Korea, 54. 2320 Massachusetts Ave NW ☎ 939-5600

Kuwait, 16. 2940 Tilden St NW ☎ 966-0702

Laos, 59. 2222 S St NW ☎ 332-6416

Latvia, 15. 4325 17th St NW ☎ 726-8213

Lebanon, 35. 2560 28th St NW ☎ 939-6300

Lesotho, 38. 2511 Massachusetts Ave NW ☎ 797-5533

Liberia, 2. 5303 Colorado Ave NW ☎ 723-0437

Lithuania, 103. 2622 16th St NW ☎ 234-5860

Luxembourg, 93. 2200 Massachusetts Ave NW ☎ 265-4171

Madagascar, 42. 2374 Massachusetts Ave NW ☎ 265-5525

Malawi, 40. 2408 Massachusetts Ave NW ☎ 797-1007

Malaysia, 50. 2401 Massachusetts Ave NW ☎ 328-2700

Mali, 83. 2130 R St NW ☎ 332-2249

Malta, 74. 2017 Connecticut Ave NW ☎ 462-3611

Mauritania, 72. 2129 Leroy Pl NW ☎ 232-5700

Mauritius, 5. 4301 Connecticut Ave NW ☎ 244-1491

Mexico, 127. 1911 Pennsylvania Ave NW ☎ 728-1600

Mongolia, 110. 2833 M St NW ☎ 333-7117

Morocco, 85. 1601 21st St NW ☎ 462-7979

Mozambique, 116. 1990 M St NW ☎ 293-7146

Myanmar (Burma), 60. 2300 S St NW ☎ 332-9044

Namibia, 99. 1605 New Hampshire Ave NW ☎ 986-0540

Nepal, 73. 2131 Leroy Pl NW ☎ 667-4550

Netherlands, 4. 4200 Wisconsin Ave NW ☎ 244-5300

New Zealand, 28. 37 Observatory Circle NW ☎ 328-4800

Nicaragua, 100. 1627 New Hampshire Ave NW ☎ 939-6570

Niger, 77. 2204 R St NW ☎ 483-4224

Nigeria, 114. 2201 M St NW ☎ 822-1500

Norway, 22. 2720 34th St NW ☎ 333-6000

Oman, 67. 2535 Belmont Rd NW ☎ 387-1980

Listed Alphabetically (cont.)

Pakistan, 52. 2315 Massachusetts Ave NW ☎ 939-6200

Panama, 34. 2862 McGill Ter NW ☎ 483-1407

Paraguay, 41. 2400 Massachusetts Ave NW ☎ 483-6960

Peru, 120. 1700 Massachusetts Ave NW ☎ 833-9860

Philippines, 121. 1600 Massachusetts Ave NW ☎ 467-9300

Poland, 104. 2640 16th St NW ☎ 234-3800

Portugal, 62. 2310 Tracy Pl NW ☎ 332-3007

Qatar, 4. 4200 Wisconsin Ave NW ☎ 274-1600

Romania, 90. 1607 23rd St NW ☎ 232-4747

Russia, 132. 1125 16th St NW ☎ 232-6020

Rwanda, 98. 1714 New Hampshire Ave NW ☎ 232-2882

San Marino, 125. 1899 L St NW ☎ 223-3517

Saudi Arabia, 115. 601 New Hampshire Ave NW ☎ 342-3800

Senegal, 71. 2112 Wyoming Ave NW ☎ 234-0540

Singapore, 13. 3501 International Pl NW ☎ 537-3100

Slovakia, 3. 4828 Linnean Ave NW ☎ 274-9100

Slovenia, 108. 1300 19th St NW ☎ 818-1650

South Africa, 31. 3051 Massachusetts Ave NW ☎ 232-4400

Spain, 113. 2375 Pennsylvania Ave NW ☎ 452-0100

Sri Lanka, 69. 2148 Wyoming Ave NW ☎ 483-4025

St Lucia, 14. 3216 New Mexico Ave NW ☎ 364-6792

Sudan, 91. 2210 Massachusetts Ave NW ☎ 338-8565

Surinam, 5. 4301 Connecticut Ave NW ☎ 244-7488

Swaziland, 10. 3007 Tilden St NW ☎ 362-6683

Sweden, 133. 1501 M St NW ☎ 467-2600

Switzerland, 19. 2900 Cathedral Ave NW ☎ 745-7900

Syria, 64. 2215 Wyoming Ave NW ☎ 232-6313

Tanzania, 78. 2139 R St NW ☎ 939-6125

Thailand, 27. 1024 Wisconsin Ave NW ☎ 944-3600

Togo, 92. 2208 Massachusetts Ave NW ☎ 234-4212

Trinidad & Tobago, 119. 1708 Massachusetts Ave NW ☎ 467-6490

Tunisia, 124. 1515 Massachusetts Ave NW ☎ 862-1850

Turkey, 118. 1714 Massachusetts Ave NW ☎ 387-3200

Uganda, 1. 5909 16th St NW ☎ 726-7100

Ukraine, 109. 3350 M St NW ☎ 333-0606

United Arab Emirates, 111. 3000 K St NW ☎ 338-6500

Uruguay, 128. 1918 F St NW ☎ 331-1313

Vatican, 24. 3339 Massachusetts Ave NW ☎ 333-7121

Venezuela, 112. 1099 30th St NW ☎ 342-2214

Yugoslavia, 49. 2410 California St NW ☎ 462-6566

Zambia, 47. 2419 Massachusetts Ave NW ☎ 265-9717

Zimbabwe, 96. 1608 New Hampshire Ave NW ☎ 332-7100

Listed by Site Number

1 American University
2 Wesley Theological Seminary
3 University of DC
4 Howard University
5 Catholic University of America
6 St Paul's College
7 Trinity College
8 Mt Vernon College
9 Georgetown University
10 Georgetown School of Nursing
11 Georgetown School of Medicine
12 Johns Hopkins School of Advanced International Studies
13 Georgetown Law Center

Listed Alphabetically

American University, 1.
4400 Massachusetts Ave NW
☎ 885-1000

Berlitz School of Languages, 15.
1050 Connecticut Ave NW
☎ 331-1160

Catholic University of America, 5.
620 Michigan Ave NE
☎ 319-5000

Gallaudet College, 14.
800 Florida Ave NE
☎ 651-5000

George Mason School of Law, 20.
3401 N Fairfax Dr, Arlington VA
☎ 703/993-8000

George Washington University, 17.
2121 I St NW
☎ 994-1000

George Washington University School of Engineering, 19.
725 23rd St NW
☎ 994-6080

George Washington University School of Medicine, 18.
2300 I St NW
☎ 994-3506

Georgetown Law Center, 13.
600 New Jersey Ave NE
☎ 662-9000

Georgetown School of Medicine, 11. 3900 Reservoir Rd NW
☎ 687-5055

Georgetown School of Nursing, 10.
3700 Reservoir Rd NW
☎ 687-5001

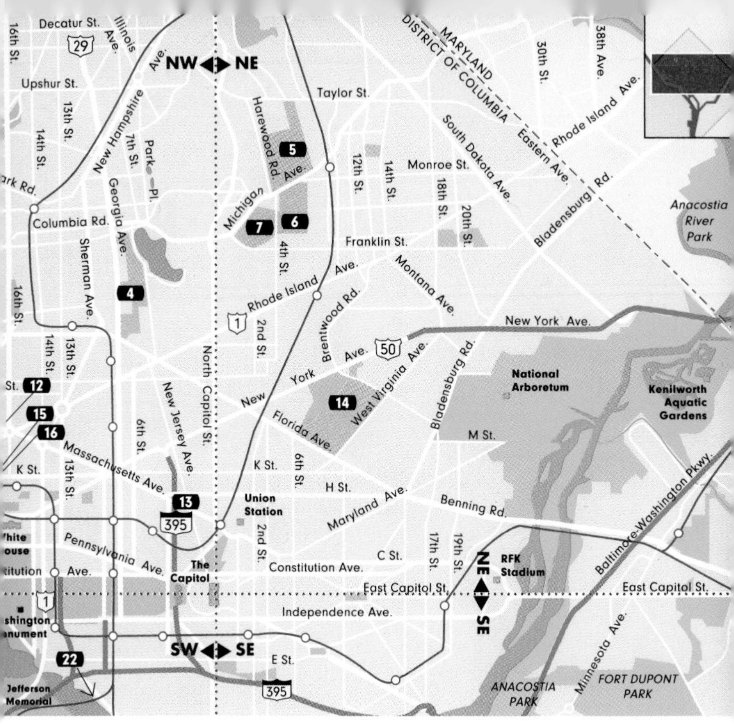

Listed by Site Numberr (cont.)

14 Gallaudet College

15 Berlitz School of Languages

16 Strayer College

17 George Washington University

18 George Washington University School of Medicine

19 George Washington University School of Engineering

20 George Mason School of Law

21 Marymount

22 National War College

Listed Alphabeticallyr (cont.)

Georgetown University, 9. O & 37th Sts NW ☎ 687-0100

Howard University, 4. 2400 6th St NW ☎ 806-6100

Johns Hopkins School of Advanced International Studies, 12. 1740 Massachusetts Ave NW ☎ 663-5600

Marymount, 21. 2807 N. Glebe Rd Arlington, VA ☎ (703) 522-5600

Mt Vernon College, 8. 2100 Foxhall Rd NW ☎ 625-0400

National War College, 22. Fort McNair St SW ☎ 475-1775

St Paul's College, 6. 3015 4th St NE ☎ 832-6262

Strayer College, 16. 1025 15th St NW ☎ 408-2400

Trinity College, 7. 1215 Michigan Ave NE ☎ 939-5000

University of DC, 3. 4200 Connecticut Ave NW ☎ 274-5000

Wesley Theological Seminary, 2. 4500 Massachusetts Ave NW ☎ 885-8600

Listed by Site Number

1 National Library of Medicine
2 National Agricultural
3 Cleveland Park
4 Petworth
5 Mt Pleasant
6 Georgetown Regional
7 Dumbarton Oaks
8 Alexander Graham Bell Society
9 Sumner School Archives
10 West End
11 Foundation Center
12 Federal Bar Foundation
13 Performing Arts
14 National Academy of Sciences
15 Organization of American States
16 DAR

Listed Alphabetically

Air & Space, 24. Independence Ave & 6th St SW ☎ 357-3133

Alexander Graham Bell Society, 8. 3417 Volta Pl NW ☎ 337-5220

American Art/Portrait Gallery, 18. G & 8th Sts NW ☎ 357-1886

American History, 21. Constitution Ave & 14th St SW ☎ 357-2414

Arts & Industries, 23. 900 Jefferson Dr SW ☎ 786-2271

Cleveland Park, 3. 3310 Connecticut Ave NW ☎ 727-1345

DAR, 16. 1776 D St NW ☎ 628-1776

Dumbarton Oaks, 7. 1703 32nd St NW ☎ 339-6981

Federal Bar Foundation, 12. 1815 H St NW ☎ 638-1956

Folger Shakespeare, 28. 201 E Capitol St SE ☎ 544-4600

Foundation Center, 11. 1001 Connecticut Ave NW ☎ 331-1400

Georgetown Regional, 6. 3260 R St NW ☎ 727-1353

Library of Congress, 27. 10 Independence Ave SE ☎ 707-5000

Martin Luther King Jr Memorial, 17. 901 G St NW ☎ 727-1111

Mt Pleasant, 5. Lamont Ave & 16th St NW ☎ 727-1361

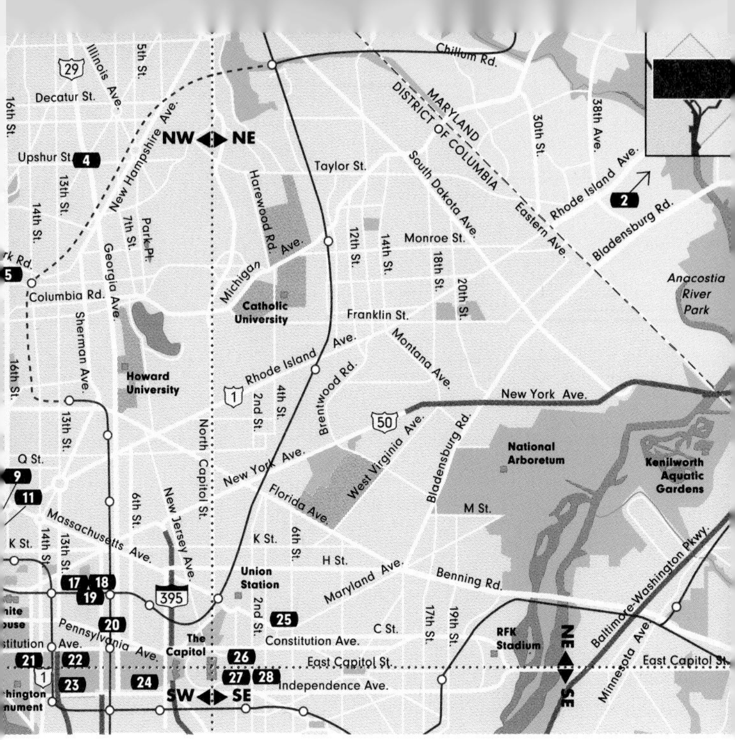

Listed by Site Number (cont.)

17 Martin Luther King Jr Memorial

18 American Art/Portrait Gallery

19 Watha T. Daniel

20 National Archives

21 American History

22 Natural History

23 Arts & Industries

24 Air & Space

25 Northeast

26 Supreme Court

27 Library of Congress

28 Folger Shakespeare

Listed Alphabetically

National Academy of Sciences, 14. 2101 Constitution Ave NW ☎ 334-2125

National Agricultural, 2. 10301 Baltimore Ave, Beltsville, MD ☎ 301/504-5755

National Archives, 20. Pennsylvania Ave & 8th St NW ☎ 501-5402

National Library of Medicine, 1. 800 Rockville Pk, Rockville, MD ☎ 301/496-6095

Natural History, 22. Constitution Ave & 10th St NW ☎ 357-1496

Northeast, 25. 330 7th St NE ☎ 727-1365

Organization of American States, 15. Constitution Ave & 19th St NW ☎ 458-6037

Performing Arts, 13. Kennedy Center, 2700 F St NW ☎ 416-8780

Petworth, 4. 4200 Georgia Ave NW ☎ 727-1373

Sumner School Archives, 9. 1201 17th St NW ☎ 727-3419

Supreme Court, 26. Maryland Ave & 1st St NE ☎ 479-3175

Watha T. Daniel, 19. 801 8th St NW ☎ 727-1228

West End, 10. 1101 24th St NW ☎ 727-1397

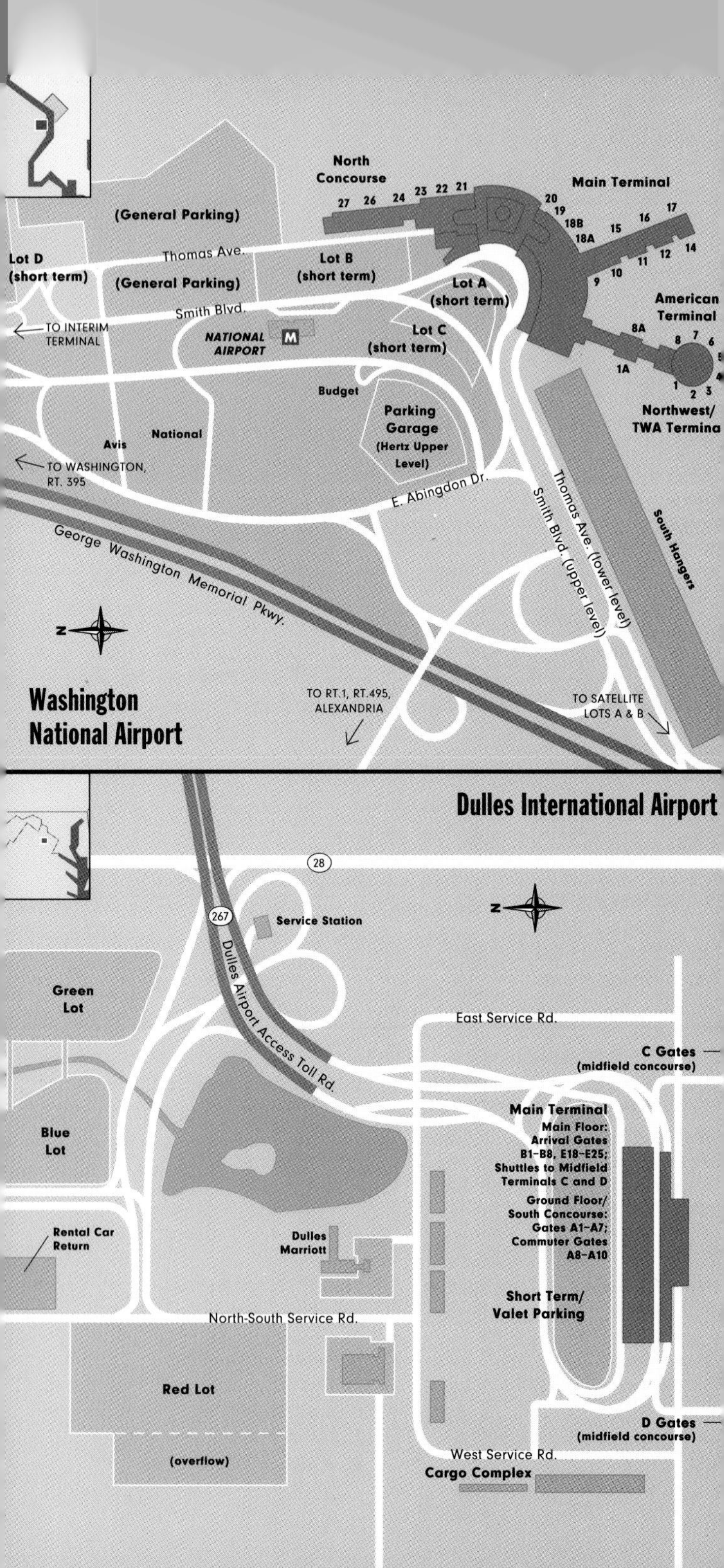

North Concourse
Main Terminal
27 26 24 23 22 21
20 19 18B 18A 15 16 17 14 12 11 10 9
(General Parking)
Lot D (short term)
Thomas Ave.
Lot B (short term)
Lot A (short term)
American Terminal
8A 8 7 6 5 4 3 2 1 1A
(General Parking)
Smith Blvd.
TO INTERIM TERMINAL
NATIONAL AIRPORT
M
Lot C (short term)
Budget
Parking Garage (Hertz Upper Level)
Northwest/ TWA Termina
Avis
National
TO WASHINGTON, RT. 395
E. Abingdon Dr.
George Washington Memorial Pkwy.
Thomas Ave. (lower level)
Smith Blvd. (upper level)
South Hangers
N
Washington National Airport
TO RT.1, RT.495, ALEXANDRIA
TO SATELLITE LOTS A & B
Dulles International Airport
28
267
Service Station
N
Green Lot
Dulles Airport Access Toll Rd.
East Service Rd.
C Gates (midfield concourse)
Blue Lot
Main Terminal
Main Floor: Arrival Gates B1–B8, E18–E25; Shuttles to Midfield Terminals C and D
Ground Floor/ South Concourse: Gates A1–A7; Commuter Gates A8–A10
Rental Car Return
Dulles Marriott
Short Term/ Valet Parking
North-South Service Rd.
Red Lot
(overflow)
D Gates (midfield concourse)
West Service Rd.
Cargo Complex

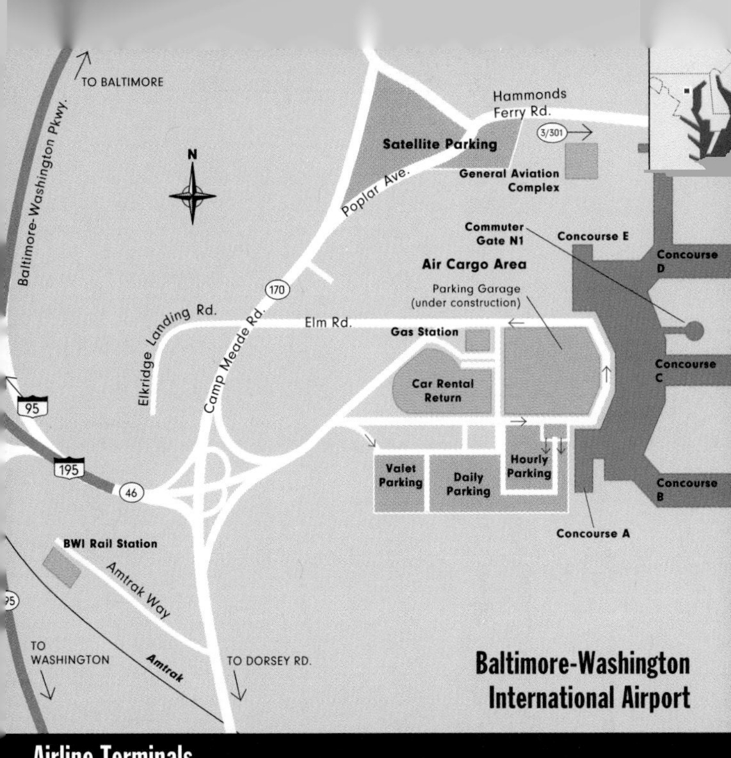

Airline Terminals

AIRLINES	NATIONAL	DULLES	BWI
Aeroflot Russian International Airlines ☎ 202/429-4922		E	
Air Canada ☎ 800/776-3000			B
Air France ☎ 800/237-2747		E	
Air Jamaica ☎ 800/523-5585			E
All Nippon (ANA) ☎ 800/235-9262		E	
America West ☎ 800/247-5692	Main		B
American ☎ 800/223-5436	Main	D	C
American Eagle ☎ 800/433-7300	Main		C
Bahamasair ☎ 800/222-4262		D	
British Airways ☎ 800/247-9297		E	
Business Express/Delta ☎ 800/221-1212	Main		B
Continental ☎ 800/525-0280	Main	D	C, B
Continental Express ☎ 800/525-0280		D	
Delta ☎ 800/221-1212	Interim	E	B
Delta Shuttle ☎ 800/221-1212	Main		
El Al Israel ☎ 800/352-5747			E
Icelandair ☎ 800/223-5500			E
KLM ☎ 800/374-7747			E
Lufthansa ☎ 800/645-3880		B	
Mexican ☎ 800/531-7921			E
Midway ☎ 800/446-4392	Main		
Midwest Express ☎ 800/452-2022	Main		
Mohawk ☎ 800/252-2144		A	
Northwest ☎ 800/225-2525	Main	A	C
Saudi Arabian ☎ 800/472-8342		E	
Southwest ☎ 800/435-9792			C
TWA ☎ 800/892-2746	Main	C	D
United ☎ 800/241-6522	Main	D,C	A,A
United Express ☎ 800/241-6522		A	A
USAir ☎ 800/428-4322	Interim	A	D
USAir Express ☎ 800/428-4322	Interim	A	D
USAir Shuttle ☎ 800/428-4322	Main		

KEY
Red Line
Blue Line
Yellow Line
Orange Line
Green Line
Proposed Extensions
Terminal
Station
Transfer Station
Metrorail Parking (fee)
(400) Parking Capacity (cars)
SHADY GROVE
(2946)
ROCKVILLE
(538)
TWINBROOK
(1075)
WHITE FLINT
(991)
GROSVENOR
(639)
MEDICAL CENTER
BETHESDA
FRIENDSHIP HEIGHTS
TENLEY TOWN
VAN NESS-UDC
CLEVELAND PARK
ROSSLYN
COURT HOUSE
CLARENDON
VIRGINIA SQ
BALLSTON
ARLINGTON CEMETERY
PENTAGON
PENTAGON CITY
WEST FALLS CHURCH
(979)
EAST FALLS CHURCH
(390)
VIENNA
(2187)
DUNN LORING
(1096)
VAN DORN ST
HUNTINGTON
(2323)
EISENHOWER
KING STREET
BRADDOCK
Darnestown Rd.
Muncaster Mill Rd
Frederick Rd.
Norbeck Rd.
W. Montgomery Ave.
Rockville Pike
Bel Pre
Georgia Av
Veirs Mill Rd.
COLUMBIA HEIGHTS
Great Falls Rd.
Seven Locks Rd.
Montrose Rd.
Randolph Rd.
Tuckerman La.
Democracy Blvd.
Bradley Blvd.
Kensington
Falls Rd.
Georgetown Pike
Bethesda
Chevy Chase
Glen Echo
Goldsboro Rd.
Bradley La.
Somerset
Potomac River
Connecticut Ave.
Wisconsin Ave.
MARYLAND
DISTRICT OF COLUMBIA
NW
Leesburg Pike
Old Dominion Dr.
George Washington Memorial Pkwy.
Dolley Madison Blvd.
Langley
Dulles Airport Access Rd.
Tysons Corner
Maple Ave.
McLean
Kirby Rd.
Canal Rd.
Massachusetts
Chain Bridge Rd.
Gallows Rd.
Lee Hwy.
Falls Church
Vienna
Arlington Blvd.
Leesburg Pike
Fairfax
Old Lee Hwy.
Beltway
Capital
ARLINGTON
King St.
VIRGINIA
Main St.
Little River Tnpk.
Annandale
Memorial Hwy.
Van Dorn St.
ALEXANDRIA
Duke St.
Braddock Rd.
Henry G. Shirley
Edsall Rd.
Old Keene Mill Rd.
N
0 2 miles
0 3 km
28
185
355
396
7
694
267
495
270
66
29
50
236
395
95
1

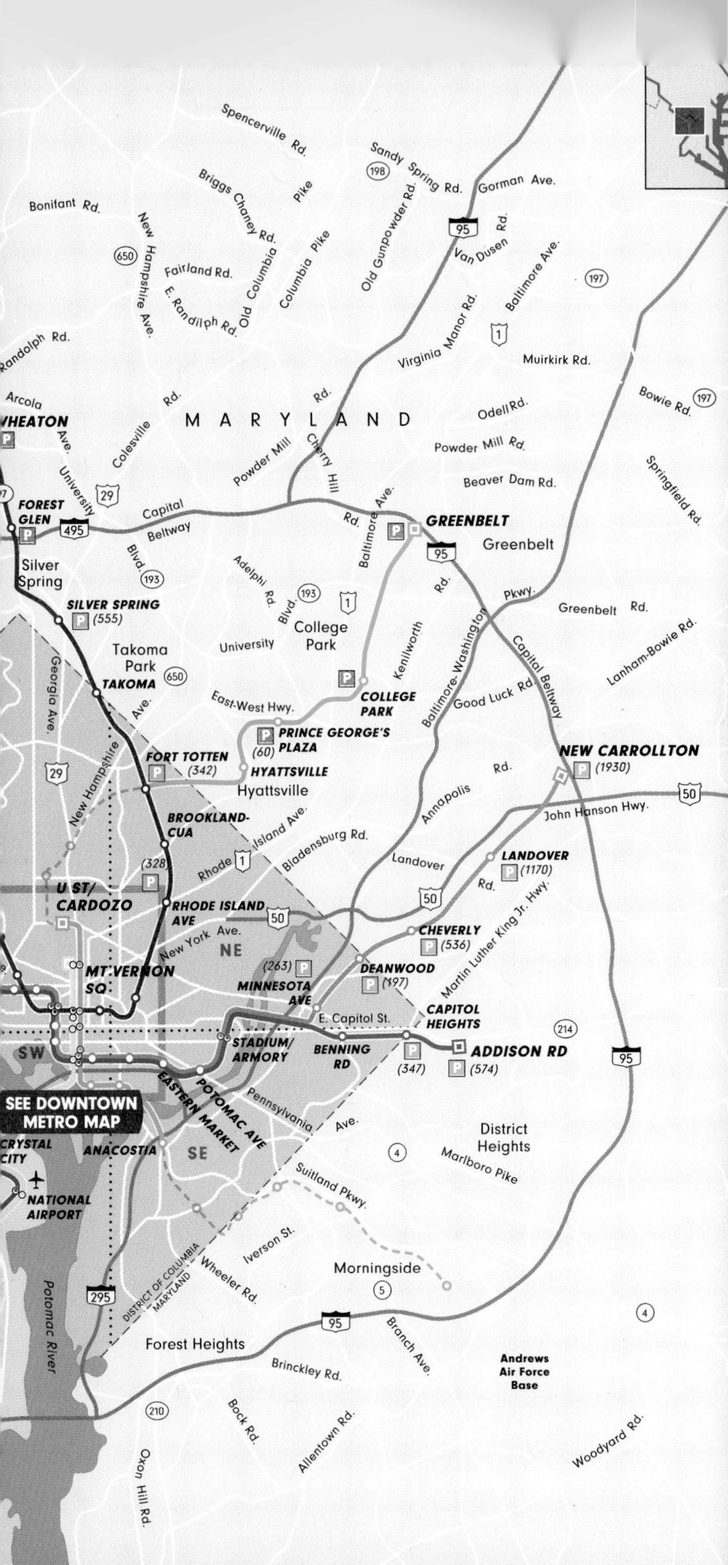

MARYLAND
WHEATON
FOREST GLEN
SILVER SPRING (555)
TAKOMA
FORT TOTTEN (342)
BROOKLAND-CUA
(328)
U ST/ CARDOZO
RHODE ISLAND AVE
MT VERNON SQ
GREENBELT
COLLEGE PARK
PRINCE GEORGE'S PLAZA (60)
HYATTSVILLE
NEW CARROLLTON (1930)
LANDOVER (1170)
CHEVERLY (536)
DEANWOOD (197)
MINNESOTA AVE (263)
CAPITOL HEIGHTS
ADDISON RD (574)
BENNING RD (347)
STADIUM/ ARMORY
POTOMAC AVE
EASTERN MARKET
ANACOSTIA
CRYSTAL CITY
NATIONAL AIRPORT
SEE DOWNTOWN METRO MAP
NE
SE
SW
Silver Spring
Takoma Park
College Park
Hyattsville
Greenbelt
District Heights
Morningside
Forest Heights
Andrews Air Force Base
Potomac River
DISTRICT OF COLUMBIA
MARYLAND
Spencerville Rd.
Sandy Spring Rd.
Gorman Ave.
Briggs Chaney Rd.
Bonifant Rd.
New Hampshire Ave.
Fairland Rd.
E. Randolph Rd.
Old Columbia Pike
Columbia Pike
Old Gunpowder Rd.
Van Dusen Rd.
Baltimore Ave.
Virginia Manor Rd.
Muirkirk Rd.
Randolph Rd.
Arcola
Colesville Rd.
Cherry Hill Rd.
Powder Mill Rd.
Odell Rd.
Bowie Rd.
Powder Mill Rd.
Beaver Dam Rd.
Springfield Rd.
University Blvd.
Capital Beltway
Adelphi Rd.
Kenilworth Rd.
Baltimore-Washington Pkwy.
Greenbelt Rd.
Lanham-Bowie Rd.
Good Luck Rd.
East-West Hwy.
Georgia Ave.
Annapolis Rd.
John Hanson Hwy.
Rhode Island Ave.
Bladensburg Rd.
Landover Rd.
Martin Luther King Jr. Hwy.
New York Ave.
E. Capitol St.
Pennsylvania Ave.
Marlboro Pike
Suitland Pkwy.
Iverson St.
Wheeler Rd.
Branch Ave.
Brinckley Rd.
Bock Rd.
Allentown Rd.
Woodyard Rd.
Oxon Hill Rd.
198
95
650
197
1
29
495
193
555
50
214
4
5
295
210

National Zoological Park
Woodley Park/ Zoo
Dupont Circle
Farragut North
Farragut West
McPherson Square
Foggy Bottom/ GWU
Columbia Heights
Naval Observatory
Normanstone Park
Dumbarton Oaks Park
Montrose Park
Oak Hill Cemetery
Kalorama Circle
Sheridan Circle
Scott Circle
Washington Circle
National Trust
Explorers Hall
Bus Terminal
George Washington University
Watergate Hotel Complex
World Bank
Old Executive Office Bldg.
White House
General Services Bldg.
Dept. of State
The Ellipse
Commerce Dept.
Theodore Roosevelt Memorial
Theodore Roosevelt Island
Vietnam Veterans Memorial
Reflecting Pool
Lincoln Memorial
Washington Monument
Tidal Basin
Jefferson Memorial
West Potomac Park
Potomac River
Rock Creek
Constitution Ave.
Independence Ave.
Massachusetts Ave.
Connecticut Ave.
New Hampshire Ave.
Virginia Ave.
Wisconsin Ave.
Rock Creek & Potomac Pkwy.
Whitehurst Fwy.
Theodore Roosevelt Br.
Arlington Memorial Br.
Kutz Br.
Outlet Br.
NW
SW
KEY
Red Line
Blue Line
Yellow Line
Orange Line
Green Line
Proposed Extensions
Terminal
Station
Entrance
0 1500 feet
0 500 meters

Kenyon St.
Irving St.
Columbia Rd.
Georgia Ave.
Irving St.
13th St.
Harvard St.
McMillan Reservoir
Michigan Ave.
North Capitol St.
Girard St.
Franklin St.
Girard St.
11th St.
Sherman Ave.
Fairmont St.
Euclid St.
9th St.
Georgia Ave.
Howard University
NW
NE
Douglas St.
Lincoln Rd.
Clifton St.
Howard Pl.
McMillan Dr.
Channing St.
Glenwood Cemetery
Channing St.
College St.
Rhode Island Ave.
Barry Pl.
6th St.
Bryant St.
2nd St.
Adams St.
Bryant St.
Adams St.
Prospect Hill Cemetery
St. Mary's Cemetery
W St.
W St.
W St.
4th St.
V St.
Flagler Pl.
V St.
5th St.
2nd St.
Summit St.
U Street/ Cardozo
Howard University
Elm St.
1st St.
U St.
U St.
Thomas St.
1
Todd St.
T St.
12th St.
11th St.
8th St.
Shaw/ Howard U
3rd St.
Seaton Pl.
T St.
S St.
S St.
Rhode Island Ave.
Randolph Pl.
2nd St.
3rd St.
13th St.
French St.
Vermont Ave.
R St.
Florida Ave.
Lincoln Rd.
R St.
29
Warner St.
New Jersey Ave.
3rd St.
Quincy Pl.
Eckington Pl.
Q St.
1
Q St.
Bates St.
Logan Circle
Franklin St.
P St.
1st St.
12th St.
11th St.
10th St.
9th St.
8th St.
7th St.
6th St.
5th St.
O St.
O St.
2nd St.
4th St.
5th St.
13th St.
Neal Pl.
York Ave.
Florida Ave.
N St.
N St.
New
1st St.
Patterson St.
29
Mt. Vernon Square/ UDC
4th St.
50
M St.
M St.
Pierce St.
Massachusetts Ave.
L St.
50
1
L St.
North Capitol St.
Bus Terminal
Mt. Vernon Square
New Jersey Ave.
K St.
K St.
Washington Convention Center
3rd St.
Parker St.
I St.
I St.
Capital Children's Museum
I St.
1
H St.
York Ave.
H St.
Massachusetts Ave.
50
G St.
Metro Center
Gallery Place
2nd St.
Union Station
2nd St.
3rd St.
4th St.
G St.
G St.
F St.
National Museum of American Art
Judiciary Square
1
Union Station
E St.
10th St.
E St.
395
Columbus Fountain
Freedom Plaza
50
D St.
Indiana Ave.
Pennsylvania Ave.
Market Pl.
Delaware Ave.
Stanton Park
C St.
3rd St.
Louisiana Ave.
Senate Office Buildings
Federal Triangle
Archives
Maryland Ave.
50
1
Natural History Museum
National Gallery of Art
Supreme Court
A St.
Natl. Museum of American History
US Capitol
NE
Madison Dr.
E. Capitol St.
SE
Smithsonian Institution
THE MALL
Jefferson Dr.
1st St.
Library of Congress
Jefferson
Smithsonian
Air & Space Museum
Independence Ave.
Maryland Ave.
New
Pennsylvania Ave.
2nd St.
C St.
Canal St.
C St.
13th St.
12th St.
D St.
Virginia
D St.
2nd
South
D St.
Eastern Mkt
12th St.
Expwy.
10th St.
Ave.
School St.
4th St.
Federal Center
St.
Ivy St.
Jersey
Capitol South
D St.
L'Enfant Plaza
E St.
Capitol St.
E St.
South Carolina Ave
Maine Ave.
Duddington Pl. SE
7th St.
395
F St.
Virginia Ave.
Garfield Park
Southwest Fwy.
G St.
G St.
395
Francis Case Memorial Br.
H St.
4th St.
Pl.
H St.
Ave.
Canal St.
H St.
3rd St.
Makemie Pl.
3rd St.
Wesley Pl.
I St.
Delaware Ave.
Half St.
I St.
Half St.
1st St.
2nd St.
2nd St. E
3rd St.
4th St.
5th St.
Maine Ave.
Water St.
K St.
K St.
Washington Canal
6th St.
L St.
L St.
Navy Yard
Waterfront
M St.
M St.
4th St.
1st St.
Washington Navy Yard

KEY
Metrorail Station
Metrorail Parking (fee)
Free Park & Ride Parking
(400) Parking Capacity (cars)
Expressway Interchange
Lakeforest Mall (100)
Shady Grove (2946)
Norbeck Rd/Rt 28 (248)
Rockville (538)
Twinbrook (1075)
Montrose/ N Bethesda (500)
White Flint (991)
Grosvenor (639)
Montgomery Mall (400)
Reston (48)
Reston Commuter Parking (350)
Greenbriar Shopping Ctr (140)
Fair Oaks Shopping Ctr (150)
West Falls Church (979)
(2187) Vienna
Dunn Loring (1096)
(391) East Falls Church
Washington Lee (300)
Four Mile Run (30)
Fairfax City/ Long-term Metered (100)
Fairfax City (45)
Canterbury Woods Park
Wakefield Rec Park
Burke Center (390)
Rolling Valley (340)
South Run District Park
Springfield Cinema (180)
Springfield Plaza (220)
Springfield United Methodist (90)
Springfield Mall (400)
Shirley Plaza (50)
Huntington (2323)
Darnestown Rd.
Frederick Rd.
Muncaster Mill Rd
Norbeck Rd.
W. Montgomery Ave.
Rockville Pike
Veirs Mill Rd.
Seven Locks Rd.
Great Falls Rd.
Montrose Rd.
Randolph Rd.
Tuckerman La.
Democracy Blvd.
Kensington
River Rd.
Potomac
Falls Rd.
Bradley Blvd.
Bradley Blvd.
Pike
Georgetown Pike
MacArthur Blvd.
Bethesda
Glen Echo
Goldsboro Rd.
Bradley La.
Chevy Chase
Somerset
Potomac River
Leesburg Pike
Old Dominion Dr.
Georgetown Pike
George Washington Memorial Pkwy.
MARYLAND
DISTRICT OF COLUMBIA
Wisconsin Ave.
Massachusetts Ave.
NW
Canal Rd.
Dolley Madison Blvd.
Langley
Dulles Airport Access Rd.
McLean
Tysons Corner
Maple Ave.
Kirby Rd.
Chain Bridge Rd.
Gallows Rd.
Lee Hwy.
Vienna
Falls Church
Lee Hwy.
Lee Hwy.
Arlington Blvd.
Leesburg Pike
Arlington Blvd.
Old Lee Hwy.
Fairfax
Gallows Rd.
Capital Beltway
VIRGINIA
King St.
ARLINGTON
Main St.
Little River Tnpk.
Annandale
Memorial Hwy.
Van Dorn St.
King St.
ALEXANDRIA
Duke St.
Braddock Rd.
Henry G. Shirley
Edsall Rd.
Old Keene Mill Rd.
N
0 2 miles
0 3 km
270
495
66
29
50
495
395
95

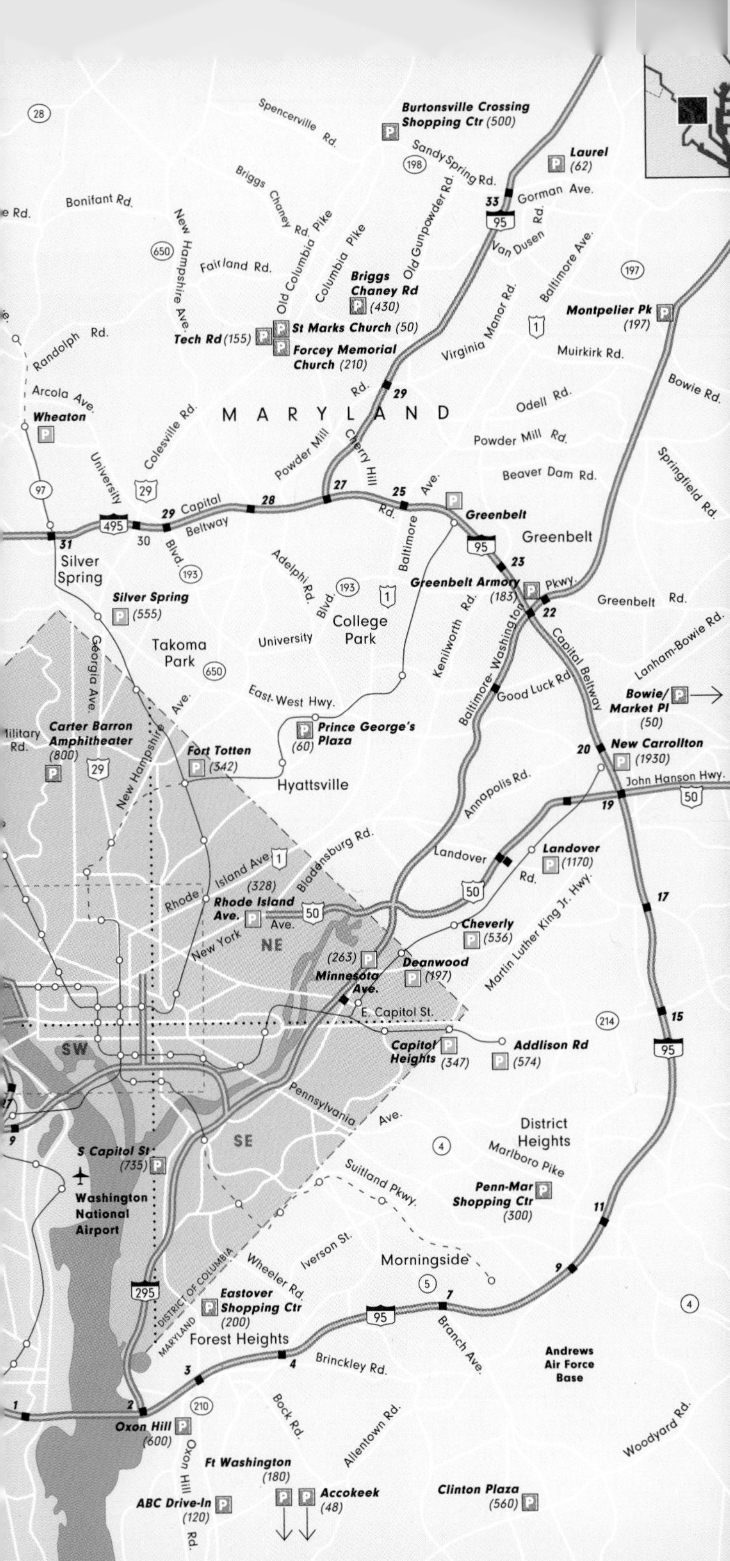

MARYLAND
Burtonsville Crossing Shopping Ctr (500)
Laurel (62)
Briggs Chaney Rd (430)
St Marks Church (50)
Tech Rd (155)
Forcey Memorial Church (210)
Montpelier Pk (197)
Wheaton
Greenbelt
Greenbelt Armory (183)
Silver Spring (555)
Bowie/ Market Pl (50)
Carter Barron Amphitheater (800)
Fort Totten (342)
Prince George's Plaza (60)
New Carrollton (1930)
Landover (1170)
Rhode Island Ave. (328)
Cheverly (536)
Minnesota Ave. (263)
Deanwood (197)
Capitol Heights (347)
Addison Rd (574)
S Capitol St (735)
Washington National Airport
Penn-Mar Shopping Ctr (300)
Eastover Shopping Ctr (200)
Oxon Hill (600)
Ft Washington (180)
Accokeek (48)
ABC Drive-In (120)
Clinton Plaza (560)
Andrews Air Force Base
Silver Spring
Takoma Park
College Park
Hyattsville
District Heights
Morningside
Forest Heights
NE
SE
SW
DISTRICT OF COLUMBIA
Capital Beltway
John Hanson Hwy.
Baltimore-Washington Pkwy.
Martin Luther King Jr. Hwy.
Pennsylvania Ave.
Suitland Pkwy.
Spencerville Rd.
Sandy Spring Rd.
Bonifant Rd.
Briggs Chaney Rd.
New Hampshire Ave.
Old Columbia Pike
Columbia Pike
Old Gunpowder Rd.
Fairland Rd.
Gorman Ave.
Van Dusen Rd.
Baltimore Ave.
Virginia Manor Rd.
Muirkirk Rd.
Bowie Rd.
Randolph Rd.
Arcola Ave.
Colesville Rd.
Powder Mill Rd.
Cherry Hill Rd.
Odell Rd.
Beaver Dam Rd.
Springfield Rd.
University Blvd.
Adelphi Rd.
Kenilworth Rd.
Greenbelt Rd.
Lanham-Bowie Rd.
Good Luck Rd
East-West Hwy.
Georgia Ave.
Military Rd.
Annapolis Rd.
Landover Rd.
Bladensburg Rd.
Rhode Island Ave
New York Ave.
E. Capitol St.
Marlboro Pike
Iverson St.
Wheeler Rd.
Branch Ave.
Brinckley Rd.
Bock Rd.
Allentown Rd.
Oxon Hill Rd.
Woodyard Rd.

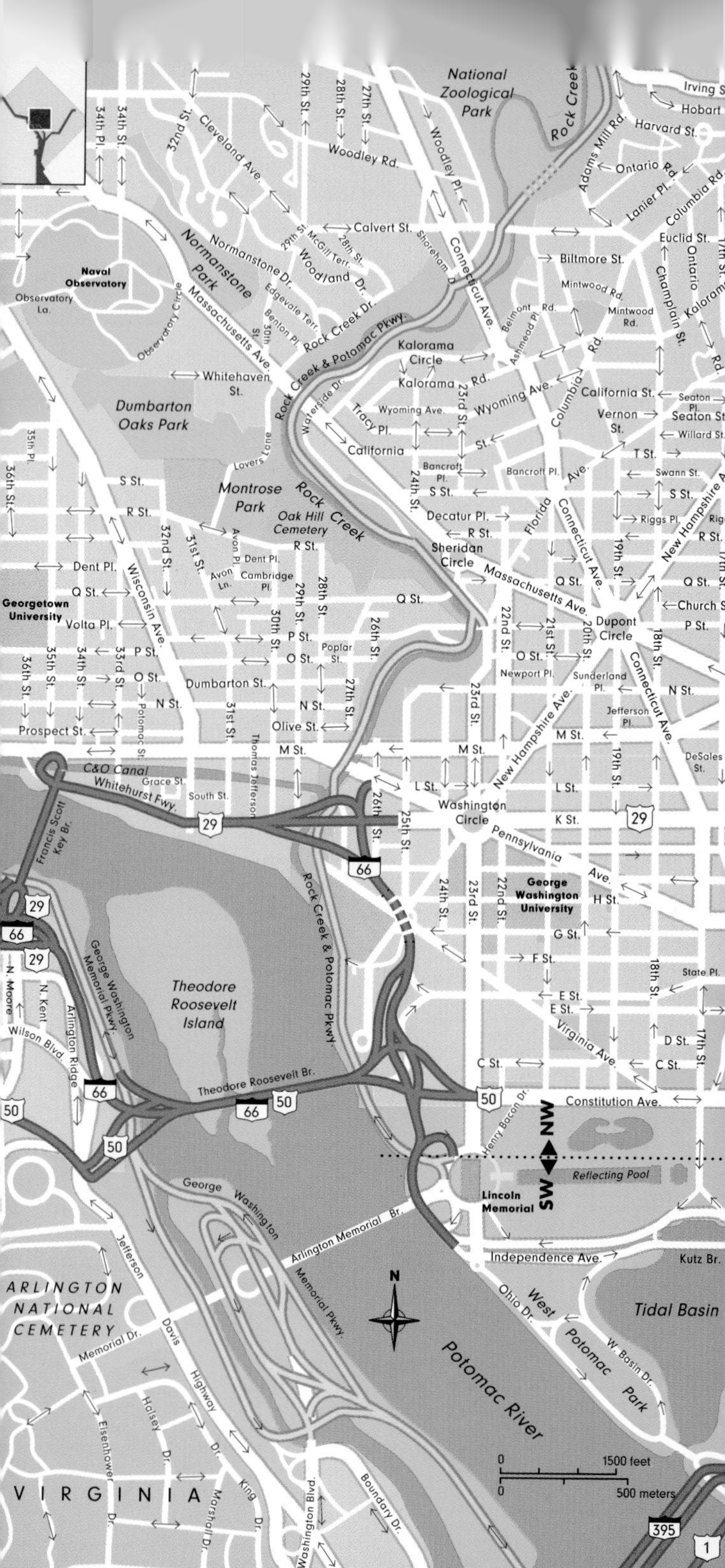
National Zoological Park
Rock Creek
Naval Observatory
Dumbarton Oaks Park
Montrose Park
Oak Hill Cemetery
Normanstone Park
Georgetown University
George Washington University
Kalorama Circle
Sheridan Circle
Dupont Circle
Washington Circle
C&O Canal
Theodore Roosevelt Island
Lincoln Memorial
Reflecting Pool
Tidal Basin
West Potomac Park
Potomac River
ARLINGTON NATIONAL CEMETERY
VIRGINIA
NW
SW
N
0 1500 feet
0 500 meters

McMillan Reservoir
Howard University
Glenwood Cemetery
Prospect Hill Cemetery
St. Mary's Cemetery
NW NE
Logan Circle
Thomas Circle
Mt. Vernon Square
Bus Terminal
Union Station
Freedom Plaza
US Capitol
THE MALL
Washington Monument
Jefferson Memorial
Washington Canal
NE SE
SW SE

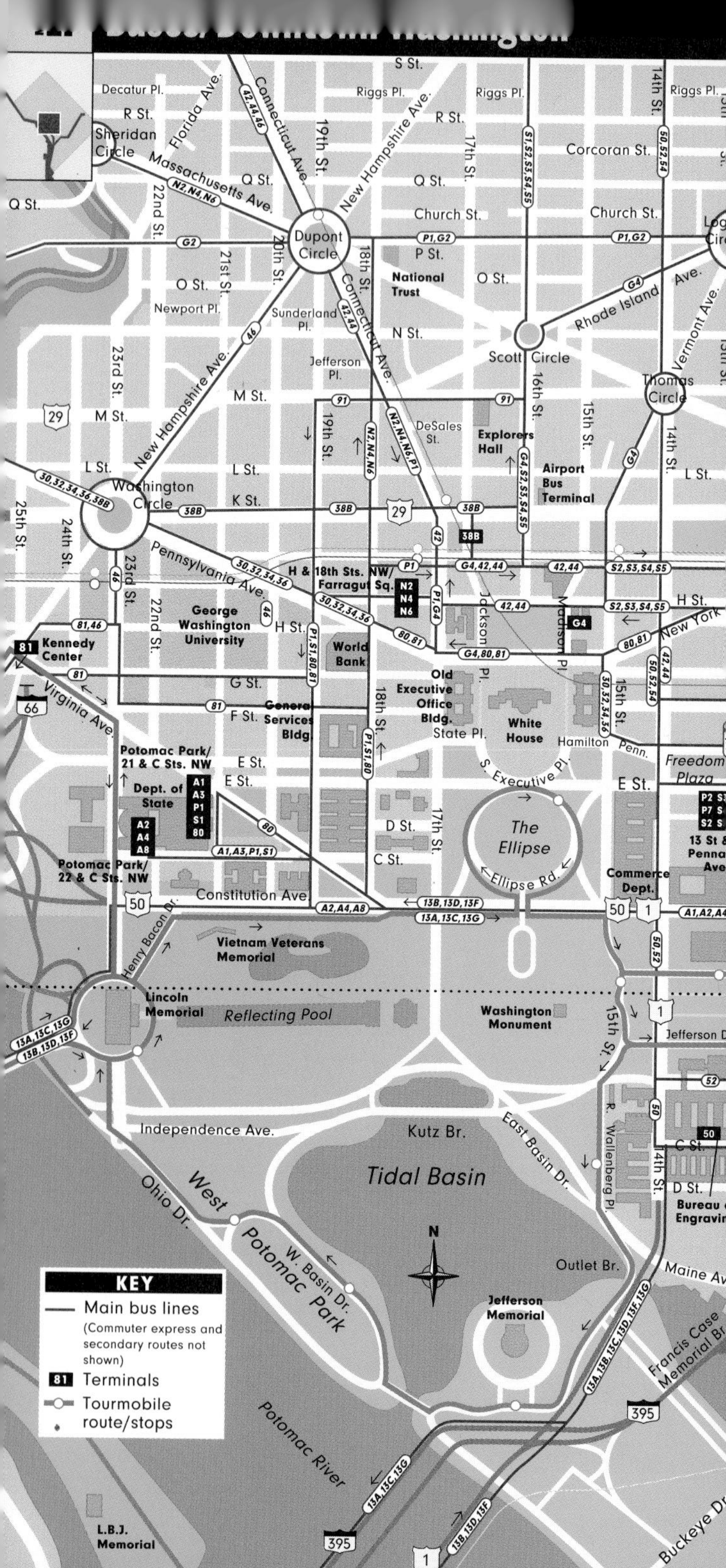
KEY
Main bus lines
(Commuter express and secondary routes not shown)
81 Terminals
Tourmobile route/stops
N
Dupont Circle
Sheridan Circle
Scott Circle
Thomas Circle
Washington Circle
National Trust
Explorers Hall
Airport Bus Terminal
H & 18th Sts. NW/ Farragut Sq.
George Washington University
World Bank
Kennedy Center
Old Executive Office Bldg.
White House
General Services Bldg.
Potomac Park/ 21 & C Sts. NW
Dept. of State
Potomac Park/ 22 & C Sts. NW
The Ellipse
Ellipse Rd.
S. Executive Pl.
Freedom Plaza
13 St & Penna Ave.
Commerce Dept.
Vietnam Veterans Memorial
Lincoln Memorial
Reflecting Pool
Washington Monument
Tidal Basin
Kutz Br.
Outlet Br.
Jefferson Memorial
West Potomac Park
Potomac River
L.B.J. Memorial
Bureau of Engraving
Francis Case Memorial Br.
Constitution Ave.
Independence Ave.
Pennsylvania Ave.
Connecticut Ave.
Massachusetts Ave.
New Hampshire Ave.
Rhode Island Ave.
Vermont Ave.
Virginia Ave.
Florida Ave.
New York
Ohio Dr.
W. Basin Dr.
East Basin Dr.
Henry Bacon Dr.
R. Wallenberg Pl.
Maine Av
Buckeye Dr
Jackson Pl.
Madison Pl.
State Pl.
Hamilton
Jefferson Pl.
DeSales St.
Sunderland Pl.
Newport Pl.
Decatur Pl.
Riggs Pl.
Corcoran St.
Church St.
S St.
R St.
Q St.
P St.
O St.
N St.
M St.
L St.
K St.
H St.
G St.
F St.
E St.
D St.
C St.
14th St.
15th St.
16th St.
17th St.
18th St.
19th St.
20th St.
21st St.
22nd St.
23rd St.
24th St.
25th St.
29
50
66
395
1

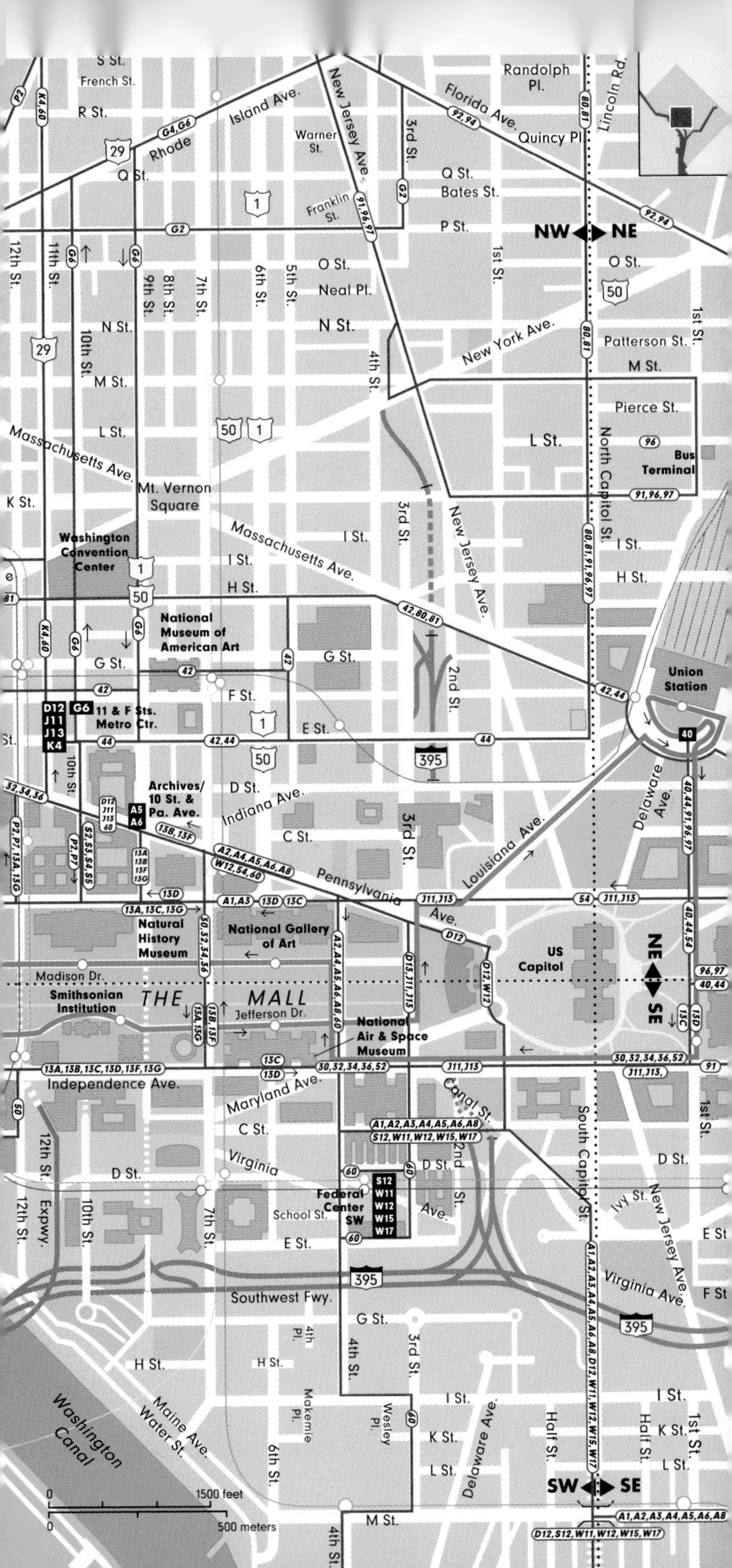

NW NE
NE SE
SW SE
THE MALL
Union Station
US Capitol
National Gallery of Art
National Air & Space Museum
Natural History Museum
Smithsonian Institution
National Museum of American Art
Washington Convention Center
Mt. Vernon Square
11 & F Sts. Metro Ctr.
Archives/ 10 St. & Pa. Ave.
Federal Center SW
Bus Terminal
Washington Canal
Massachusetts Ave.
New York Ave.
Pennsylvania Ave.
Independence Ave.
Maryland Ave.
Louisiana Ave.
Delaware Ave.
New Jersey Ave.
Rhode Island Ave.
Florida Ave.
Virginia Ave.
Maine Ave.
Water St.
Southwest Fwy.
North Capitol St.
South Capitol St.
Madison Dr.
Jefferson Dr.
Indiana Ave.
Canal St.
12th St. Expwy.
1500 feet
500 meters

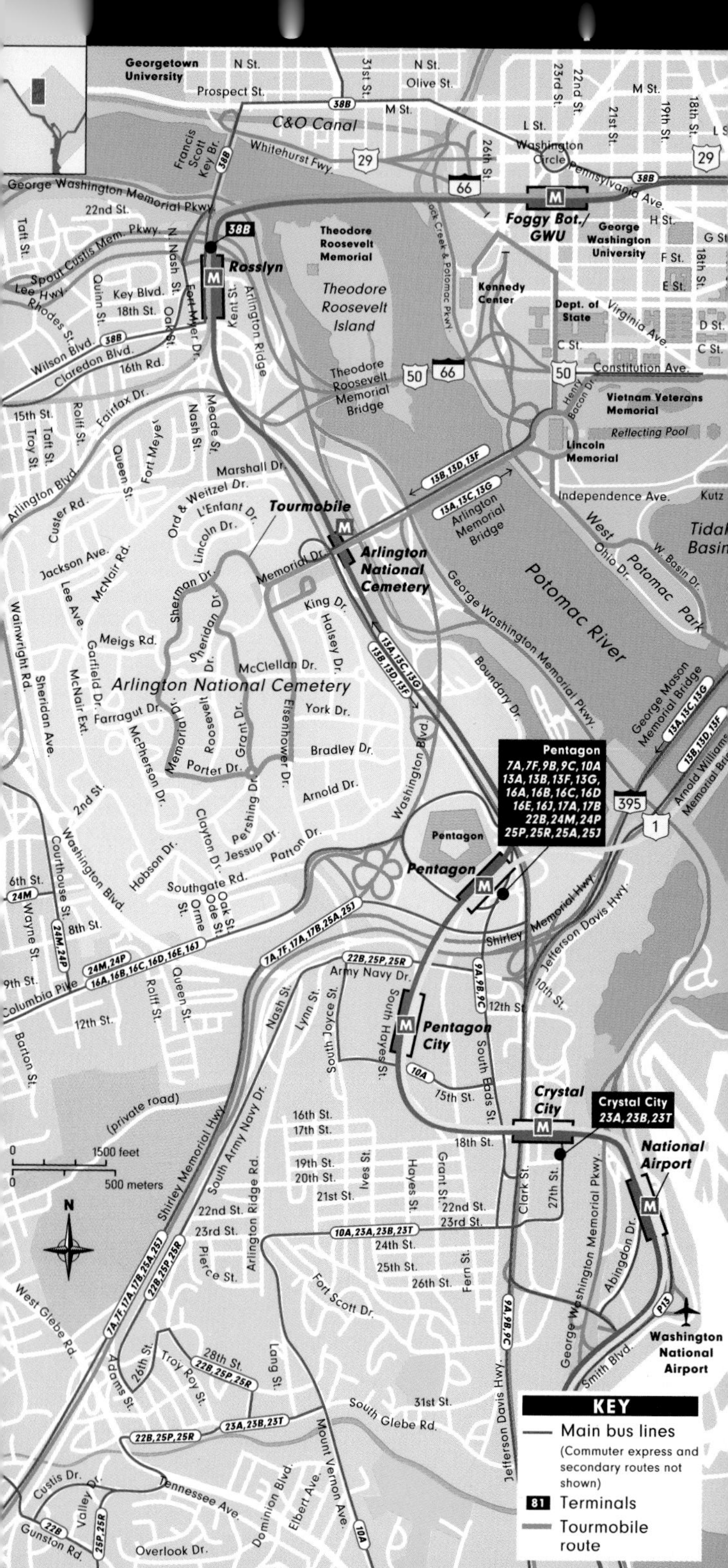

Georgetown University
N St.
Prospect St.
31st St.
Olive St.
M St.
38B
C&O Canal
Francis Scott Key Br.
Whitehurst Fwy.
29
26th St.
L St.
Washington Circle
23rd St.
22nd St.
21st St.
19th St.
18th St.
Pennsylvania Ave.
66
George Washington Memorial Pkwy.
22nd St.
Taft St.
Spout Custis Mem. Pkwy.
N. Nash St.
Rosslyn
Theodore Roosevelt Memorial
Rock Creek & Potomac Pkwy.
Foggy Bot./ GWU
George Washington University
H St.
G St.
F St.
E St.
Lee Hwy.
Rhodes St.
Quinn St.
Key Blvd.
18th St.
Oak St.
Fort Myer Dr.
Kent St.
Arlington Ridge
Theodore Roosevelt Island
Kennedy Center
Dept. of State
Virginia Ave.
D St.
C St.
Wilson Blvd.
Clarendon Blvd.
16th Rd.
Theodore Roosevelt Memorial Bridge
50
Constitution Ave.
Henry Bacon Dr.
Vietnam Veterans Memorial
Reflecting Pool
Lincoln Memorial
15th St.
Rolfe St.
Fairfax Dr.
Taft St.
Troy St.
Queen St.
Fort Meyer
Nash St.
Meade St.
Marshall Dr.
13B,13D,13F
13A,13C,13G
Arlington Memorial Bridge
Independence Ave.
Kutz
Arlington Blvd.
Custer Rd.
Ord & Weitzel Dr.
L'Enfant Dr.
Lincoln Dr.
Tourmobile
Arlington National Cemetery
Memorial Dr.
West Potomac Park
Ohio Dr.
W. Basin Dr.
Tidal Basin
Jackson Ave.
McNair Rd.
Lee Ave.
Sherman Dr.
Sheridan Dr.
King Dr.
Halsey Dr.
George Washington Memorial Pkwy.
Potomac River
Wainwright Rd.
Meigs Rd.
Garfield Dr.
McNair Ext.
Sheridan Ave.
McClellan Dr.
Arlington National Cemetery
Boundary Dr.
George Mason Memorial Bridge
Farragut Dr.
McPherson Dr.
Memorial Dr.
Roosevelt
Grant Dr.
Eisenhower Dr.
York Dr.
Bradley Dr.
Washington Blvd.
Pentagon
7A,7F,9B,9C,10A
13A,13B,13F,13G,
16A,16B,16C,16D
16E,16J,17A,17B
22B,24M,24P
25P,25R,25A,25J
Arnold Williams Memorial Bridge
395
1
Porter Dr.
Pershing Dr.
Arnold Dr.
2nd St.
Clayton Dr.
Jessup Dr.
Patton Dr.
Pentagon
Courthouse St.
Washington Blvd.
Hobson Dr.
Southgate Rd.
6th St.
24M
Wayne St.
8th St.
24M,24P
Orme St.
Ode St.
Oak St.
7A,7F,17A,17B,25A,25J
Shirley Memorial Hwy.
Jefferson Davis Hwy.
Shirley
9th St.
Columbia Pike
16A,16B,16C,16D,16E,16J
Rolfe St.
Queen St.
22B,25P,25R
Army Navy Dr.
9A,9B,9C
12th St.
10th St.
12th St.
Nash St.
Lynn St.
South Joyce St.
South Hayes St.
Pentagon City
South Eads St.
Barton St.
10A
15th St.
Crystal City
Crystal City
23A,23B,23T
(private road)
16th St.
17th St.
18th St.
0
1500 feet
500 meters
Shirley Memorial Hwy.
South Army Navy Dr.
Arlington Ridge Rd.
19th St.
20th St.
21st St.
Ives St.
Hayes St.
Grant St.
Clark St.
27th St.
National Airport
George Washington Memorial Pkwy.
N
22nd St.
23rd St.
22nd St.
23rd St.
10A,23A,23B,23T
24th St.
Abingdon Dr.
7A,7F,17A,17B,25A,25J
22B,25P,25R
Pierce St.
25th St.
26th St.
Fern St.
West Glebe Rd.
Fort Scott Dr.
9A,9B,9C
P13
Washington National Airport
Smith Blvd.
Adams St.
26th St.
28th St.
22B,25P,25R
Troy Roy St.
Lang St.
Jefferson Davis Hwy.
31st St.
South Glebe Rd.
23A,23B,23T
22B,25P,25R
Mount Vernon Ave.
Curtis Dr.
Valley Dr.
Tennessee Ave.
Dominion Blvd.
Elbert Ave.
22B
25P,25R
Gunston Rd.
Overlook Dr.
10A
KEY
Main bus lines
(Commuter express and secondary routes not shown)
81 Terminals
Tourmobile route

Chevy Chase Circle
L2,L4,L5
Friendship Heights
E2,E4,E6,L8,
N1,N2,N6,N8,
T2,T6,
30,32,34,36
Friendship Heights
MARYLAND
D.C.
Fort Reno Park
Tenleytown
37,E7
Tenleytown
Tenley Circle
University of the District of Columbia
Van Ness/ UDC
VanNess/UDC
L6,L7
Howard University Law School
Sunshine Valley Park
Newlands Park
Melvin Park
Sidwell Friends School
Naval Security Station
Glover Archbold Park
McLean Gardens
X3,96
Cleveland Park
Washington Cathedral
Wesley Heights
N3
Glover Park
D1,D2,D6
Naval Observatory
Wisconsin Ave.
Connecticut Ave.
Nebraska Ave.
Massachusetts Ave.
Military Rd.
1200 feet
400 meters
N

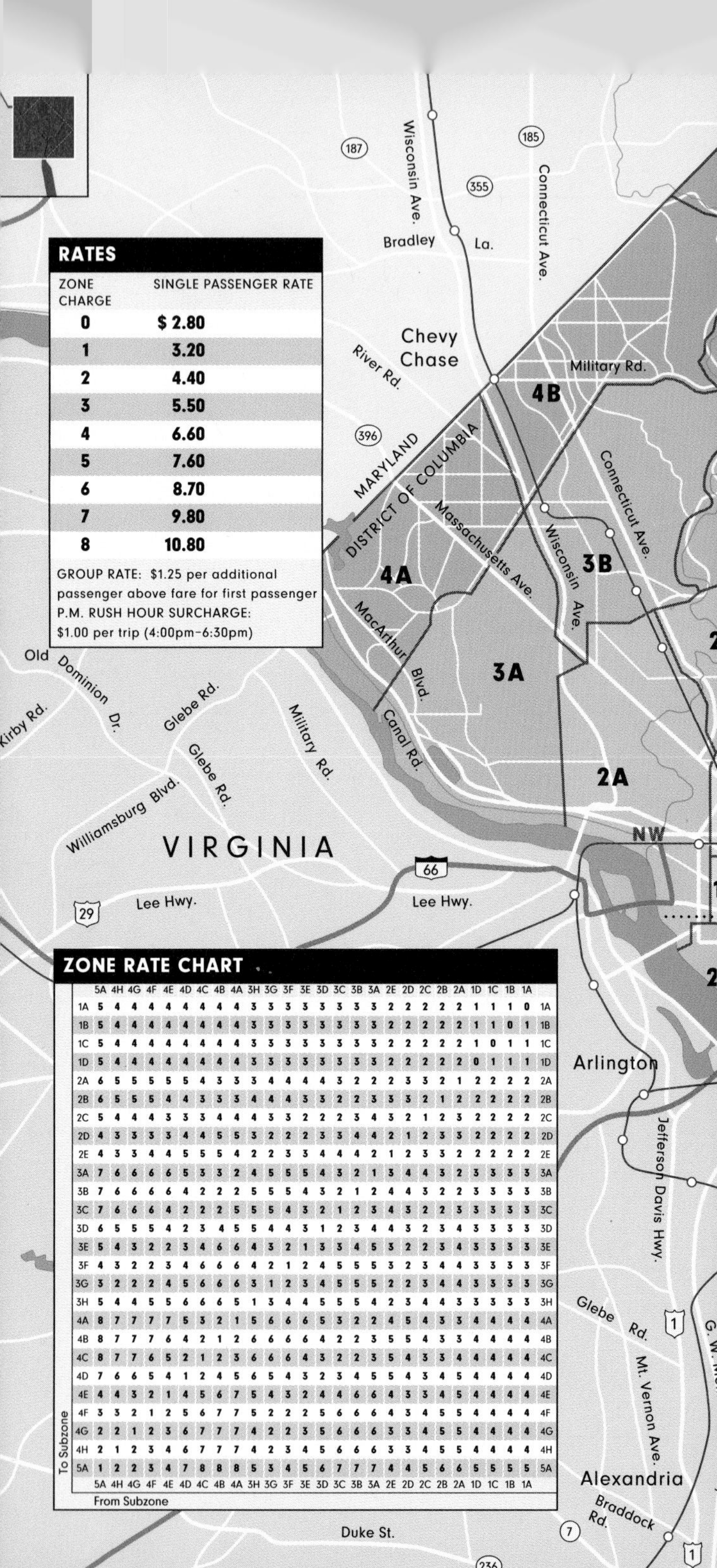

RATES

ZONE CHARGE	SINGLE PASSENGER RATE
0	$ 2.80
1	3.20
2	4.40
3	5.50
4	6.60
5	7.60
6	8.70
7	9.80
8	10.80

GROUP RATE: $1.25 per additional passenger above fare for first passenger

P.M. RUSH HOUR SURCHARGE: $1.00 per trip (4:00pm–6:30pm)

ZONE RATE CHART

To Subzone	5A	4H	4G	4F	4E	4D	4C	4B	4A	3H	3G	3F	3E	3D	3C	3B	3A	2E	2D	2C	2B	2A	1D	1C	1B	1A	
1A	5	4	4	4	4	4	4	4	4	3	3	3	3	3	3	3	3	2	2	2	2	2	1	1	1	0	1A
1B	5	4	4	4	4	4	4	4	4	3	3	3	3	3	3	3	3	2	2	2	2	2	1	1	0	1	1B
1C	5	4	4	4	4	4	4	4	4	3	3	3	3	3	3	3	3	2	2	2	2	2	1	0	1	1	1C
1D	5	4	4	4	4	4	4	4	4	3	3	3	3	3	3	3	3	2	2	2	2	2	0	1	1	1	1D
2A	6	5	5	5	5	5	4	3	3	3	4	4	4	4	3	2	2	2	3	3	2	1	2	2	2	2	2A
2B	6	5	5	5	4	4	3	3	3	4	4	4	3	3	2	2	3	3	3	2	1	2	2	2	2	2	2B
2C	5	4	4	4	3	3	3	4	4	4	3	3	2	2	2	3	4	3	2	1	2	3	2	2	2	2	2C
2D	4	3	3	3	3	4	4	5	5	3	2	2	2	3	3	4	4	2	1	2	3	3	2	2	2	2	2D
2E	4	3	3	4	4	5	5	5	4	2	2	3	3	4	4	4	2	1	2	3	3	2	2	2	2	2	2E
3A	7	6	6	6	6	5	3	3	2	4	5	5	5	4	3	2	1	3	4	4	3	2	3	3	3	3	3A
3B	7	6	6	6	6	4	2	2	2	5	5	5	4	3	2	1	2	4	4	3	2	2	3	3	3	3	3B
3C	7	6	6	6	4	2	2	2	5	5	5	4	3	2	1	2	3	4	3	2	2	3	3	3	3	3	3C
3D	6	5	5	5	4	2	3	4	5	5	4	4	3	1	2	3	4	4	3	2	3	4	3	3	3	3	3D
3E	5	4	3	2	2	3	4	6	6	4	3	2	1	3	3	4	5	3	2	2	3	4	3	3	3	3	3E
3F	4	3	2	2	3	4	6	6	6	4	2	1	2	4	5	5	5	3	2	3	4	4	3	3	3	3	3F
3G	3	2	2	2	4	5	6	6	6	3	1	2	3	4	5	5	5	2	2	3	4	4	3	3	3	3	3G
3H	5	4	4	5	5	6	6	6	5	1	3	4	4	5	5	5	4	2	3	4	4	3	3	3	3	3	3H
4A	8	7	7	7	7	5	3	2	1	5	6	6	6	5	3	2	2	4	5	4	3	3	4	4	4	4	4A
4B	8	7	7	7	6	4	2	1	2	6	6	6	6	4	2	2	3	5	5	4	3	3	4	4	4	4	4B
4C	8	7	7	6	5	2	1	2	3	6	6	6	4	3	2	2	3	5	4	3	3	4	4	4	4	4	4C
4D	7	6	6	5	4	1	2	4	5	6	5	4	3	2	3	4	5	5	4	3	4	5	4	4	4	4	4D
4E	4	4	3	2	1	4	5	6	7	5	4	3	2	4	4	6	6	4	3	3	4	5	4	4	4	4	4E
4F	3	3	2	1	2	5	6	7	7	5	2	2	2	5	6	6	6	4	3	4	5	5	4	4	4	4	4F
4G	2	2	1	2	3	6	7	7	7	4	2	2	3	5	6	6	6	3	3	4	5	5	4	4	4	4	4G
4H	2	1	2	3	4	6	7	7	7	4	2	3	4	5	6	6	6	3	3	4	5	5	4	4	4	4	4H
5A	1	2	2	3	4	7	8	8	8	5	3	4	5	6	7	7	7	4	4	5	6	6	5	5	5	5	5A
	5A	4H	4G	4F	4E	4D	4C	4B	4A	3H	3G	3F	3E	3D	3C	3B	3A	2E	2D	2C	2B	2A	1D	1C	1B	1A	

From Subzone

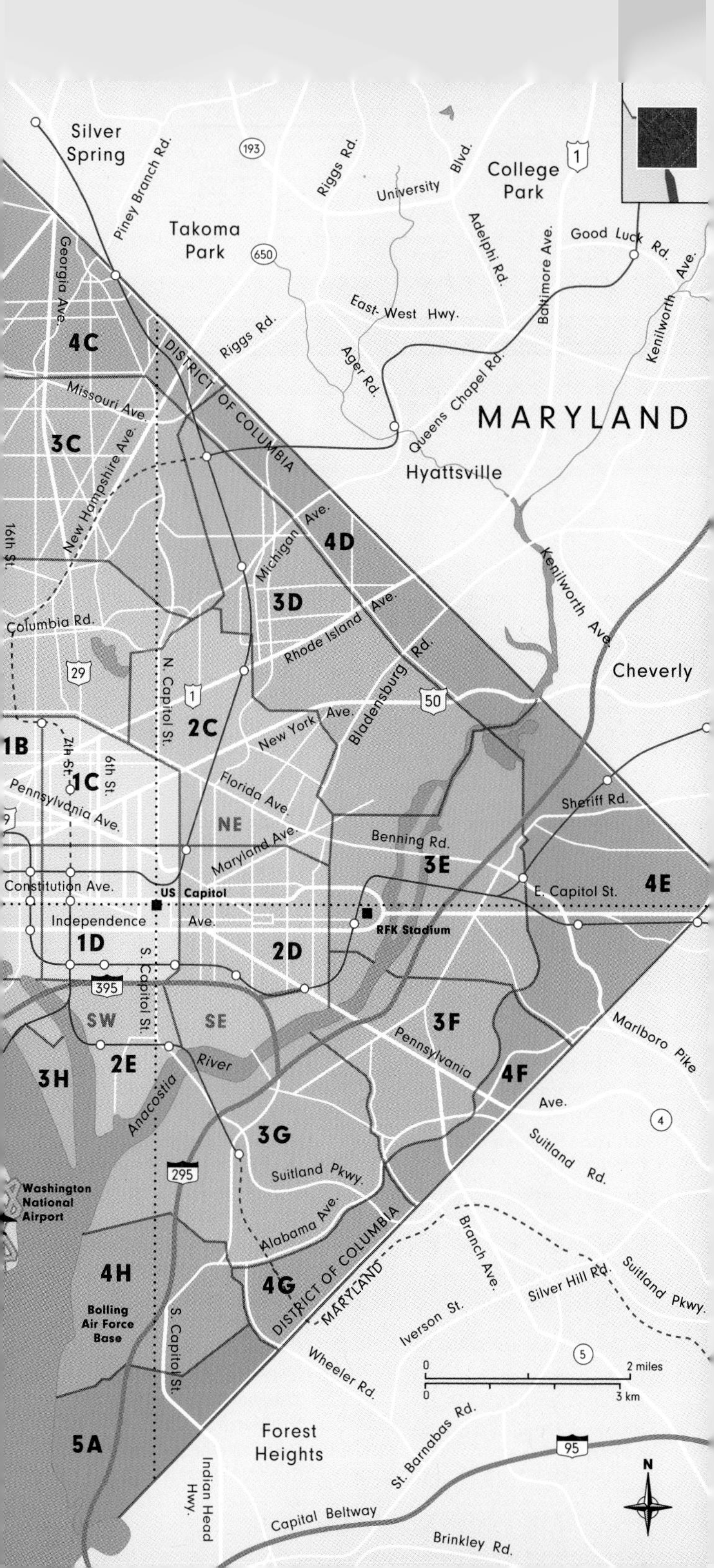

Silver Spring
Takoma Park
College Park
MARYLAND
Hyattsville
Cheverly
DISTRICT OF COLUMBIA
4C
3C
4D
3D
2C
1B
1C
NE
3E
4E
1D
2D
SW
SE
3F
4F
3H
2E
3G
4H
4G
5A
Piney Branch Rd.
Riggs Rd.
University Blvd.
Adelphi Rd.
Baltimore Ave.
Good Luck Rd.
Kenilworth Ave.
East-West Hwy.
Ager Rd.
Queens Chapel Rd.
Georgia Ave.
Missouri Ave.
New Hampshire Ave.
16th St.
Michigan Ave.
Rhode Island Ave.
Bladensburg Rd.
Columbia Rd.
N. Capitol St.
New York Ave.
Florida Ave.
7th St.
6th St.
Pennsylvania Ave.
Maryland Ave.
Benning Rd.
Sheriff Rd.
Constitution Ave.
US Capitol
E. Capitol St.
Independence Ave.
RFK Stadium
S. Capitol St.
Anacostia River
Pennsylvania Ave.
Marlboro Pike
Suitland Rd.
Suitland Pkwy.
Alabama Ave.
Washington National Airport
Bolling Air Force Base
Branch Ave.
Silver Hill Rd.
Iverson St.
Wheeler Rd.
St. Barnabas Rd.
Forest Heights
Indian Head Hwy.
Capital Beltway
Brinkley Rd.
193
650
1
29
50
395
295
95
4
5
0
2 miles
3 km
N

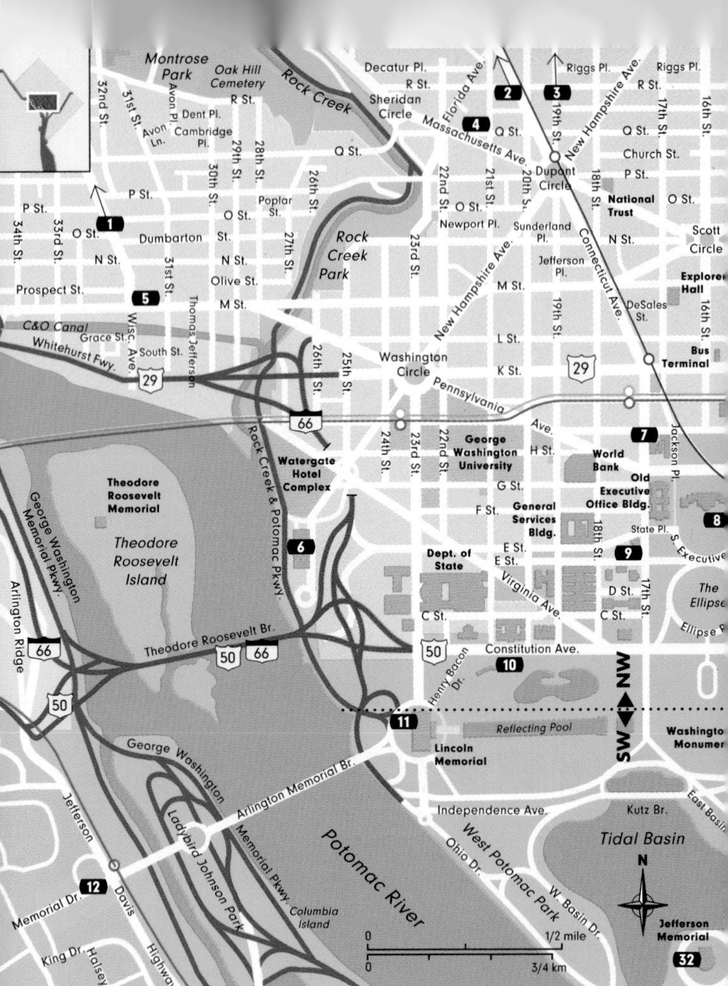

Listed Alphabetically

Adams-Morgan, 3.
Columbia Rd & 18th St NW

Arlington National Cemetery, 12.
Arlington, VA

Bureau of Engraving & Printing, 24.
1400 C St SW

Corcoran Gallery of Art, 9.
New York Ave & 17th St NW

Ford's Theatre, 15. 511 10th St NW

Freer Gallery, 25.
Jefferson Dr & 12th St SW

Georgetown, 5.
Wisconsin Ave & M St NW

Hirshhorn Museum & Sculpture Gardens, 28.
Independence Ave & 7th St SW

Jefferson Memorial, 32.
W Potomac Park SW

Kennedy Center, 6. New Hampshire Ave & Rock Creek Pkwy NW

Lincoln Memorial, 11.
Potomac Park SW

National Air & Space Museum, 29.
Independence Ave & 6th St SW

National Arboretum, 14.
3501 New York Ave NE

National Archives, 22.
Constitution Ave & 8th St NW

National Building Museum (Pension Bldg), 18. F & 4th Sts NW

National Gallery of Art, 30.
Constitution Ave & 7th St NW

Listed Alphabetically (cont.)

National Museum of African Art, 27.
950 Independence Ave SW

National Museum of American Art, 16. G & 8th Sts NW

National Museum of American History, 20. Constitution Ave & 14th St NW

National Museum of Natural History, 21. Constitution Ave & 10th St NW

National Museum of Women in the Arts, 13. 1250 New York Ave NW

National Portrait Gallery, 17.
F & 8th Sts NW

National Zoo, 2.
3000 Connecticut Ave NW

Pentagon, 33. off I-395, Arlington, VA

Phillips Collection, 4. 1600 21st StNW

Renwick Gallery, 7.
Pennsylvania Ave & 17th St NW

Smithsonian Castle, 26.
1000 Jefferson Dr SW

Union Station, 19.
50 Massachusetts Ave & 1st St NE

US Capitol, 31. 1 1st St NE

US Holocaust Memorial Museum, 23.
200 Raoul Wallenberg Pl SW

Vietnam Veterans Memorial, 10.
Constitution Ave & 21st St NW

Washington National Cathedral, 1.
Wisconsin & Massachusetts Aves NW

White House, 8.
1600 Pennsylvania Ave NW

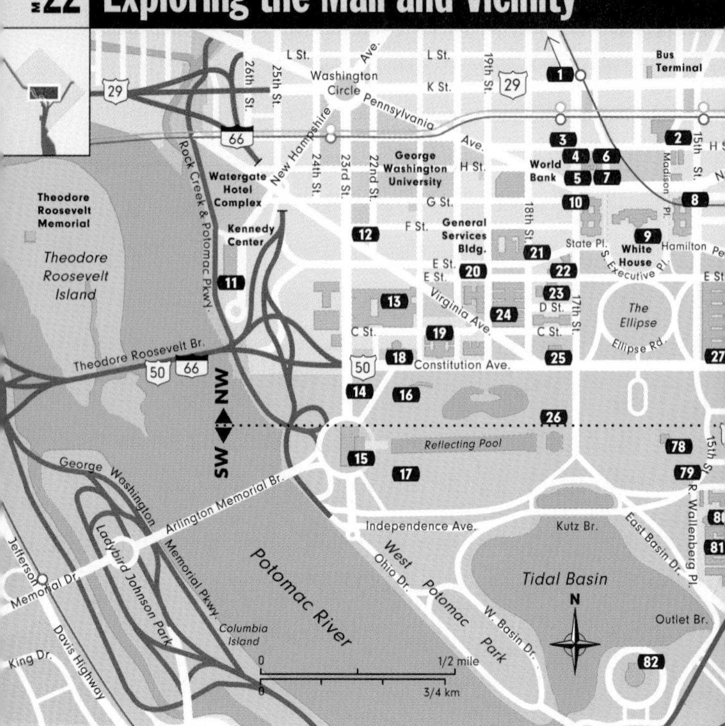

Listed by Site Number

1 Church Street Theatre
2 Veterans Admin
3 Wilderness Society
4 New Executive Office Building
5 Renwick Gallery
6 Decatur House
7 Blair House
8 Treasury
9 White House
10 Old Executive Office Building
11 Kennedy Center
12 Pan American Health Organization
13 State Department
14 Vietnam Women's Memorial
15 Lincoln Memorial
16 Vietnam Veterans Memorial
17 Korean War Veteran's Memorial
18 National Academy of Sciences
19 Federal Reserve
20 Civil Service
21 Octagon House
22 Corcoran Gallery
23 DAR Museum
24 Dept of the Interior
25 Organization of American States
26 Constitution Gardens
27 Dept of Commerce
28 Customs Service
29 Interstate Commerce Commission
30 National Museum of American History
31 National Museum of Natural History
32 National Gallery of Art W
33 National Gallery of Art E
34 Department of Labor
35 US Courthouse
36 Federal Trade Commission
37 National Archives
38 Justice Department
39 Internal Revenue Service
40 The Pavilion-Old Post Office
41 FBI
42 Ford's Theatre
43 National Portrait Gallery
44 National Museum of American Art
45 DC Government
46 Alcohol, Tobacco & Firearms
47 Capital Children's Museum
48 Government Printing Office
49 National Capital Post Office
50 Union Station
51 National Building Museum
52 DC Superior Court
53 Executive Office of the Mayor
54 US Tax Court
55 Hart Senate Office Building

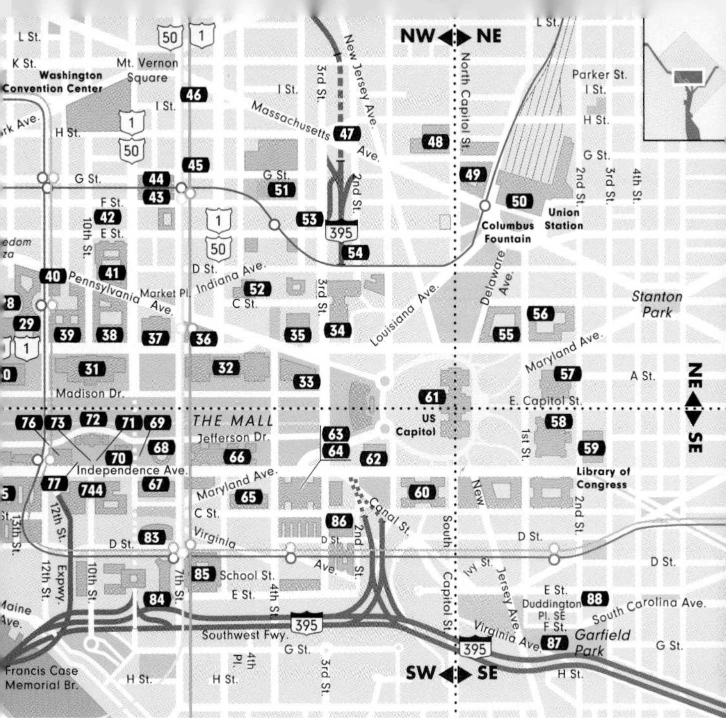

Listed by Site Number (cont.)

55 Russell Senate Office Building

56 Dirksen Senate Office Building

57 Supreme Court

58 Library of Congress

59 Folger Shakespeare Library

60 Rayburn House Office Building

61 US Capitol

62 US Botanic Gardens

63 Voice of America

64 Department of Health & Human Services

65 Education Department

66 National Air & Space Museum

67 Federal Aviation Administration

68 Hirshhorn Museum

69 Sculpture Gardens

70 Arts and Industries Building

71 National Museum of African Art

72 Smithsonian Castle

73 Enid Haupt Memorial Garden

74 Energy Department/ Forrestal Building

75 Department of Agriculture

76 Freer Gallery

77 Sackler Gallery

78 Washington Monument

79 Sylvan Theater

80 US Holocaust Memorial Museum

81 Bureau of Engraving & Printing

82 Jefferson Memorial

83 General Services Administration

84 Department of Housing & Urban Development

85 Department of Transportation

86 Food & Drug Administration

87 Cannon House Office Building

88 National Aeronautics & Space Administration

Listed Alphabetically

Alcohol, Tobacco & Firearms, 45. 650 Massachusetts Ave NW ☎ 927-7777

Arts and Industries Bldg, 69. 900 Jefferson Dr SW ☎ 357-2700

Blair House, 7. 1651 Pennsylvania Ave NW ☎ 879-7880

Bureau of Engraving & Printing, 80. 1400 C St SW ☎ 622-2000

Cannon House Office Building, 86. 25 Independence Ave SE ☎ 224-3121

Capital Children's Museum, 46. 800 3rd St NE ☎ 543-8600

Church Street Theatre, 1. 1742 Church St NW ☎ 265-3767

Civil Service, 19. 1900 E St NW ☎ 606-0500

Constitution Gardens, 25. Between Washington Monument & Lincoln Memorial

Corcoran Gallery, 21. New York Ave & 17th St NW ☎ 638-3211

Customs Service, 27. 1301 Constitution Ave NW ☎ 927-6724

DAR Museum, 22. 1776 D St NW ☎ 879-3254

DC Government, 44. 613 G St NW ☎ 727-1000

DC Superior Court, 51. 500 Indiana Ave NW ☎ 879-1010

Decatur House, 6. 748 Jackson Pl NW ☎ 842-0920

Department of Agriculture, 74. 1200 Independence Ave SW ☎ 720-2791

Department of Commerce, 26. 1400 Constitution Ave NW ☎ 482-2000

Department of Health & Human Services, 63. 200 Independence Ave SW ☎ 619-0257

Department of Housing & Urban Development, 83. 451 7th St SW ☎ 708-1422

Department of the Interior, 23. 1849 C St NW ☎ 208-3100

Department of Labor, 33. 200 Constitution Ave NW ☎ 219-6666

Department of Transportation, 84. 400 7th St SW ☎ 366-4000

Dirksen Senate Office Building, 55. 100 Constitution Ave NE ☎ 224-3121

Education Department, 64. 400 Maryland Ave SW ☎ 401-2000

Energy Dept/Forrestal Building, 73. 1000 Independence Ave SW ☎ 586-5000

Enid Haupt Memorial Garden, 72. 1050 Independence Ave SW ☎ 357-2700

Executive Office of the Mayor, 52. 411 4th St NW ☎ 727-2980

FBI, 40. 900 Pennsylvania Ave NW ☎ 324-3000

Federal Aviation Administration, 66. 800 Independence Ave SW ☎ 366-4000

Federal Reserve, 18. 2000 Constitution Ave NW ☎ 452-3000

Federal Trade Commission, 35. 600 Pennsylvania Ave NW ☎ 326-2222

Folger Shakespeare Library, 58. 201 E Capitol St SE ☎ 544-4600

Food & Drug Administration, 85. 200 C St SW ☎ 301/443-1544

Ford's Theatre, 41. 511 10th St NW ☎ 426-6924

Freer Gallery, 75. Jefferson Dr & 12th St SW ☎ 357-2700

General Services Administration, 82. 700 D St SW ☎ 708-5082

Government Printing Office, 47. 732 N Capitol St NW ☎ 512-0000

Hart Senate Office Building, 54. 120 Constitution Ave NE ☎ 224-3121

Hirshhorn Museum, 67. Independence Ave & 7th St SW ☎ 357-2700

Internal Revenue Service, 38. 1111 Constitution Ave NW ☎ 622-5000

Interstate Commerce Commission, 28. 1200 Constitution Ave NW ☎ 927-7600

Jefferson Memorial, 81. W Potomac Park SW ☎ 426-6821

Justice Department, 37. 900 Constitution Ave NW ☎ 514-2000

Kennedy Center, 11. New Hampshire Ave & Rock Creek Pkwy ☎ 467-4600

Korean War Veteran's Memorial, 17. W. Potomac Park SW ☎ 426-6841

Library of Congress, 57. 10 Independence Ave SE ☎ 707-5000

Lincoln Memorial, 15. W Potomac Park SW ☎ 426-6841

National Academy of Sciences, 17. 2101 Constitution Ave NW ☎ 334-2000

Listed Alphabetically (cont.)

National Aeronautics & Space Administration, 87. 300 E St SE ☎ 358-0000

National Air & Space Museum, 65. Independence Ave & 6th St SW ☎ 357-2700

National Archives, 36. 800 Constitution Ave NW ☎ 501-5402

National Building Museum (Pension Bldg), 50. 401 F St NW ☎ 272-2448

National Capital Post Office, 48. 2 Massachusetts Ave NE ☎ 523-2628

National Gallery of Art E, 32. Constitution Ave & 4th St NW ☎ 737-4215

National Gallery of Art W, 31. Constitution Ave & 6th St NW ☎ 737-4215

National Museum of African Art, 70. 950 Independence Ave SW ☎ 357-2700

National Museum of American Art, 43. G & 8th Sts NW ☎ 357-2700

National Museum of American History, 29. Constitution Ave & 14th St NW ☎ 357-2700

National Museum of Natural History, 30. Constitution Ave & 10th St NW ☎ 357-2700

National Portrait Gallery, 42. F & 8th Sts NW ☎ 357-2700

New Executive Office Building, 4. 725 17th St NW ☎ 395-3000

Octagon House, 20. 1799 New York Ave NW ☎ 638-3105

Old Executive Office Building, 10. 1700 Pennsylvania Ave NW ☎ 395-3000

Organization of American States, 24. Constitution Ave & 19th St NW ☎ 458-6037

Pan American Health Organization, 12. 525 23rd St NW ☎ 861-3200

The Pavilion-Old Post Office, 39. 1100 Pennsylvania Ave NW ☎ 289-4224

Rayburn House Office Building, 59. 50 Independence Ave SW ☎ 224-3121

Renwick Gallery, 5. Pennsylvania Ave & 17th St NW ☎ 357-2700

Russell Senate Office Building, 54. 120 Constitution Ave NE ☎ 224-3121

Sackler Gallery, 76. 1050 Independence Ave SW ☎ 357-2700

Sculpture Gardens, 68. Independence Ave & 8th St NW ☎ 357-2700

Smithsonian Castle, 71. 1000 Jefferson Dr SW ☎ 357-2700

State Dept, 13. 2201 C St NW ☎ 647-4000

Supreme Court, 56. 1 First Ave NE ☎ 479-3000

Sylvan Theater, 78. Independence Ave & 15th St SW ☎ 426-6841

Treasury, 8. 1500 Pennsylvania Ave NW ☎ 622-2000

Union Station, 49. 50 Massachusetts Ave NE ☎ 371-9441

US Botanic Gardens, 61. Maryland Ave & First St SW ☎ 225-8333

US Capitol, 60. 1 First St NW ☎ 224-3121

US Courthouse, 34. 333 Constitution Ave NW ☎ 273-0300

US Holocaust Memorial Museum, 79. 200 Raoul Wallenberg Pl SW ☎ 488-0400

US Tax Court, 53. 400 2nd St NW ☎ 606-8700

Veterans Administration, 2. 810 Vermont Ave NW ☎ 273-5400

Vietnam Veterans Memorial, 16. Constitution Ave & 21st St NW ☎ 426-6841

Vietnam Women's Memorial, 14. Constitution Gardens, Constitution Ave & 23rd St NW ☎ 426-6841

Voice of America, 62. 330 Independence Ave SW ☎ 619-4700

Washington Monument, 77. The Mall & 15th St NW ☎ 426-6841

White House, 9. 1600 Pennsylvania Ave NW ☎ 456-7041

Wilderness Society, 3. 900 17th St NW ☎ 833-2300

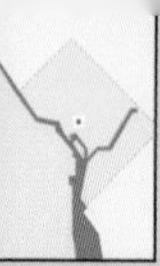

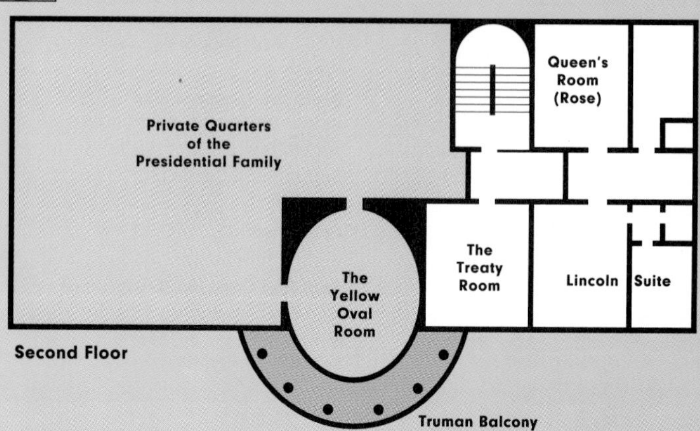

Second Floor

Main Floor

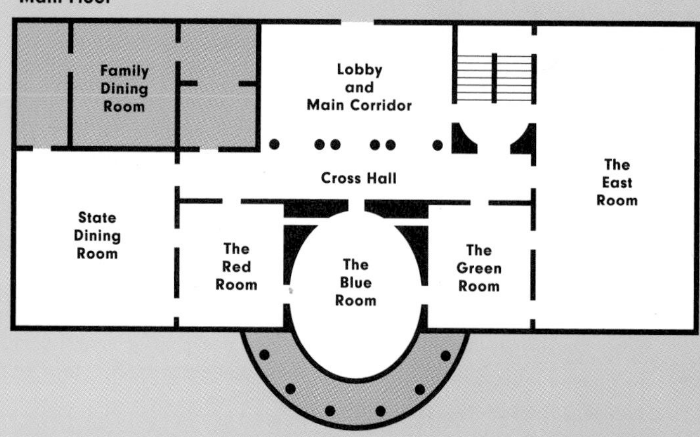

Ground Floor

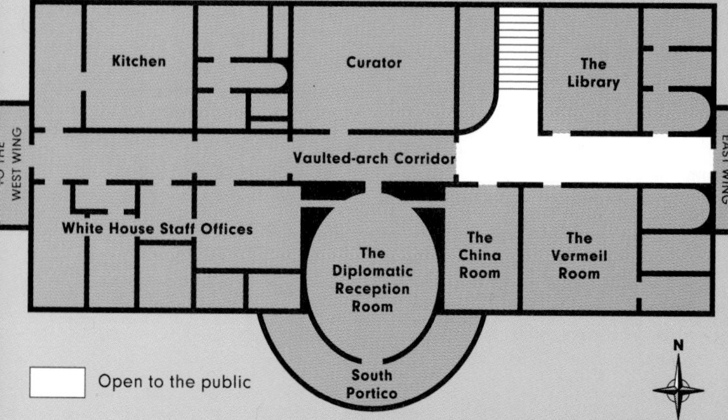

Open to the public

1
2
3
4
5
6
7
8
9
10
11
12
13
14
15
16
17
18
N
Open to public
0
60 feet
0
20 meters

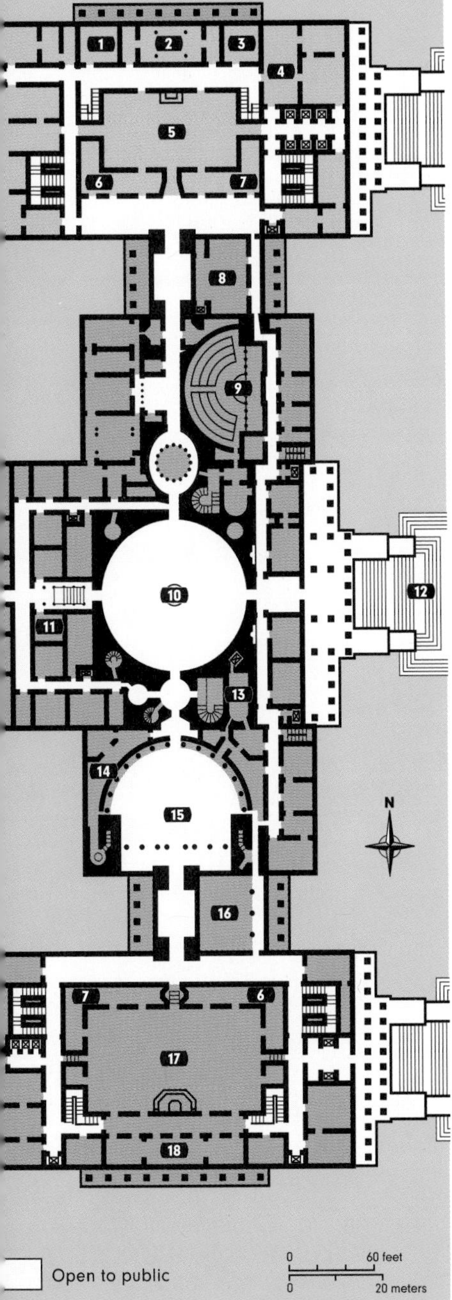

Listed by Site Number

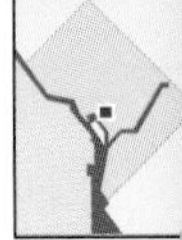

1 President's Room

2 Marble room (Senators' Retiring Room)

3 Ceremonial Office of the Vice President

4 Senators' Reception Room

5 Senate Chamber

6 Democratic Cloakrooms

7 Republican Cloakrooms

8 Senators' Conference Room

9 Old Senate Chamber

10 Rotunda

11 Prayer Room

12 East Front

13 Congresswomen's Suite

14 House Document Room

15 Statuary Hall

16 House Reception Room

17 House Chamber

18 Representatives' Retiring Rooms

Calvert St.
Lanier Pl.
Columbia Rd.
Fuller St.
14th St.
Fairmont St.
11th St.
Sherman Ave.
Georgia Ave.
Euclid St.
Euclid St.
9th St.
Biltmore St.
Ontario
17th St.
Clifton St.
Clifton St.
Mintwood Rd.
Champlain St.
Kalorama Rd.
Chapin St.
Belmont St.
Belmont Rd.
Mintwood Rd.
Crescent Pl.
Belmont St.
Barry Pl.
Ashmead Pl.
Belmont St.
Florida Ave.
Kalorama Circle
W St.
8th St.
Kalorama Rd.
15th St.
V St.
Wyoming Ave.
Columbia
California St.
Seaton Pl.
Wyoming Ave.
23rd St.
Vernon St.
Seaton St.
U St.
Willard St.
Caroline St.
Wallach St.
12th St.
California
T St.
T St.
24th St.
Bancroft Pl.
Bancroft Pl.
Ave.
Swann St.
New Hampshire Ave.
16th St.
Swann St.
S St.
S St.
Decatur Pl.
Florida
Riggs Pl.
Riggs Pl.
Johnson Ave.
14th St.
Riggs Pl.
13th St.
Vermont Ave.
French St.
R St.
R St.
R St.
Sheridan Circle
19th St.
17th St.
Corcoran St.
29
Massachusetts Ave.
Q St.
Q St.
Q St.
Q St.
Church St.
Church St.
Logan Circle
Ave.
26th St.
22nd St.
21st St.
20th St.
Dupont Circle
P St.
18th St.
Rock Creek
O St.
National Trust
O St.
Rhode Island
Newport Pl.
Sunderland Pl.
Scott Circle
13th St.
12th St.
11th St.
10th St.
9th St.
8th St.
7th St.
23rd St.
N St.
N St.
Jefferson Pl.
29
Connecticut Ave.
New Hampshire Ave.
M St.
M St.
16th St.
15th St.
Thomas Circle
M St.
M St.
DeSales St.
Explorers Hall
Massachusetts Ave.
L St.
50
19th St.
L St.
L St.
L St.
Bus Terminal
26th St.
25th St.
Washington Circle
K St.
29
K St.
Washington Convention Center
Mt. Vernon Square
Pennsylvania Ave.
66
24th St.
23rd St.
22nd St.
George Washington University
H St.
World Bank
Jackson Pl.
Madison Pl.
15th St.
H St.
New York Ave.
H St.
1
50
Watergate Hotel Complex
G St.
14th St.
G St.
Kennedy Center
F St.
General Services Bldg.
18th St.
State Pl.
White House
Hamilton
F St.
10th St.
E St.
Penn. Freedom Plaza
E St.
E St.
Dept. of State
E St.
E St.
Executive Pl.
E St.
D St.
Pennsylvania
Market Pl.
Ave.
Virginia Ave.
D St.
17th St.
The Ellipse
C St.
C St.
Ellipse Rd.
66
50
Constitution Ave.
Commerce Dept.
50
1
Henry Bacon Dr.
Vietnam Veterans Memorial
NW
National Museum of American History
Natural History Museum
Madison Dr.
Smithsonian Institution
THE
Reflecting Pool
SW
1
Washington Monument
Lincoln Memorial
15th St.
Jefferson Dr.
Independence Ave.
Arlington Memorial Br.
R. Wallenberg Pl.
Independence Ave.
Kutz Br.
East Basin Dr.
C St.
14th St.
13th St.
12th St.
D St.
D St.
D St.
Ohio Dr.
West
Tidal Basin
Expwy.
12th St.
10th St.
7th St.
Potomac
W. Basin Dr.
Outlet Br.
Maine Ave.
Columbia Island
Park
Jefferson Memorial
Potomac River
H St.
Francis Case Memorial Br.
395
Maine Ave.
Water St.
Washington Canal
Boundary Dr.
L.B.J. Memorial
East Potomac Park
Buckeye Dr.
395
1
N
0
1500 feet
0
500 meters
Pentagon
1
2
3
4
5
6
7
8
9
10
11
12
13
14
15
19
20
21
22
23
24
25
27
28
29
30
31
32
33
37
38
39
40
41
44
45

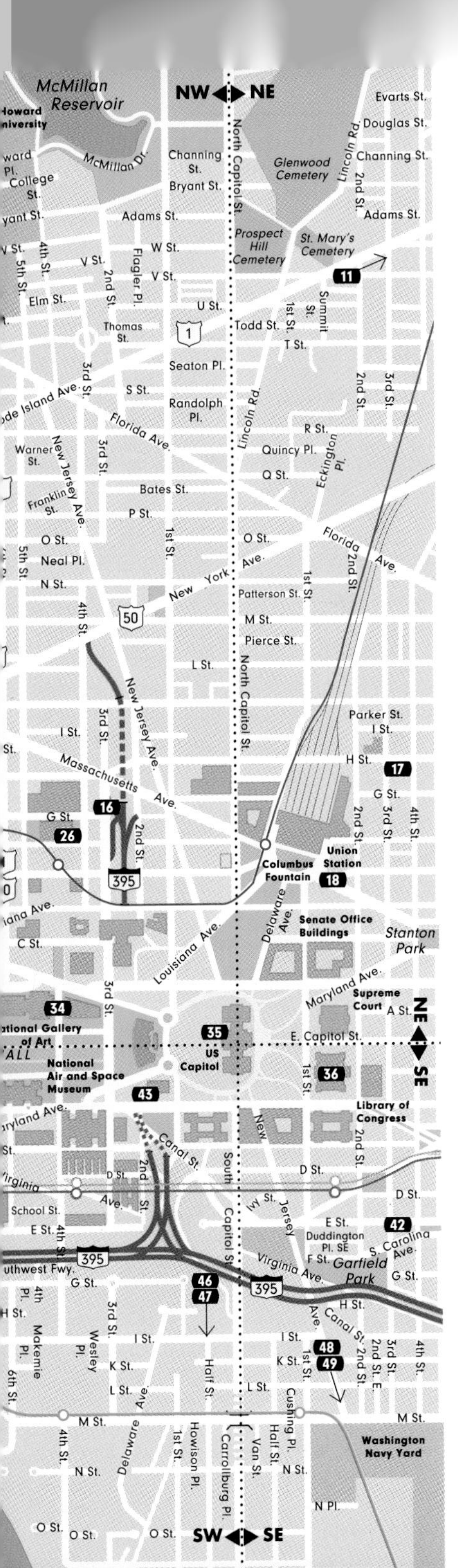

Listed by Site Number

1 Nat'l Zoo Park
2 Hillwood
3 Dolls' House & Toy
4 Naval Observatory
5 Textile
6 W Wilson House
7 Dumbarton Oaks
8 Phillips Collection
9 Jewish War Veterans
10 B'nai B'rith Klutznick
11 Nat'l Geographic
12 Bethune
13 Renwick Gallery
14 Decatur House
15 Women in Arts
16 Jewish Hist Soc
17 Nat'l Learning Ctr
18 Nat'l Postal Museum
19 Octagon House
20 White House
21 Corcoran Gallery
22 American Art
23 Nat'l Portrait Gallery
24 Ford's Theatre
25 FBI
26 National Building
27 Dept of the Interior
28 DAR
29 Mod Latin Amer Art
30 National Aquarium
31 American History
32 Natural History
33 National Archives
34 Nat'l Gallery of Art
35 US Capitol
36 Library of Congress
37 Smithsonian (Info)
38 Sackler Gallery
39 African Art
40 American Indian
40 Arts and Industries
41 Hirshhorn
42 Air & Space
43 US Botanic Gardens
44 US Holocaust Mem
45 Engraving & Printing
46 Anacostia
47 Frederick Douglass
48 Marine Corps
49 Navy

Listed Alphabetically

African Art (Nat'l Mus), 39. 950 Independence Ave SW ☎ 357-2700

Air & Space (National Museum), 42. Independence Ave & 6th St SW ☎ 357-2700

American Art (National Museum), 22. G & 8th Sts NW ☎ 357-2700

American History (National Museum), 31. Constitution Ave & 14th St NW ☎ 357-2700

American Indian (National Museum), 40. 900 Jefferson Dr SW ☎ 357-1300

Anacostia, 46. 1901 Fort Pl SE ☎ 287-3369

Arts and Industries, 40. 900 Jefferson Dr SW ☎ 357-2700

B'nai B'rith Klutznick, 10. 1640 Rhode Island Ave NW ☎ 857-6583

Bethune, 12. 1318 Vermont Ave NW ☎ 332-1233

Bureau of Engraving & Printing, 45. 1400 C St SW ☎ 622-2000

Corcoran Gallery, 21. New York Ave & 17th St NW ☎ 638-3211

DAR, 28. 1776 D St NW ☎ 879-3254

Decatur House, 14. 748 Jackson Pl NW ☎ 842-0920

Department of the Interior, 27. 1849 C St NW ☎ 208-3100

Dolls' House & Toy, 3. 5236 44th St NW ☎ 244-0024

Dumbarton Oaks, 7. 1703 32nd St NW ☎ 339-6401

FBI, 25. Pennsylvania Ave & 9th St NW ☎ 324-3000

Ford's Theatre, 27. 511 10th St NW ☎ 426-6924

Frederick Douglass Nat'l Historic Site, 47. 1411 W St SE ☎ 426-5961

Hillwood, 2. 4155 Linnean Ave NW ☎ 686-5807

Hirshhorn, 41. Independence Ave & 7th St SW ☎ 357-2700

Jewish Historical Society, 16. 701 3rd St NW ☎ 789-0900

Jewish War Veterans National Memorial, 9. 1811 R St NW ☎ 265-6280

Library of Congress, 36. 101 Independence Ave SE ☎ 707-5000

Marine Corps, 48. Navy Yard, M & 9th Sts SE ☎ 433-3534

Museum of Modern Latin American Art, 29. 201 18th St NW ☎ 458-6019

Nat'l Aquarium, 30. Constitution Ave & 14th St NW ☎ 482-2825

Nat'l Archives, 33. Constitution Ave & 8th St NW ☎ 501-5402

National Building (Pension Bldg), 26. 401 F St NW ☎ 272-2448

Nat'l Gallery of Art, 34. Constitution Ave & 6th St NW ☎ 737-4215

National Geographic, 11. M & 17th Sts NW ☎ 857-7588

National Learning Center, 17. 800 3rd St NE ☎ 543-8600

National Portrait Gallery, 23. F & 8th Sts NW ☎ 357-2700

National Postal Museum, 18. 1st & Massachusetts Aves NE ☎ 357-1300

National Zoological Park, 1. 3001 Connecticut Ave NW ☎ 673-4800

Natural History (National Museum), 32. Constitution Ave & 10th St NW ☎ 357-2700

Naval Observatory, 4. Massachusetts Ave & 34th St NW ☎ 653-1507

Navy, 49. Navy Yard, M & 9th Sts SE ☎ 433-2651

Octagon House, 19. 1799 New York Ave NW ☎ 638-3105

Phillips Collection, 8. 1600 21st St NW ☎ 387-2151

Renwick Gallery, 13. Pennsylvania Ave & 17th St NW ☎ 357-2700

Sackler Gallery, 38. 1050 Independence Ave SW ☎ 357-2700

Smithsonian Institution (Info Ctr), 37. 1000 Jefferson Dr NW ☎ 357-2700

Textile, 5. 2320 S St NW ☎ 667-0441

US Botanic Gardens, 43. Maryland Ave & 1st St SW ☎ 225-8333

US Capitol, 38. 1st St NW ☎ 224-3121

US Holocaust Memorial, 44. 200 Raoul Wallenberg Pl SW ☎ 488-0400

White House, 20. 1600 Pennsylvania Ave NW ☎ 456-7041

Women in Arts (National Museum), 15. 1250 New York Ave NW ☎ 783-5000

Woodrow Wilson House, 6. 2340 S St NW ☎ 387-4062

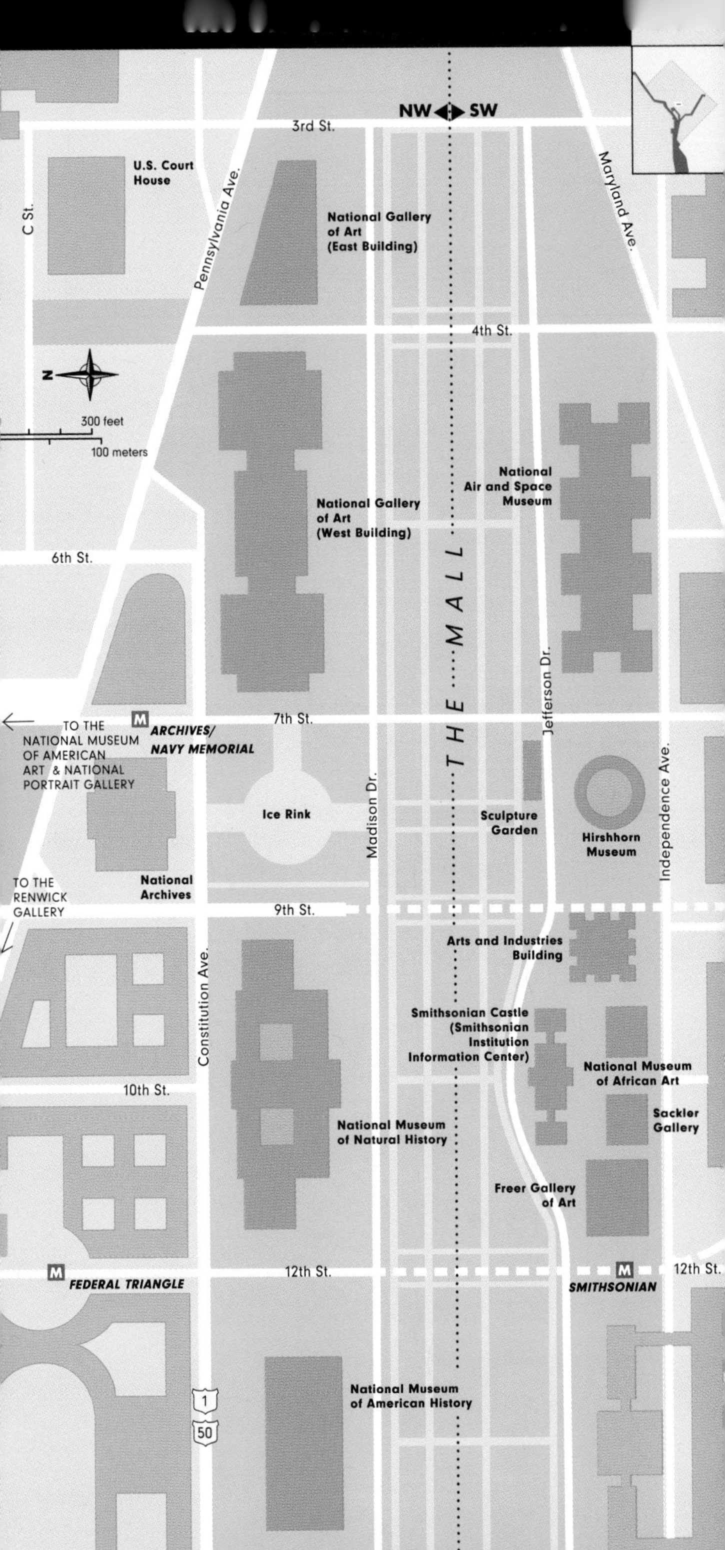

NW SW
3rd St.
U.S. Court House
C St.
Pennsylvania Ave.
National Gallery of Art (East Building)
Maryland Ave.
4th St.
N
300 feet
100 meters
National Air and Space Museum
National Gallery of Art (West Building)
6th St.
THE MALL
Jefferson Dr.
TO THE NATIONAL MUSEUM OF AMERICAN ART & NATIONAL PORTRAIT GALLERY
M
ARCHIVES/ NAVY MEMORIAL
7th St.
Madison Dr.
Independence Ave.
Ice Rink
Sculpture Garden
Hirshhorn Museum
TO THE RENWICK GALLERY
National Archives
9th St.
Arts and Industries Building
Constitution Ave.
Smithsonian Castle (Smithsonian Institution Information Center)
National Museum of African Art
10th St.
Sackler Gallery
National Museum of Natural History
Freer Gallery of Art
M
FEDERAL TRIANGLE
12th St.
M
12th St.
SMITHSONIAN
1
50
National Museum of American History

National Gallery of Art/West Building

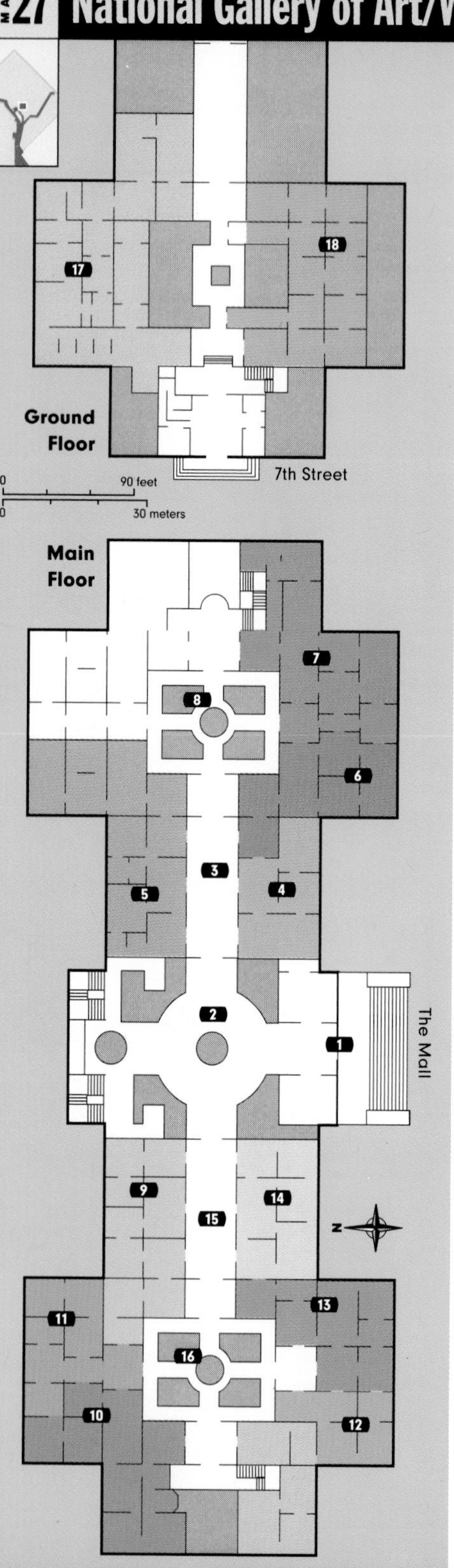

Listed by Site Number

1 Mall Entrance
2 Rotunda
3 East Sculpture Hall
4 French Painting (17th & 18th Century)
5 French Painting (19th Century)
6 British Painting
7 American Painting
8 East Garden Court
9 Renaissance Painting (Florence & Central Italy)
10 Renaissance Painting (Venice & Northern Italy)
11 Italian Furniture & Sculpture
12 Italian Painting (17th & 18th Century)
13 Spanish Painting
14 Flemish & German Painting
15 Dutch Painting
16 West Sculpture Hall
17 European Sculpture (West Garden Court)
18 Sculpture & Decorative Arts

National

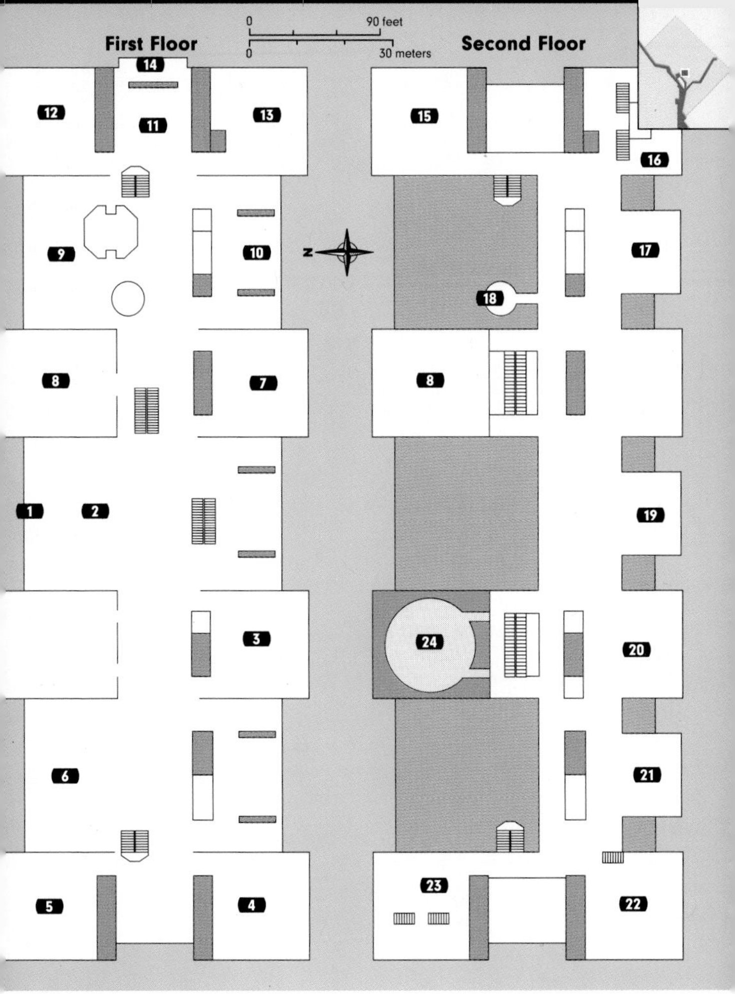
First Floor
Second Floor
0
90 feet
0
30 meters
N
1
2
3
4
5
6
7
8
9
10
11
12
13
14
15
16
17
18
19
20
21
22
23
24

Listed by Site Number

1 Main Entrance
2 Milestones of Flight
3 Early Flight
4 Golden Age of Flight
5 Vertical Flight
6 Air Transportation
7 Flight Tests
8 Langley Theater
9 Space Hall
10 Looking at Earth
11 Lunar Rovers
12 Space Flight & Rockets
13 Astronomical Devices
14 Dining Room
15 Flight in the Computer Age
16 Art and Flying
17 Apollo Equipment & Artifacts
18 Skylab Workshop
19 Pioneers of Flight
20 Planetary Exploration
21 World War I Aviation
22 World War II Aviation
23 Naval Aviation
24 Einstein Planetarium

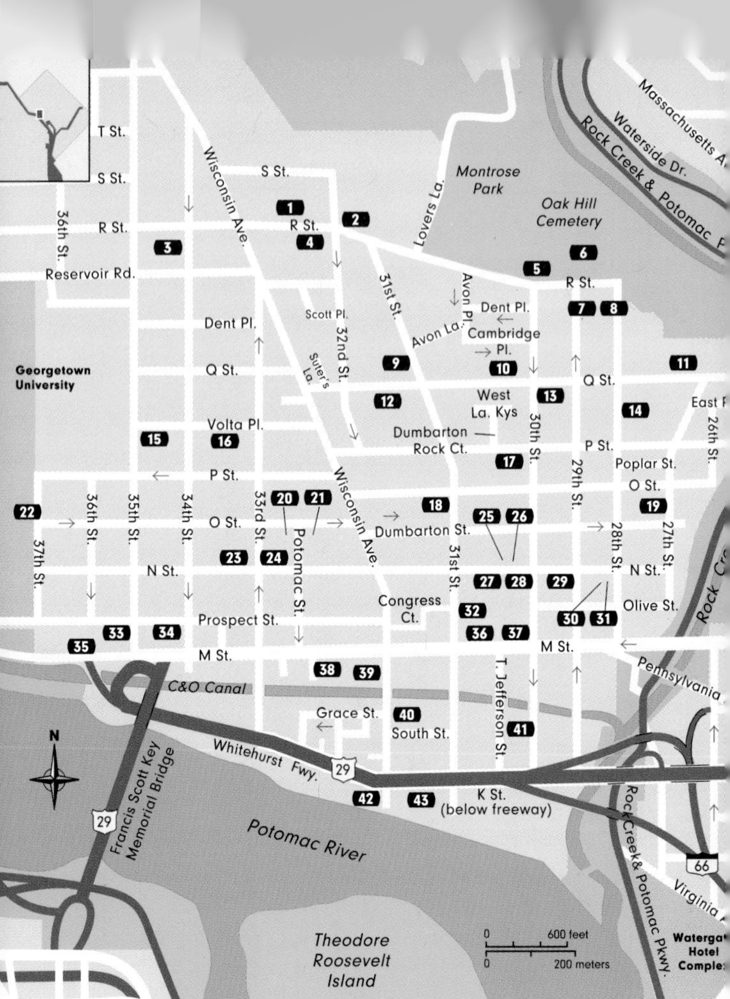

Listed by Site Number

1 Dougall House
2 Dumbarton Oaks
3 Mackall-Worthington House
4 Scott-Grant House
5 Oak Hill Cemetery Gatehouse
6 Oak Hill Cemetery
7 Mackall Square
8 Evermay
9 Tudor Place
10 Cooke's Row
11 Dumbarton House
12 Bowie-Sevier House
13 Francis Dodge House
14 Miller House
15 Alexander Melville Bell House
16 Pomander Walk
17 Linthicum House
18 Christ Church
19 Trentman House
20 Bodisco House
21 St John's Church
22 Georgetown Univ
23 Cox's Row
24 Smith Row
25 Loughboro-Paterson House
26 Wheatley House
27 Riggs-Riley House
28 Laird-Dunlop House
29 Foxall House
30 Decatur House
31 Gannt-Williams House
32 Custom House
33 Prospect House
34 Halcyon House
35 Exorcist Steps
36 Old Stone House
37 Thomas Sim Lee Corner
38 Georgetown Park
39 Vigilant Firehouse
40 Grace Epis. Church
41 C & O Canal (Barge)
42 Washington Harbour
43 Dodge Warehouse

Listed Alphabetically

Alexander Melville Bell House, 15.
152 35th St NW

Bodisco House, 20.
3322 O St NW

Bowie-Sevier House, 12.
3124 Q St NW

C & O Canal (Barge), 41.
1055 Thomas Jefferson St NW

Christ Church, 18.
O & 31st Sts NW

Cooke's Row, 10.
3007-29 Q St NW

Cox's Row, 23.
3327-39 N St NW

Custom House, 32.
1221 31st St NW

Decatur House, 30.
2812 N St NW

Dodge Warehouse, 43.
Wisconsin Ave & K St NW

Dougall House, 1.
3259 R St NW

Dumbarton House, 11.
2715 Q St NW

Dumbarton Oaks, 2.
1703 32nd St NW

Evermay, 8.
1628 28th St NW

Exorcist Steps, 35.
M & 36th Sts NW

Foxall House, 29.
2908 N St NW

Francis Dodge House, 13.
1517-37 30th St NW

Gannt-Williams House, 31.
2806 N St NW

Georgetown Park, 38.
3222 M St NW

Georgetown University, 22.
O & 37th Sts NW

Grace Episcopal Church, 40.
1041 Wisc Ave NW

Halcyon House, 34.
3400 Prospect St NW

Laird-Dunlop House, 28.
3014 N St NW

Linthicum House, 17.
3019 P St NW

Loughboro-Paterson House, 25.
3039-41 N St NW

Mackall Square, 7.
1633 29th St NW

Mackall-Worthington House, 3.
1686 34th St NW

Miller House, 14.
1524 28th St NW

Oak Hill Cemetery Gatehouse, 5.
R & 30th Sts NW

Oak Hill Cemetery, 6.
R & 30th Sts NW

Old Stone House, 36.
3051 M St NW

Pomander Walk, 16.
Volta Pl NW

Prospect House, 33.
3508 Prospect St NW

Riggs-Riley House, 27.
3038 N St NW

Scott-Grant House, 4.
3238 R St NW

Smith Row, 24.
3255-63 N St NW

St John's Church, 21.
3240 O St NW

Thomas Sim Lee Corner, 37.
3001-9 M St NW

Trentman House, 19.
1350 27th St NW

Tudor Place, 9.
1644 31st St NW

Vigilant Firehouse, 39.
1066 Wisconsin Ave NW

Washington Harbour, 42.
3020 K St NW

Wheatley House, 26.
3041-3 N St NW

Listed by Site Number

1 Church of Jesus Christ of Latter-Day Saints

2 Franciscan Monastery

3 St Paul's Rock Creek

4 National Presbyterian

5 Adas Israel Synagogue

6 Metropolitan Memorial Methodist

7 Washington Hebrew Congregation

8 Washington National Cathedral

9 Cathedral of St Sophia

10 St Stephen Church

11 Central Presbyterian

12 National Baptist Memorial

13 All Souls Unitarian

14 First Church of Christ, Scientist

15 Islamic Center Mosque

16 Georgetown Lutheran

17 Holy Trinity Cathedral

18 St John's Church Georgetown Parish

19 Mt Zion United Methodist

20 Friends Meeting of Washington

21 Foundry Methodist

22 First Baptist

23 Grace Evangelical & Reformed

24 St Matthew's Cathedral

25 Metropolitan African Methodist Episcopal

26 National City Christian

27 Luther Place Memorial

28 Shiloh Baptist-Family Life Center

29 Mt Vernon Place Methodist

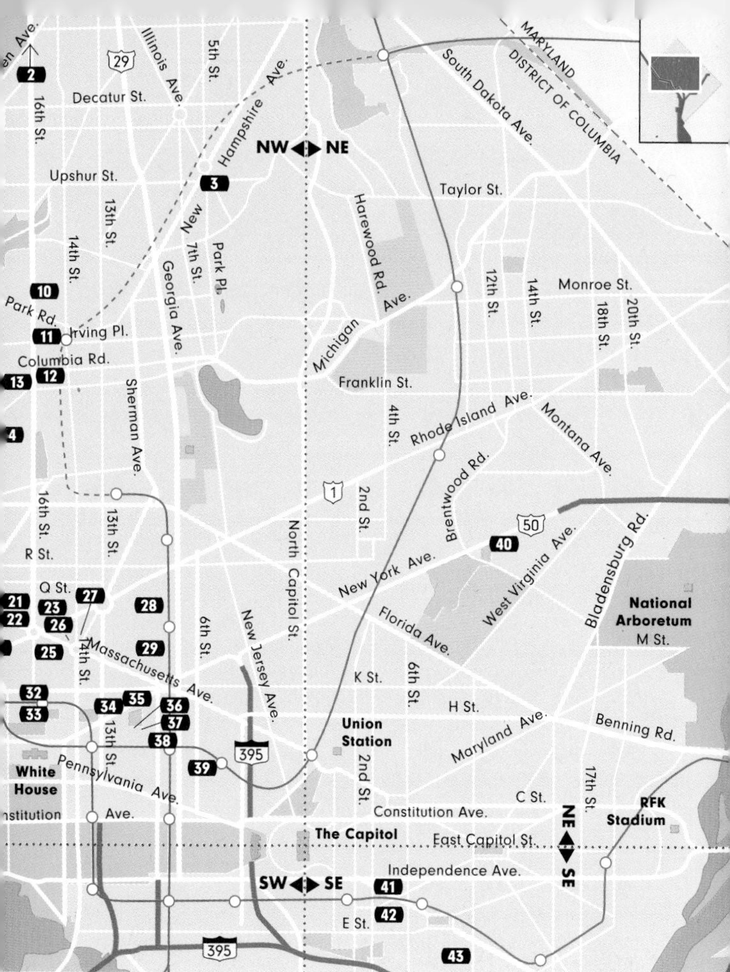

Listed by Site Number (cont.)

30 St Mary's Episcopal
31 Western Presbyterian
32 Third Christ, Scientist
33 St John's Episcopal
34 Church of the Epiphany
35 Asbury Methodist
36 St Patrick's Cathedral
37 First Congregational
38 Calvary Baptist
39 St Mary's Catholic
40 New York Ave Presbyterian
41 Capitol Hill Presbyterian
42 Ebenezer United Methodist
43 Christ Church

Listed Alphabetically

Adas Israel Synagogue, 5.
2850 Quebec St NW
☏ 362-4433. Jewish

All Souls Unitarian, 13.
2835 16th St NW ☏ 332-5266

Asbury Methodist, 35.
926 11th St NW ☏ 628-0009

Calvary Baptist, 38.
755 8th St NW ☏ 347-8355

Capitol Hill Presbyterian, 41.
201 4th St SE ☏ 547-8676

Cathedral of St Sophia, 9.
Massachusetts Ave & 36th St NW
☏ 333-4730. Greek Orthodox

Central Presbyterian, 11.
Irving Pl & 15th St NW (site only)

Christ Church, 43.
620 G St SE ☏ 547-9300. Episcopal

Church of Jesus Christ of Latter-Day Saints, 1. 1000 Stonybrook Dr, Kensington, MD ☏ 301/589-1435. Mormon

Church of the Epiphany, 34.
1317 G St NW ☏ 347-2635. Episcopal

Ebenezer United Methodist, 42.
400 D St SE ☏ 544-9539

First Baptist, 22.
1328 16th St NW ☏ 387-2206

First Church of Christ, Scientist, 14.
1770 Euclid St NW ☏ 265-1390

First Congregational, 37.
945 G St NW ☏ 628-4317.
United Church of Christ

Foundry Methodist, 21.
1500 16th St NW ☏ 332-4010

Franciscan Monastery, 2.
1400 Quincy St NE ☏ 526-6800.
Roman Catholic

Friends Meeting of Washington, 20.
2111 Florida Ave NW ☏ 483-3310.
Quaker

Georgetown Lutheran, 16.
1556 Wisconsin Ave NW ☏ 337-9070

Grace Evangelical & Reformed, 23.
1405 15th St NW ☏ 387-3131.
United Church of Christ

Holy Trinity Church, 17.
3513 N St NW ☏ 337-2840.
Roman Catholic

Islamic Center Mosque, 15. 2551 Massachusetts Ave NW ☏ 332-8343

Luther Place Memorial, 27.
1226 Vermont Ave NW ☏ 667-1377.
Lutheran

Metro Memorial Methodist, 6.
3401 Nebraska Ave NW ☏ 363-4900

Metropolitan African Methodist Episcopal, 25.
1518 M St NW ☏ 331-1426

Mt Vernon Place Methodist, 29.
900 Massachusetts Ave NW
☏ 347-9620

Mt Zion United Methodist, 19.
1334 29th St NW ☏ 234-0148

National Baptist Memorial, 12.
1501 Columbia Rd NW ☏ 265-1410

National City Christian, 26.
5 Thomas Circle NW ☏ 232-0323.
Disciples of Christ

National Presbyterian, 4.
4101 Nebraska Ave NW ☏ 537-0800

New York Ave Presbyterian, 40.
1313 New York Ave NW ☏ 393-3700

Shiloh Baptist-Family Life Center, 28.
1510 9th St NW ☏ 232-4200

St John's Church Georgetown Parish, 18.
3240 O St NW ☏ 338-1796. Episcopal

St John's Episcopal, 33.
1525 H St NW ☏ 347-8766

St Mary's Catholic, 39.
727 5th St NW ☏ 289-7770

St Mary's Episcopal, 30.
728 23rd St NW ☏ 333-3985

St Matthew's Cathedral, 24.
1725 Rhode Island Ave NW
☏ 347-3215. Roman Catholic

St Patrick's Cathedral, 36.
619 10th St NW
☏ 347-2713. Roman Catholic

St Paul's Rock Creek, 3.
Rock Creek Church Rd & Webster St NW
☏ 726-2080. Episcopal

St Stephen Church, 10.
1525 Newton St NW
☏ 232-0900. Episcopal

Third Church of Christ, Scientist, 32.
900 16th St NW ☏ 833-3325

Washington Hebrew Congregation, 7. 3935 Macomb St NW ☏ 362-7100. Jewish

Washington National Cathedral, 8.
3001 Wisconsin & Massachusetts Aves NW ☏ 537-6200. Episcopal

Western Presbyterian, 31.
2401 Virginia Ave NW ☏ 835-8383

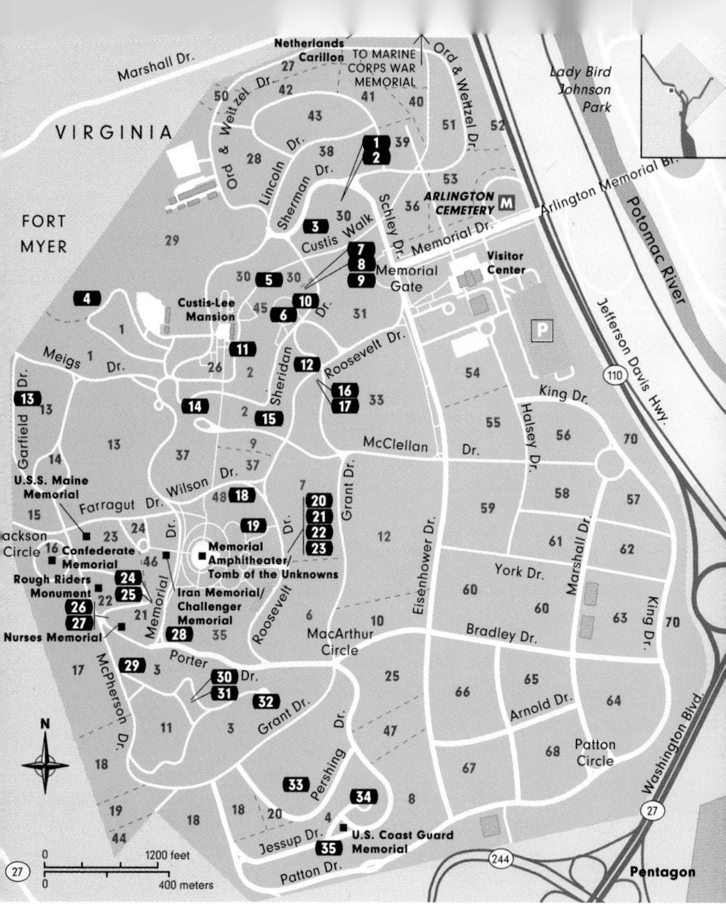

Listed Alphabetically

Abrams, Gen Creighton, 28
Barrow, T Sgt Joe L, 23
Bonesteel, Gen Chas III, 29
Boyington, Col "Pappy", 18
Bradley, Gen Omar, 1
Brown, Gen George S, 25
Bryan, Col William Jennings, 34
Byrd, R Adm Richard E, 16
Chaffee, Lt Comdr Roger, 30
Chennault, Lt Gen Claire Lee, 14
Decker, Gen George H, 22
Douglas, Justice William O, 6
Grissom, Lt Col Virgil I, 31
Halsey, Adm William Jr, 15
Holmes, Capt Oliver Wendell, 5
James, Gen Daniel, 12
Kennedy, Pres John F, 8
Kennedy, Robert F, 10
Kennedy Onassis, Jacqueline, 9
L'Enfant, Pierre Charles, 17
Leahy, Adm William D, 13
Lincoln, Capt Robt Todd, 3
Louis, Joe, 19
Marshall, Gen George C, 21
Murphy, Audie, 27
Peary, R Adm Robert E, 35
Pershing, Gen George, 33
Reed, Maj Walter, 32
Rickover, Adm Hyman, 7
Scobee, Comdr Francis, 24
Sheridan, Gen Philip H, 11
Smith, Capt Michael, 20
Taft, Pres William H, 2
Wainwright, Gen Jonathan, 4
Warren, Chief Justice Earl, 26

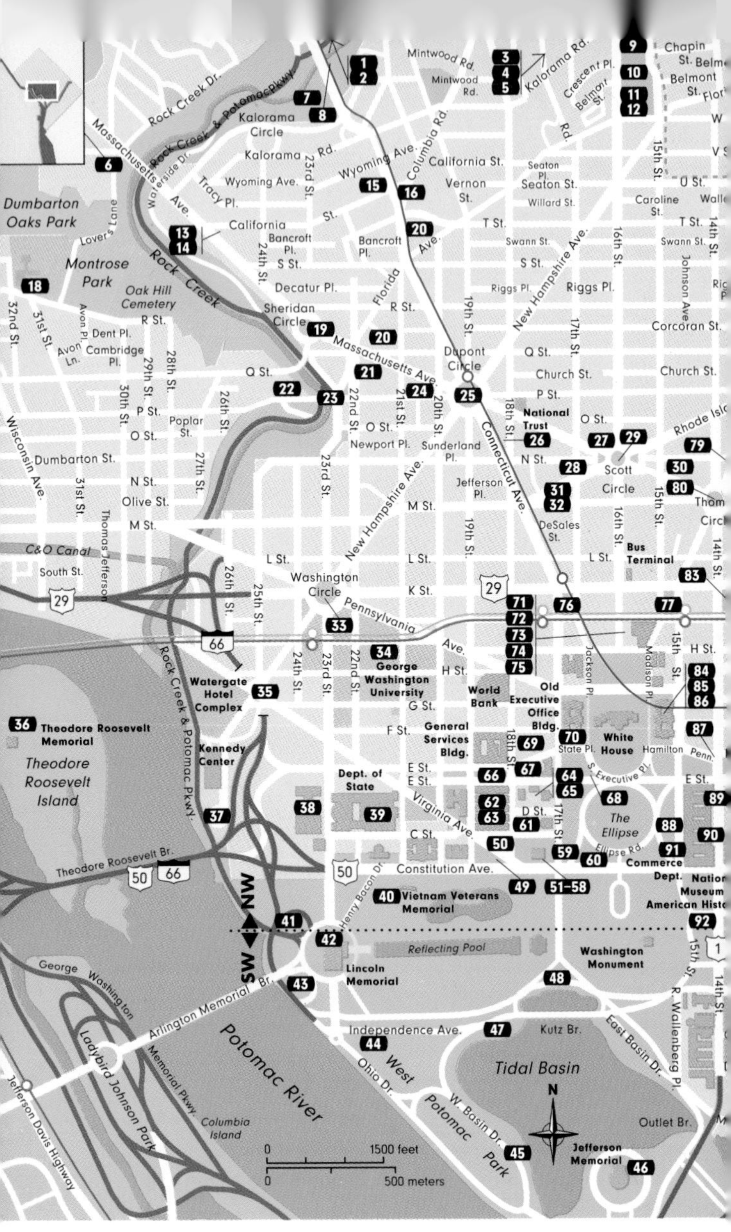

Listed by Site Number

1 Eurythmy
2 Orbit
3 Cardinal James Gibbons
4 Guglielmo Marconi Memorial
5 Francis Asbury
6 St Dominic
7 Christ, the Light of the World
8 St Jerome the Priest
9 Sir Winston Churchill
10 Perry Lions
11 Bairstow Eagle Lampposts
12 Serenity
13 Dante
14 Joan of Arc
15 Pres James Buchanan
16 The Prophet
17 Robert Emmett
18 Habitat
19 Gen George B McClellan

Listed by Site Number (cont.)

20 Cubi XI

21 Pebble Garden Fountain

22 Gen Philip Sheridan

23 Braque Bird

24 Hercules, Buddha, & Sphinx

25 Buffaloes & Indian Heads

26 Taras Shevchenko

27 Balinese Demons

28 Dupont Memorial Fountain

29 John Witherspoon

30 Australian Seal

31 Daniel Webster

32 Lt Gen Winfield Brevet Scott

33 Dr Samuel Hahnemann

34 Henry Wadsworth Longfellow

35 Nuns of the Battlefield

Listed by Site Number (cont.)

36 Pres George Washington
37 Ascension
38 Benito Juarez
39 Pres Theodore Roosevelt
40 America & War & Peace
41 Dr Benjamin Rush
42 The Expanding Universe Fountain
43 Vietnam Veterans Memorial
44 Arts of Peace
45 Lincoln Memorial
46 Arts of War
47 John Ericsson
48 Japanese Pagoda
49 Jefferson Memorial
50 Japanese Lantern
51 John Paul Jones Memorial
52 Jose Gernasio Ortegas
53 Gen Simon Bolivar
54 Queen Isabella I
55 South America
56 North America
57 Aztec Fountain
58 The Prophet Daniel
59 Jose Cecilio Del Valle
60 Cordell Hull
61 Xochipilli, Aztec God of Flowers
62 Bullfinch Gatehouses
63 2nd Division Monument
64 DAR Founders
65 Negro Mother & Child
66 Abe Lincoln, Rail Joiner
67 Red Cross Men & Women Killed in Service
68 Jane A Delano & the Nurses Who Died
69 Gen John Rawlins
70 Canova Lions
71 Butt-Millet Memorial
72 Members of the American Institute of Architecture
73 First Division Memorial
74 Gen Kosciuszko
75 Gen Lafayette
76 Pres Andrew Jackson
77 Baron von Steuben
78 Comte de Rochambeau
79 Adm David Farragut
80 Maj Gen James B McPherson
81 Gen John A Logan
82 Martin Luther
83 Maj Gen George Thomas
84 Edmund Burke
85 Samuel Gompers Memorial
86 Commodore John Barry
87 Albert Gallatin
88 Alexander Hamilton
89 Gen William Tecumseh Sherman
90 Pulaski Statue Freedom Plaza
91 Settlers of the District of Columbia
92 Boy Scout Memorial
93 Straus Statue
94 Bullfinch Gatehouses
95 The Gwenfritz
96 Three Red Lines
97 Infinity
98 Uncle Beazley
99 Joseph Henry
100 Andrew Jackson Downing (Urn)
101 The Burghers of Calais
102 Mellon Fountain
103 Man Controlling Trade
104 Acroterion Eagles
105 Robert Francis Kennedy
106 Capt Nathan Hale
107 Benjamin Franklin
108 Pegasus & Bellerophon
109 Gen Winfield Scott Hancock
110 Temperance Fountain
111 Past and Future
112 GAR Memorial
113 Abraham Lincoln
114 Joseph Darlington Fountain
115 Gen Albert Pike
116 Sir William Blackstone
117 Trylon of Freedom
118 Acacia Griffins
119 Pres Robert A Taft Memorial
120 Pres Ulysses S Grant Memorial
121 Peace Monument
122 Pres James Garfield
123 Bartholdi Fountain
124 The Majesty of Law & Spirit
125 Greek Vases
126 Christopher Columbus Memorial Fountain
127 Thomas Hopkins Gallaudet
128 Edward Miner Gallaudet
129 Equal Justice Under Law
130 The Court of Neptune Fountain
131 Ethnological Heads
132 Gen Nathanael Greene
133 Shakespeare Scenes
134 Puck Fountain
135 Olive Risley Seward
136 Emancipation Group
137 Mary McLeod Bethune

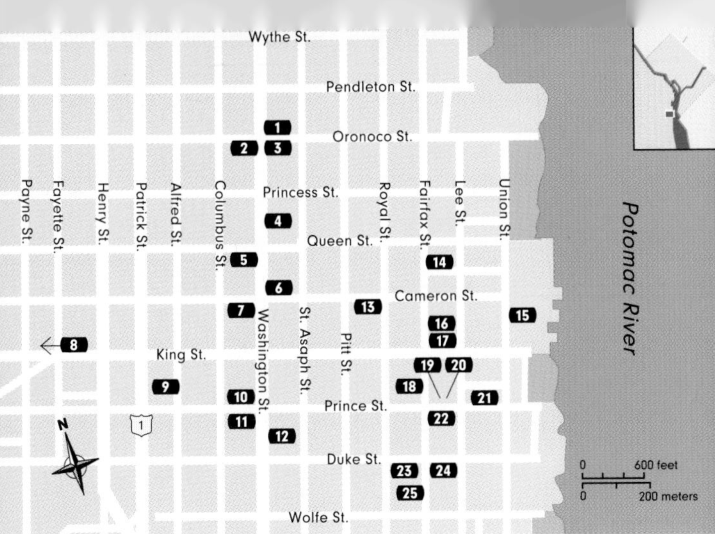

Listed by Site Number

1 Robert E Lee House
2 Edmund Jennings Lee House
3 Fendall-John L Lewis House
4 Brockett's Row
5 Lloyd House
6 Yeaton-Fairfax House
7 Christ Church
8 George Washington Masonic Nat'l Mem
9 Friendship Fire Co
10 William Fowle House
11 Lyceum
12 Lloyd's Row
13 Gadsby's Tavern Museum
14 Gentry Row
15 Torpedo Factory Arts Center
16 Carlyle House
17 Ramsay House
18 Stabler-Leadbeater Apothecary Shop
19 Thompson-Marshburn House
20 Athenaeum
21 Captain's Row
22 Dr Wm Brown House
23 St Mary's Church
24 Dr James Craik House
25 Old Presbyterian Meeting House

Listed Alphabetically

Athenaeum, 20. 201 Prince St

Brockett's Row, 4. 301-7 N Washington St

Captain's Row, 21. Prince St

Carlyle House, 16. 121 N Fairfax St

Christ Church, 7. 118 N Washington St

Dr James Craik House, 24. 210 Duke St

Dr William Brown House, 22. 212 S Fairfax St

Edmund Jennings Lee House, 2. Oronoco & N Washington Sts

Fendall-John L Lewis House, 3. 614 Oronoco St

Friendship Fire Co, 9. 107 S Alfred St

Gadsby's Tavern Museum, 13. 134-138 N Royal St

Gentry Row, 14. Prince St

George Washington Masonic National Memorial, 8. 101 Callahan Dr

Lloyd House, 5. Queen & N Washington Sts

Lloyd's Row, 12. 220-228 S Washington St

Lyceum, 11. 201 S Washington St

Old Presbyterian Meeting House, 25. 321 S Fairfax St

Ramsay House (Visitor's Center), 17. King & N Fairfax Sts

Robert E Lee House, 1. 607 Oronoco St

St Mary's Church, 23. 310 Duke St

Stabler-Leadbeater Apothecary Shop, 18. 105-107 S Fairfax St

Thompson-Marshburn House, 19. 211 N Fairfax St

Torpedo Factory Arts Center, 15. 105 N Union St

William Fowle House, 10. 711 Prince St

Yeaton-Fairfax House, 6. 607 Cameron St

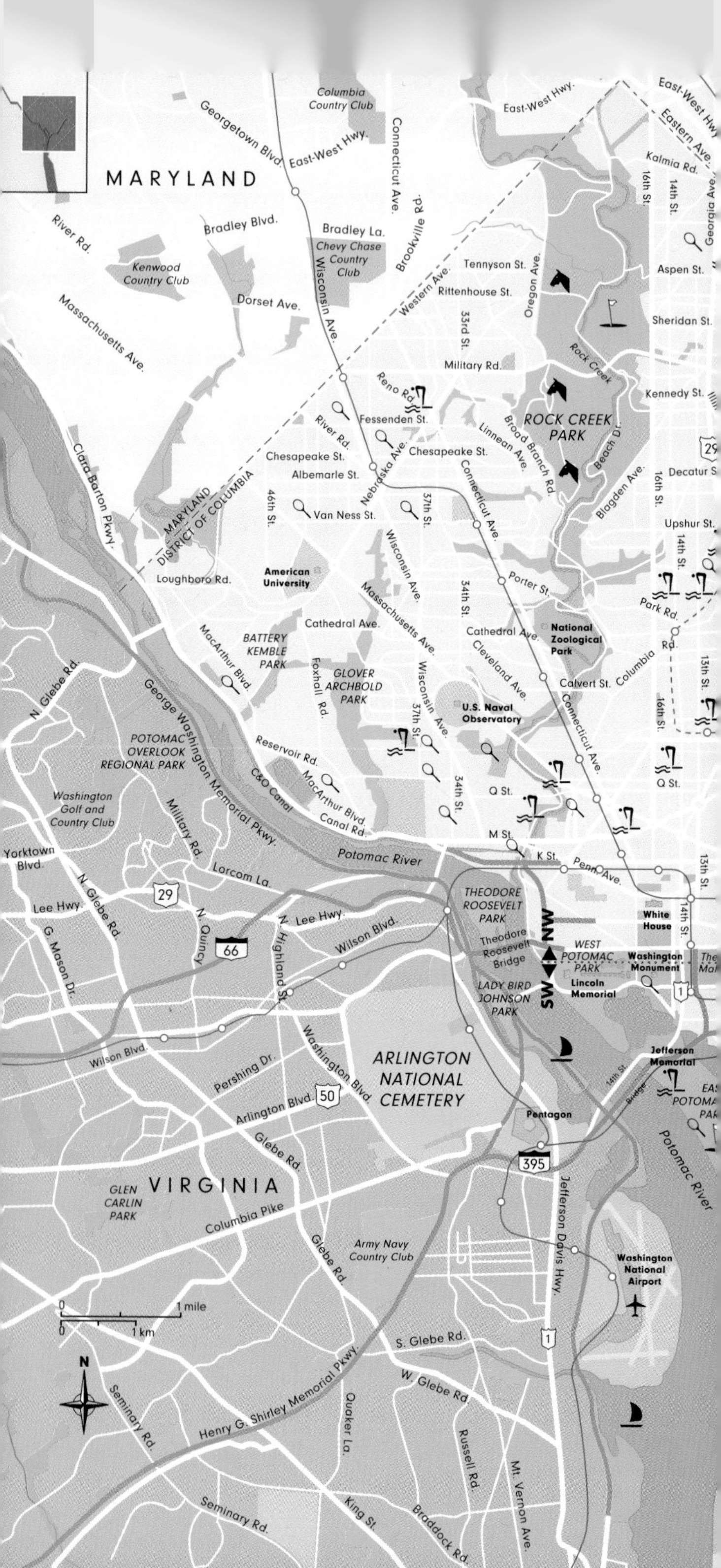

MARYLAND
DISTRICT OF COLUMBIA
VIRGINIA
Columbia Country Club
Chevy Chase Country Club
Kenwood Country Club
ROCK CREEK PARK
American University
BATTERY KEMBLE PARK
GLOVER ARCHBOLD PARK
National Zoological Park
U.S. Naval Observatory
POTOMAC OVERLOOK REGIONAL PARK
Washington Golf and Country Club
THEODORE ROOSEVELT PARK
Theodore Roosevelt Bridge
WEST POTOMAC PARK
LADY BIRD JOHNSON PARK
White House
Washington Monument
Lincoln Memorial
Jefferson Memorial
ARLINGTON NATIONAL CEMETERY
Pentagon
GLEN CARLIN PARK
Army Navy Country Club
Washington National Airport
Potomac River
C&O Canal
Georgetown Blvd.
East-West Hwy.
Eastern Ave.
Kalmia Rd.
Connecticut Ave.
Brookville Rd.
Bradley Blvd.
Bradley La.
River Rd.
Wisconsin Ave.
Western Ave.
Tennyson St.
Rittenhouse St.
Oregon Ave.
Aspen St.
Sheridan St.
Dorset Ave.
Massachusetts Ave.
33rd St.
Military Rd.
Rock Creek
Reno Rd.
Kennedy St.
Fessenden St.
Broad Branch Rd.
Linnean Ave.
Beach Dr.
Chesapeake St.
Albemarle St.
Nebraska Ave.
Decatur St.
Blagden Ave.
16th St.
14th St.
13th St.
Georgia Ave.
Clara Barton Pkwy.
46th St.
Van Ness St.
37th St.
Upshur St.
Loughboro Rd.
Porter St.
Park Rd.
34th St.
Cathedral Ave.
Columbia Rd.
MacArthur Blvd.
Foxhall Rd.
Cleveland Ave.
Calvert St.
N. Glebe Rd.
George Washington Memorial Pkwy.
Reservoir Rd.
Canal Rd.
Q St.
M St.
K St.
Penn. Ave.
Military Rd.
Yorktown Blvd.
Lorcom La.
Lee Hwy.
N. Quincy
N. Highland St.
Wilson Blvd.
G. Mason Dr.
Washington Blvd.
Pershing Dr.
Arlington Blvd.
Glebe Rd.
Columbia Pike
14th St. Bridge
Jefferson Davis Hwy.
S. Glebe Rd.
W. Glebe Rd.
Henry G. Shirley Memorial Pkwy.
Seminary Rd.
Quaker La.
Russell Rd.
Mt. Vernon Ave.
King St.
Braddock Rd.
29
66
50
395
1
NW
SW
0
1 mile
0
1 km
N

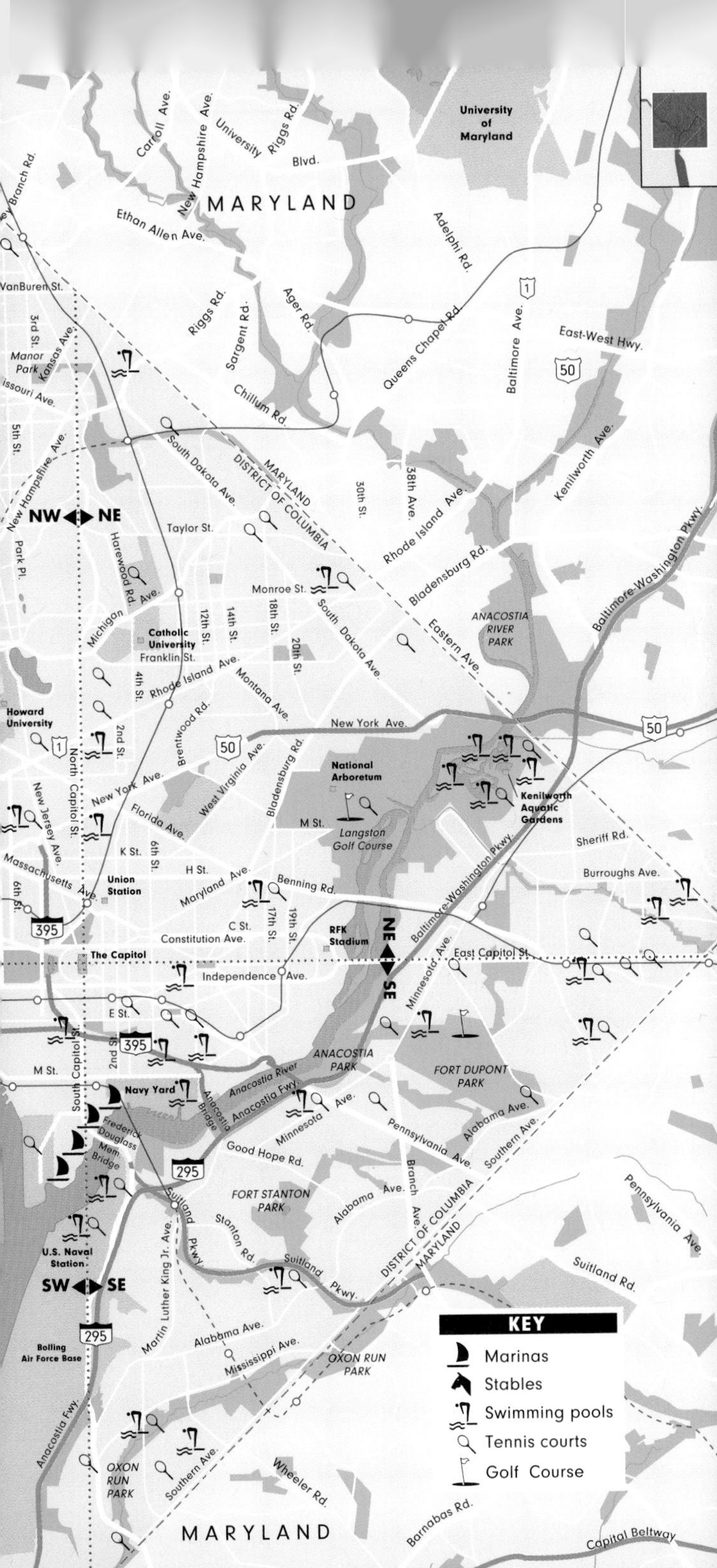

MARYLAND
University of Maryland
NW ◀▶ NE
NE ◀▶ SE
SW ◀▶ SE
Catholic University
Howard University
National Arboretum
Langston Golf Course
Kenilworth Aquatic Gardens
ANACOSTIA RIVER PARK
Union Station
The Capitol
RFK Stadium
ANACOSTIA PARK
FORT DUPONT PARK
Navy Yard
FORT STANTON PARK
U.S. Naval Station
Bolling Air Force Base
OXON RUN PARK
DISTRICT OF COLUMBIA
MARYLAND
KEY
Marinas
Stables
Swimming pools
Tennis courts
Golf Course

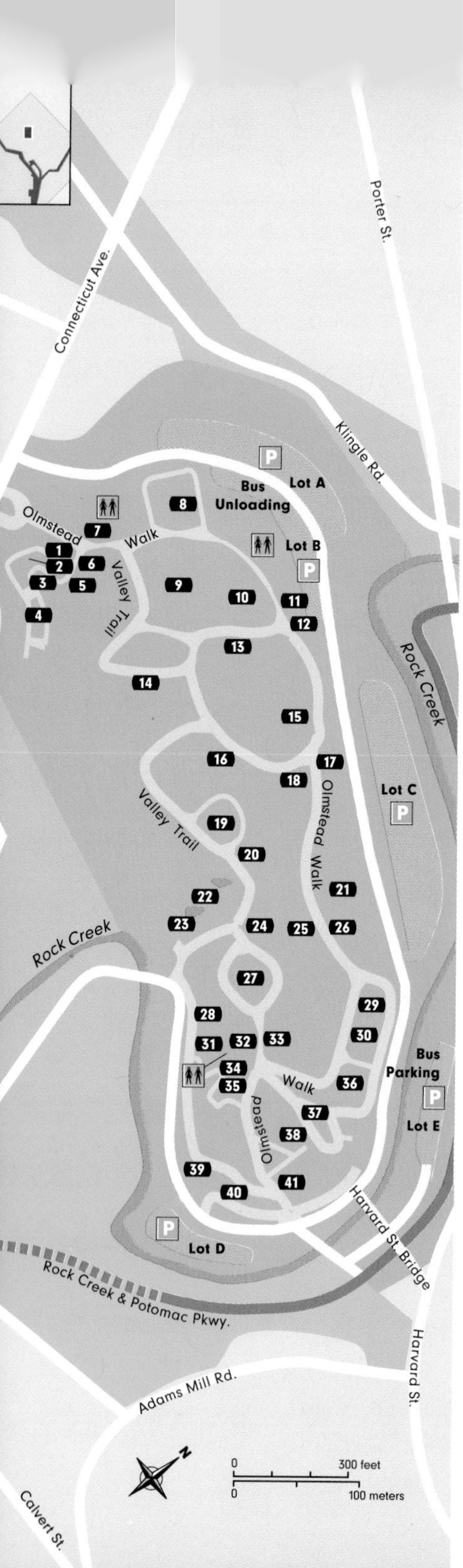

Listed by Site Number

1 Tapir
2 Hoofed Animals
3 Great Flight Cage
4 Bird House
5 Wetlands
6 Bongos
7 Gift Shop
8 Zebras
9 Australia Pavilion
10 Pandas & Panda Cafe
11 Food & Gift Shops
12 Information & Strollers
13 Elephants & Giraffes
14 Birds
15 Hippos & Rhinos
16 Free Ranging Tamarins
17 Beavers & Otters
18 Concession Stand
19 Bison
20 Wolves
21 Small Mammal House
22 Seals & Sea Lions
23 Spectacled Bears
24 Seal Gift Shop
25 Gibbon Ridge
26 Great Ape House
27 Bears
28 Pumas & Jaguars
29 Invertebrates
30 Reptile House
31 Future Amazonia Exhibit
32 Prairie Dogs
33 Monkey Island
34 Police & First Aid
35 Mane Restaurant
36 Monkey House
37 Lion-Tiger Hill
38 Bats
39 Vegetable Garden
40 Waterfowl
41 Information & Strollers

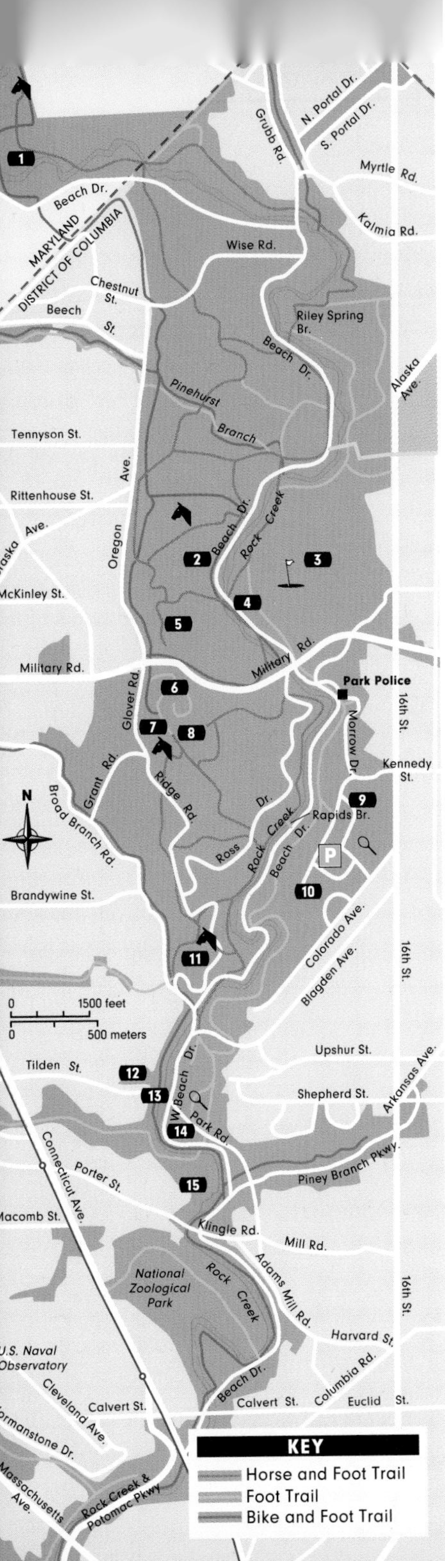

Listed by Site Number

1 Candy Cane City
2 Park Police Stables
3 Public Golf Course
4 Miller Cabin
5 Fort De Russey
6 Planetarium
6 Rock Creek Nature Center
7 Dog Training
7 Park Headquarters
8 Horse Center
9 Brightwood Rec Area
10 Carter Barron Amphitheater
11 Equitation Field
12 Art Barn
13 Pierce Mill
14 Jusserand Memorial
15 Klingle Mansion

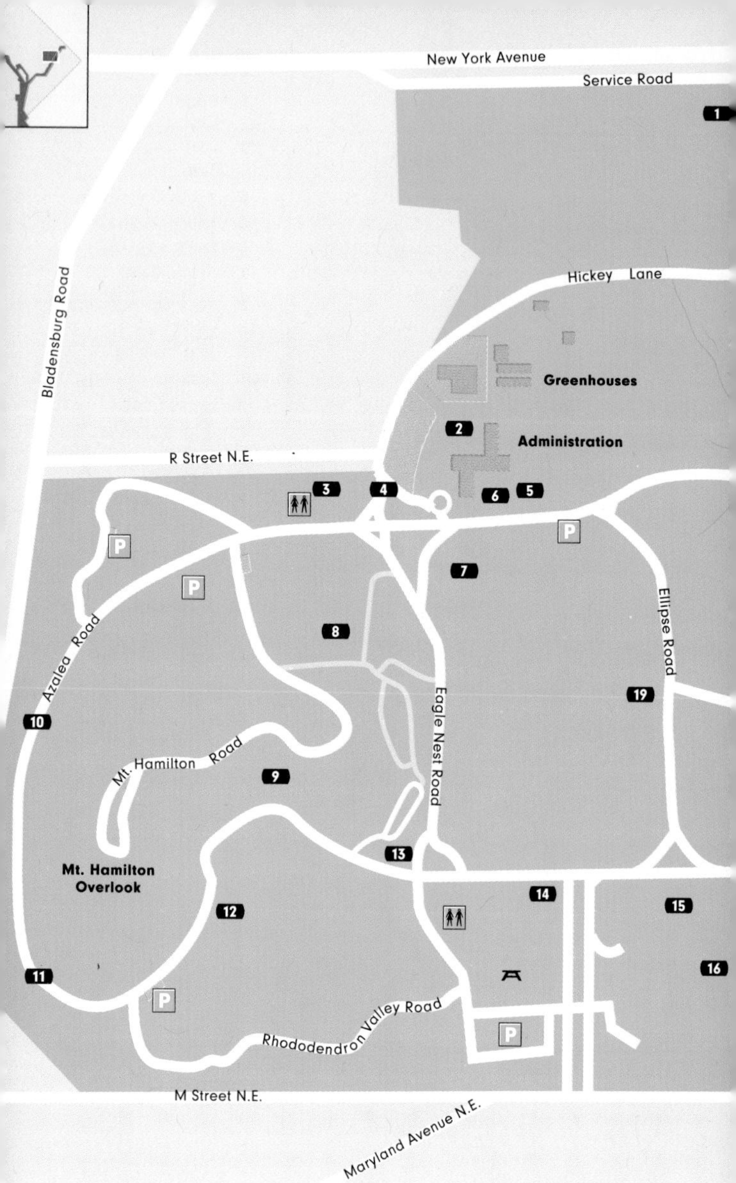

New York Avenue
Service Road
Hickey Lane
Greenhouses
Administration
Bladensburg Road
R Street N.E.
Azalea Road
Ellipse Road
Eagle Nest Road
Mt. Hamilton Road
Mt. Hamilton Overlook
Rhododendron Valley Road
M Street N.E.
Maryland Avenue N.E.

Listed by Site Number

1 Wildflower Fields
2 Court of Honor
3 Information Center
4 Baker Garden
5 Japanese Garden
6 Aquatic Gardens
7 Herb Garden
8 Lee Azalea Garden
9 Azalea Hillside
10 Crab Apples
11 Viburnum
12 Azalea Valley
13 Morrison Azalea Garden
14 Buchheister Bird Garden
15 Shade Trees
16 Shade Trees
17 Washington Youth Gardens
18 Fern Valley
19 National Capitol Columns

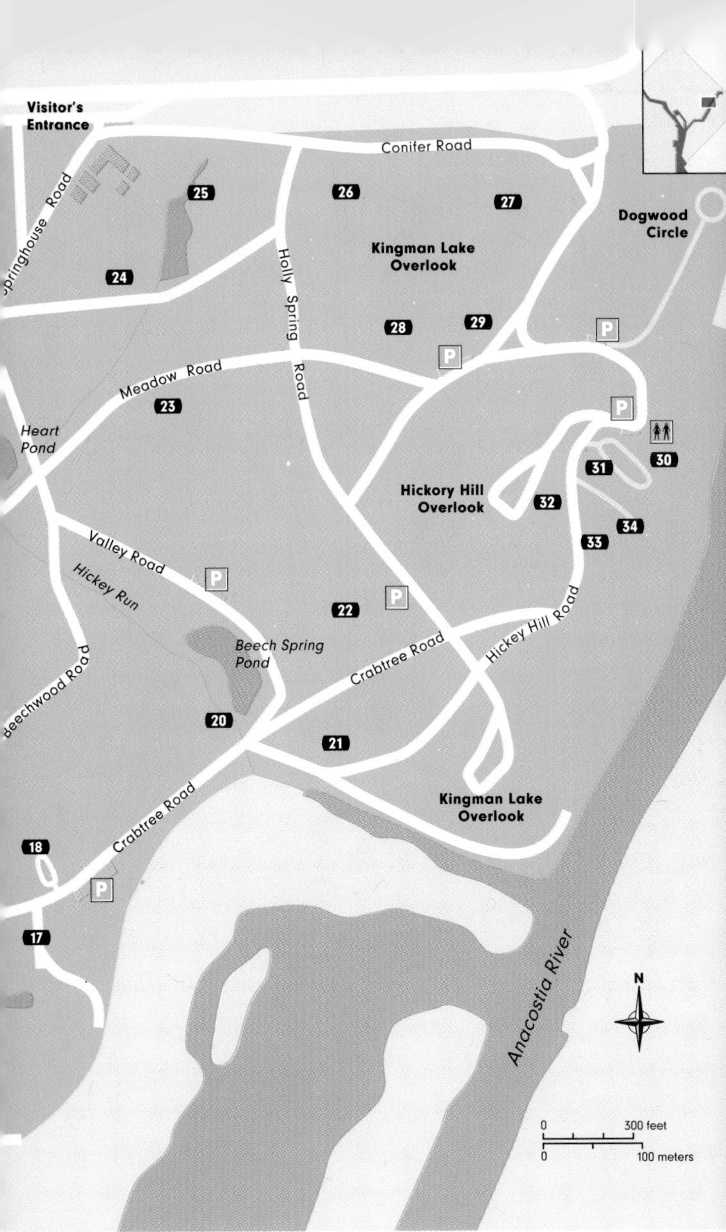

Listed by Site Number (cont.)

20 Beech Pond Gazebo
21 Crab Apples
22 Magnolias
23 Crape Myrtles
24 Legumes
25 Spring Houses
26 Japanese Maples
27 Dwarf Conifer Collection
28 Watnong Conifer Collection
29 Dawn Redwoods
30 Japanese Collections
31 Chadwick Overlook
32 Korean Mountain
33 Chinese Collections
34 Garden Club Gazebo

MARYLAND
DISTRICT OF COLUMBIA
VIRGINIA
ROCK CREEK PARK
BATTERY KEMBLE PARK
GLOVER ARCHBOLD PARK
POTOMAC OVERLOOK REGIONAL PARK
THEODORE ROOSEVELT PARK
WEST POTOMAC PARK
LADY BIRD JOHNSON PARK
ARLINGTON NATIONAL CEMETERY
EAST POTOMAC PARK
GLEN CARLIN PARK
American University
National Zoological Park
U.S. Naval Observatory
White House
Washington Monument
Lincoln Memorial
Jefferson Memorial
Pentagon
Washington National Airport
Rock Creek Bike Trail
Washington & Old Dominion Bike Trail
Mt. Vernon Bike Trail
Potomac River
C&O Canal
Theodore Roosevelt Bridge
14th St. Bridge
NW
SW
0
1 mile
0
1 km
N

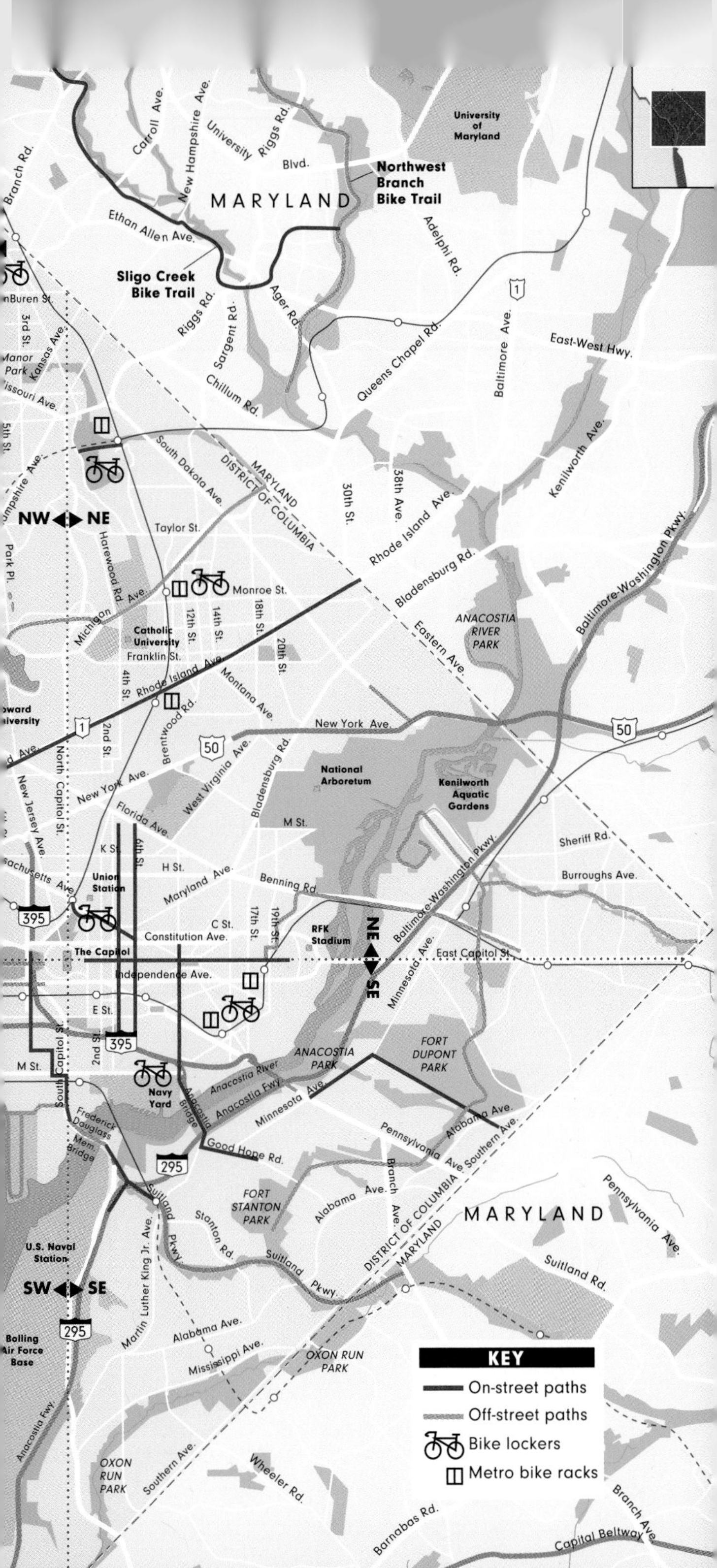

MARYLAND
University of Maryland
Northwest Branch Bike Trail
Sligo Creek Bike Trail
NW ◀▶ NE
Catholic University
Howard University
National Arboretum
Kenilworth Aquatic Gardens
ANACOSTIA RIVER PARK
Union Station
The Capitol
RFK Stadium
NE ◀▶ SE
ANACOSTIA PARK
FORT DUPONT PARK
Navy Yard
FORT STANTON PARK
U.S. Naval Station
SW ◀▶ SE
Bolling Air Force Base
OXON RUN PARK
MARYLAND
DISTRICT OF COLUMBIA
KEY
On-street paths
Off-street paths
Bike lockers
Metro bike racks

SEE DETAIL MAP OPPOSITE
Swains Lock (Lock 21)
1 mile
1 km
Great Falls Park Visitor Center
Great Falls Tavern Visitor Center
Great Falls Park
Falls Rd.
189
Maryland Gold Mine site
River Rd.
N
Old Angler's Inn
190
Old Dominion Dr.
MARYLAND
MacArthur Blvd.
193
738
Carderock
495
Capital Beltway
Lock 14
Lock 13
Lock 12
Seven Locks
Lock 11
495
Lock 10
Lock 9
Lock 8
Washington Dulles Access and Toll Rd.
Old Georgetown Pike
George Washington Memorial Pkwy.
Dolley Madison Blvd.
123
George Washington Memorial Parkway
Lock 7
McLEAN
267
396
Chain Bridge Rd.
BETHESDA
Little Falls Dam
VIRGINIA
Old Dominion Dr.
Lock 6
River Rd.
Lock 5
Little Falls
309
Massachusetts Ave.
Chain Bridge
Canal Rd.
MacArthur Blvd.
Lee Hwy.
ARLINGTON
Wisconsin Ave.
29
Abner Cloud House
Fletcher's Boathouse
DISTRICT OF COLUMBIA
Lee Hwy.
66
Rock Cree Park
Potomac River
Lee Hwy.
GEORGETOWN
50
Key Bridge
Locks 1–4
Arlington Blvd.
50
16th
New Hampshire Ave.
27

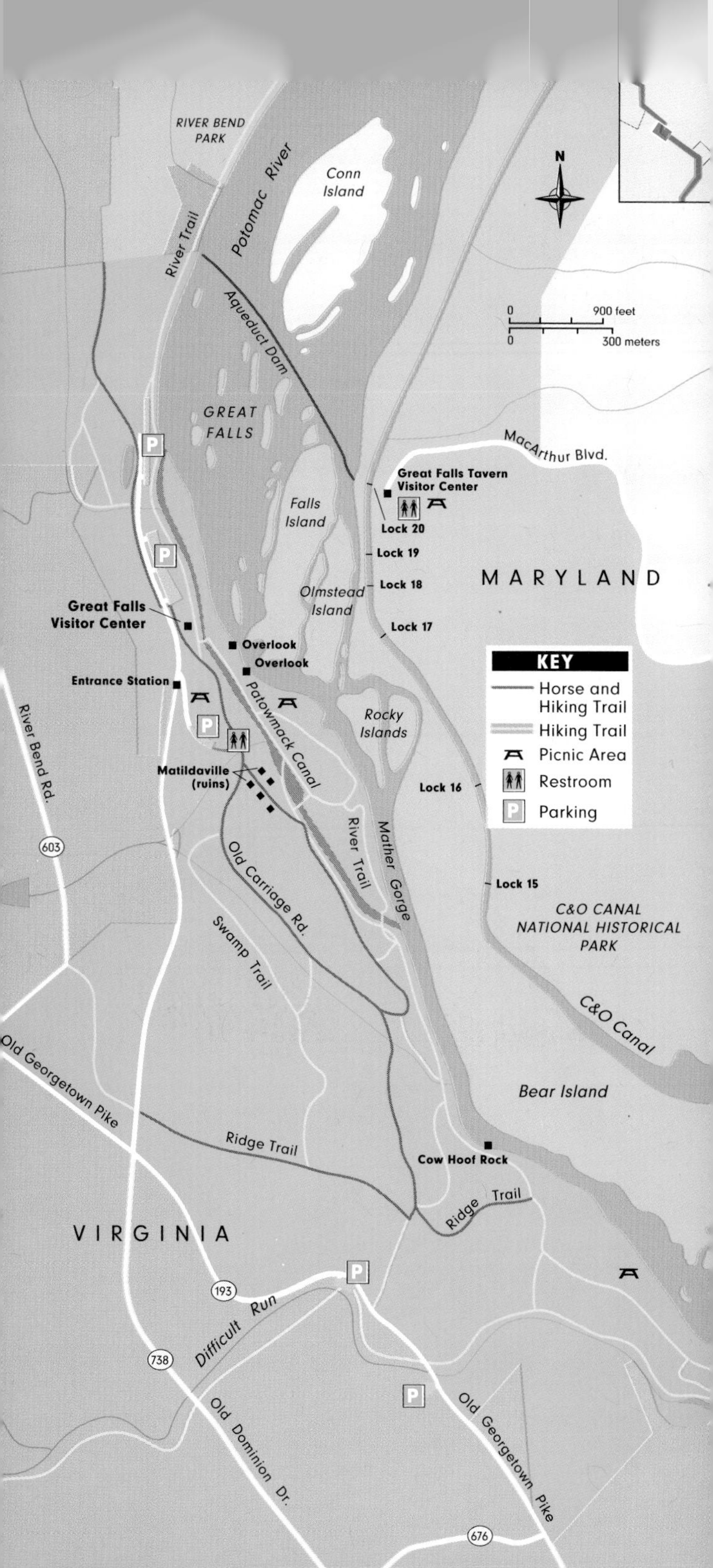

RIVER BEND PARK
Potomac River
Conn Island
River Trail
Aqueduct Dam
GREAT FALLS
N
0 900 feet
0 300 meters
MacArthur Blvd.
Great Falls Tavern Visitor Center
Falls Island
Lock 20
Lock 19
Lock 18
Olmstead Island
MARYLAND
Great Falls Visitor Center
Lock 17
Overlook
Overlook
Entrance Station
KEY
Horse and Hiking Trail
Hiking Trail
Picnic Area
Restroom
Parking
Patowmack Canal
Rocky Islands
River Bend Rd.
Matildaville (ruins)
Lock 16
603
River Trail
Mather Gorge
Old Carriage Rd.
Lock 15
C&O CANAL NATIONAL HISTORICAL PARK
Swamp Trail
C&O Canal
Old Georgetown Pike
Bear Island
Ridge Trail
Cow Hoof Rock
Ridge Trail
VIRGINIA
193
Difficult Run
738
Old Dominion Dr.
Old Georgetown Pike
676

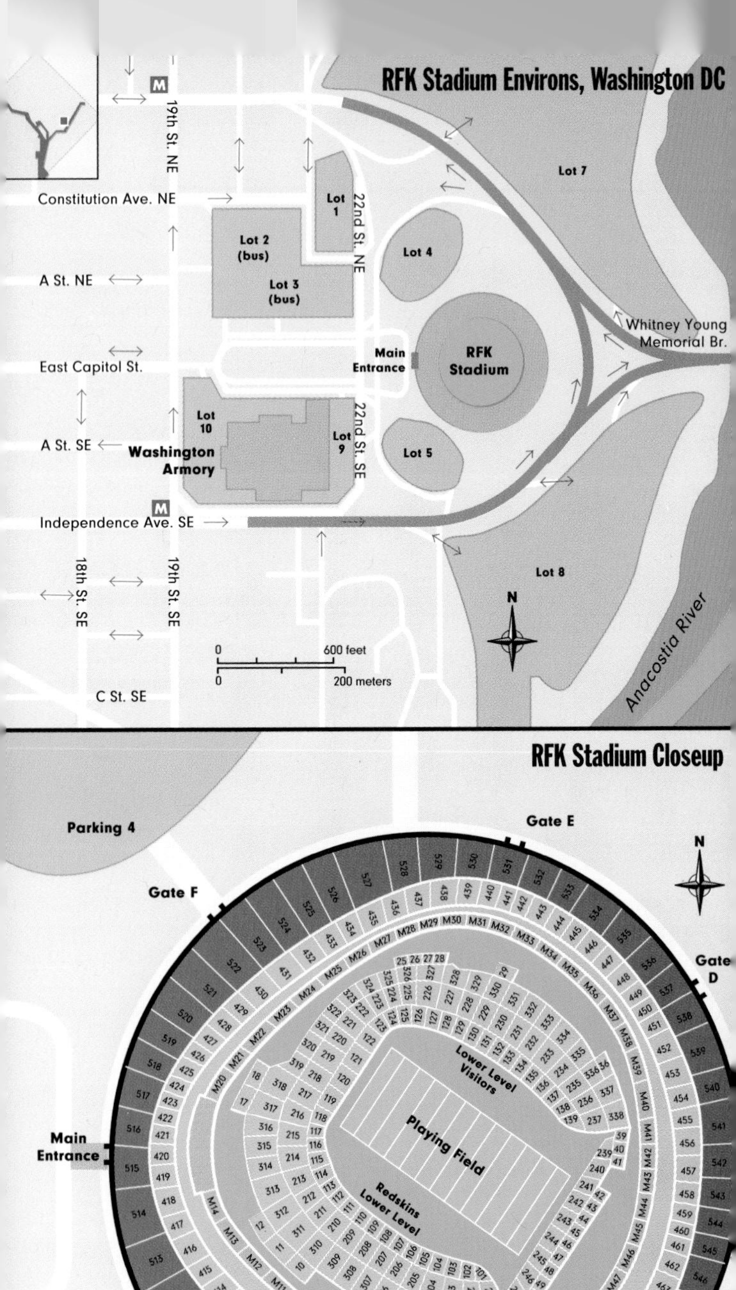

RFK Stadium Environs, Washington DC
19th St. NE
Constitution Ave. NE
Lot 1
Lot 2 (bus)
Lot 3 (bus)
22nd St. NE
Lot 4
Lot 7
A St. NE
Whitney Young Memorial Br.
Main Entrance
RFK Stadium
East Capitol St.
Lot 10
Lot 9
Lot 5
A St. SE
Washington Armory
22nd St. SE
Independence Ave. SE
Lot 8
18th St. SE
19th St. SE
N
0
600 feet
0
200 meters
Anacostia River
C St. SE
RFK Stadium Closeup
Parking 4
Gate E
N
Gate F
Gate D
Lower Level Visitors
Playing Field
Main Entrance
Redskins Lower Level
Mezzanine
Upper Level
Gate C
Gate A
Gate B
Parking 5

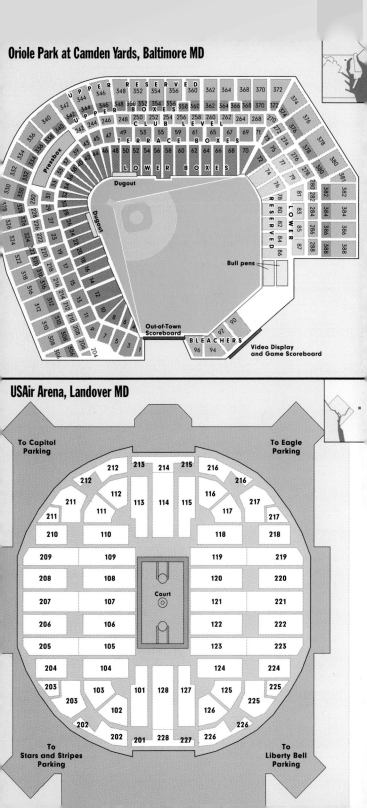

Oriole Park at Camden Yards, Baltimore MD

UPPER RESERVED
UPPER BOXES
CLUB LEVEL
TERRACE BOXES
LOWER BOXES
Pressbox
Dugout
Dugout
LOWER RESERVED
Bull pens
Out-of-Town Scoreboard
BLEACHERS
Video Display and Game Scoreboard

USAir Arena, Landover MD

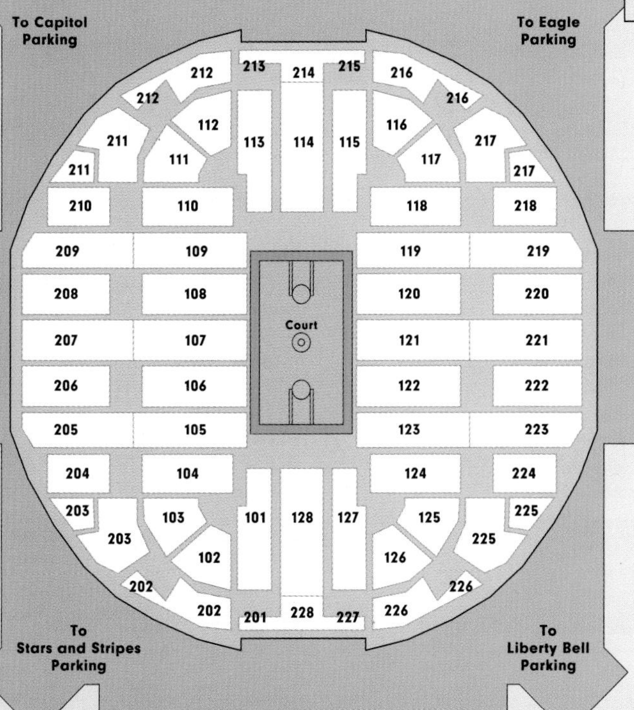

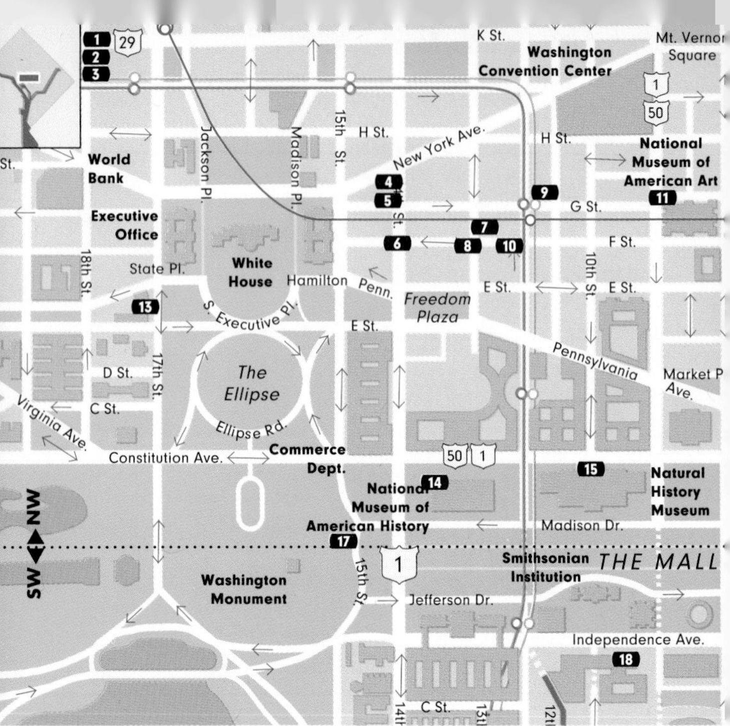

Listed by Site Number

1 Filene's Basement
2 Brooks Brothers
3 Border Books
4 Jacobs Gardner Supply
5 CVS
6 Arpelli Leather Goods
6 B. Dalton Books
6 Footlocker
6 Limited
6 Sharper Image
6 Software Etc
6 Sunglasses Hut
6 Victoria's Secret
7 Banana Republic
8 The Shops at National Place
9 Hecht's
10 Olsson's
11 National Museum of American Art Shop
12 Union Station

Listed Alphabetically

Arpelli Leather Goods, 6. 14th & F Sts NW ☎ 737-6080

B. Dalton Books, 6. 14th & F Sts NW ☎ 393-1468

Banana Republic, 7. 601 13th St NW ☎ 638-2724

Border Books, 3. 1801 K St NW ☎ 466-4999

Brooks Brothers, 2. 1804 L St NW ☎ 659-4650

Corcoran Gallery, 13. 500 17th St NW ☎ 638-3211

CVS Drug Store, 5. 717 14th St NW ☎ 737-9525

Filene's Basement, 1. 1133 Connecticut Ave NW ☎ 872-8430

Footlocker, 6. 14th & F Sts NW ☎ 783-2093

Hecht's, 9. 1201 G St NW ☎ 628-6661

Jacobs Gardner Supply, 4. 1400 New York Ave NW ☎ 347-2257

Limited, 6. 14th & F Sts NW ☎ 628-8221

National Air & Space Museum Shop, 19. Independence & 6th Aves SW ☎ 357-2700

National Aquarium Gift Shop, 14. Constitution & 14th Sts NW ☎ 482-3679

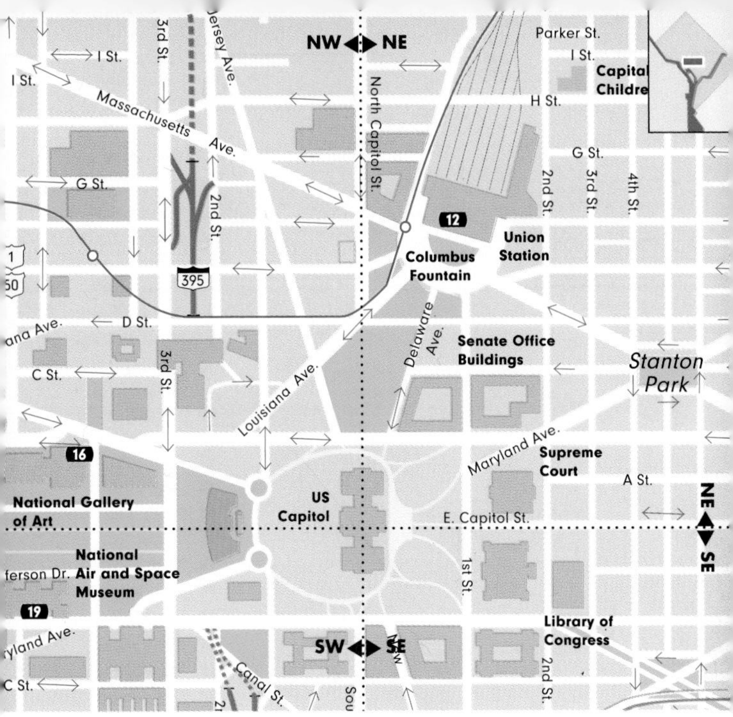

Listed by Site Number (cont.)

13 Corcoran Gallery

14 National Aquarium Gift Shop

14 National Museum of American History Shop

15 National Museum of Natural History Shop

16 National Gallery of Art Museum Shop

17 Washington Monument Gift Shop

18 National Museum of African Art Shop

19 National Air & Space Museum Shop

Listed Alphabetically (cont.)

National Gallery of Art Museum Shop, 16. Constitution & 4th Sts NW ☎ 737-4215

National Museum of American Art Shop, 11. G & 8th Sts NW ☎ 357-2700

National Museum of American History Shop, 14. Constitution & 14th Sts NW ☎ 357-2700

National Museum of African Art Shop, 18. 950 Independence Ave SW ☎ 357-2700

National Museum of Natural History Shop, 15. Constitution & 10th St NW ☎ 357-2700

Olsson's Records/Books, 10. 1200 F St NW ☎ 247-3686

Sharper Image, 6. 14th & F Sts NW ☎ 626-6340

The Shops at National Place, 8. 13th & F Sts NW ☎ 783-9090

Software Etc, 6. 14th & F Sts NW ☎ 737-7607

Sunglasses Hut, 6. 14th & F Sts NW ☎ 628-0787

Union Station, 12. 50 Massachusetts Ave NE ☎ 289-1908

Victoria's Secret, 6. 14th & F Sts NW ☎ 347-3535

Washington Monument Gift Shop, 17. The Mall & 15th St NW ☎ 426-6839

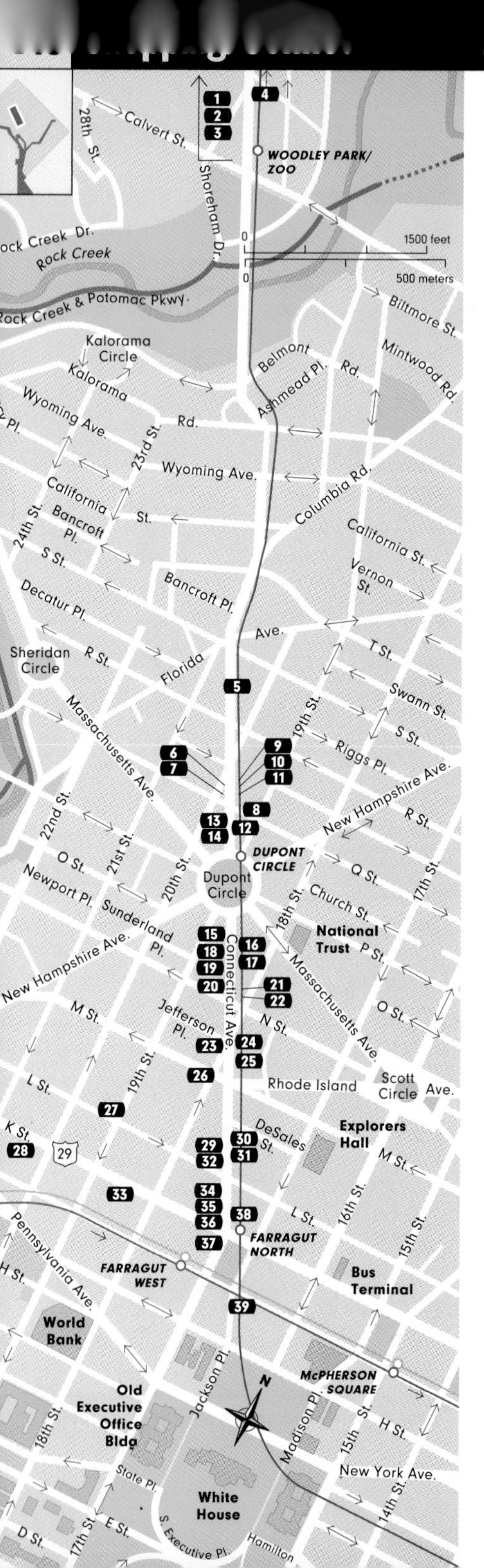

Listed by Site Number

1 Cheshire Cat
2 Politics & Prose
3 Kitchen Bazaar
4 CVS Drug Store
5 Newsroom
6 Americana West Gallery
7 Cherishables
8 Dupont Flowers
9 Lambda Rising
10 Melody Record Shop
11 Toast & Strawberries
12 Kramerbooks
13 Beadazzled
14 Kemp Mill Record Shops
15 Benetton
16 Written Word
17 Card Gallery
18 Betsy Fisher
19 Shoe Scene
20 Nature Food Center
21 Olsson's Books & Records
22 Copenhaver
23 Kid's Closet
24 Talbots
25 Britches of Georgetown
26 Chocolate Moose
27 Jos A Bank Clothiers
28 Supercrown
29 Brookstone Co
30 Burberrys
31 Tiny Jewel Box
32 Rizik Bros Inc
33 Beau Monde
34 Party 'N Paper
34 Victoria's Secret
35 Parade of Shoes
36 The Limited
37 Nine West
38 Custom Shop Shirtmakers
39 The Map Store

Listed Alphabetically

Americana West Gallery, 6. 1630 Connecticut Ave NW ☎ 265-1630

Beadazzled, 13. 1522 Connecticut Ave NW ☎ 265-2323

Beau Monde, 33. 1814 K St NW ☎ 466-7070

Benetton, 15. 1350 Connecticut Ave NW ☎ 659-1222

Betsy Fisher, 18. 1224 Connecticut Ave NW ☎ 785-1975

Britches of Georgetown, 25. 1219 Connecticut Ave NW ☎ 347-8994

Brookstone Co, 29. 1140 Connecticut Ave NW ☎ 293-9290

Burberrys, 30. 1155 Connecticut Ave NW ☎ 463-3000

Card Gallery, 17. 1363 Connecticut Ave NW ☎ 223-9230

Cherishables, 7. 1608 20th St NW ☎ 785-4087

Cheshire Cat, 1. 5512 Connecticut Ave NW ☎ 244-3956

Chocolate Moose, 26. 1800 M St NW ☎ 463-0992

Copenhaver, 22. 1301 Connecticut Ave NW ☎ 232-1200

Custom Shop Shirtmakers, 38. 1033 Connecticut Ave NW ☎ 659-8250

CVS Drug Store, 4. 3327 Connecticut Ave NW ☎ 966-7210

Dupont Flowers, 8. 1900 Q St NW ☎ 797-7600

Jos A Bank Clothiers, 27. 1118 19th St NW ☎ 466-2282

Kemp Mill Record Shops, 14. 1518 Connecticut Ave NW ☎ 332-8247

Kid's Closet, 23. 1226 Connecticut Ave NW ☎ 429-9247

Kitchen Bazaar, 3. 4401 Connecticut Ave NW ☎ 244-1550

Kramerbooks, 12. 1517 Connecticut Ave NW ☎ 387-1400

Lambda Rising, 9. 1625 Connecticut Ave NW ☎ 462-6969

The Limited, 36. 1024 Connecticut Ave NW ☎ 955-5710

The Map Store, 39. 1636 I St NW ☎ 628-2608

Melody Record Shop, 10. 1623 Connecticut Ave NW ☎ 232-4002

Nature Food Center, 20. 1330 Connecticut Ave NW ☎ 775-2573

Newsroom, 5. 1753 Connecticut Ave NW ☎ 332-1489

Nine West, 37. 1008 Connecticut Ave NW ☎ 452-9163

Olsson's Books & Records, 21. 1307 19th St NW ☎ 785-1133

Parade of Shoes, 35. 1020 Connecticut Ave NW ☎ 872-8581

Party 'N Paper, 34. 1050 Connecticut Ave NW ☎ 429-0555

Politics & Prose, 2. 5015 Connecticut Ave NW ☎ 364-1919

Rizik Bros Inc, 32. 1100 Connecticut Ave NW ☎ 223-4050

Shoe Scene, 19. 1330 Connecticut Ave NW ☎ 659-2194

Supercrown, 28. 2020 K St NW ☎ 659-2030

Talbots, 24. 24 Connecticut Ave NW ☎ 887-6973

Tiny Jewel Box, 31. 1143 Connecticut Ave NW ☎ 393-2747

Toast & Strawberries, 11. 1608 20th St NW ☎ 234-2424

Victoria's Secret, 34. 1050 Connecticut Ave NW ☎ 293-7530

Written Word, 16. 1365 Connecticut Ave NW ☎ 223-1400

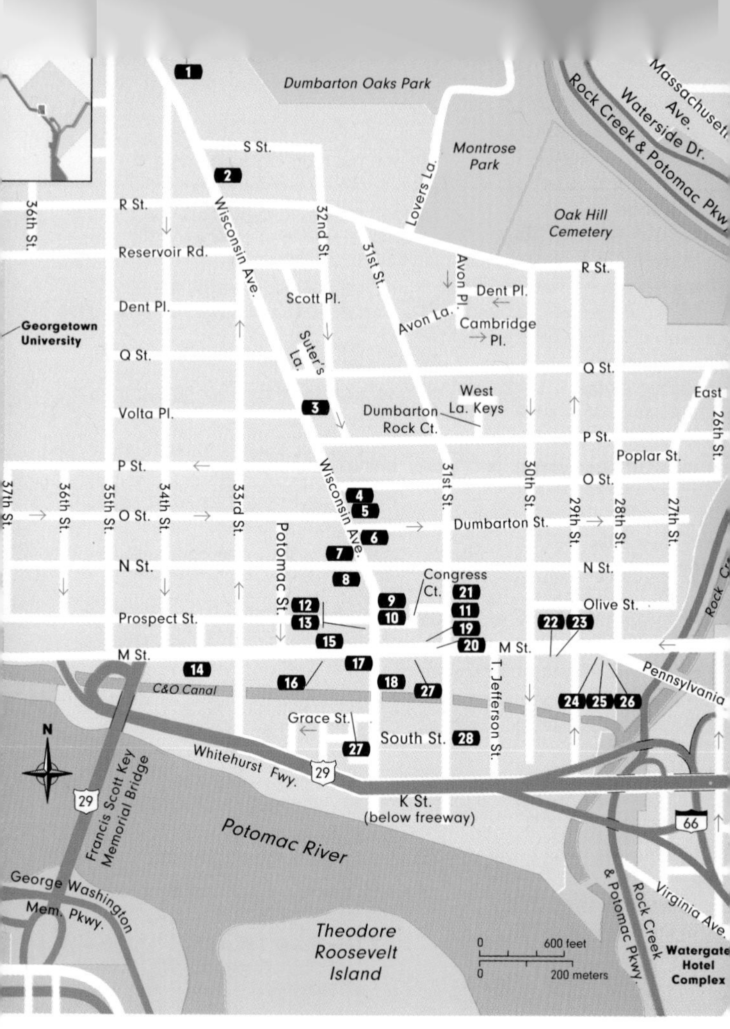

Listed by Site Number

1 Benetton
2 Miller & Arney Antiques
3 Santa Fe Style
4 Little Caledonia
5 Appalachian Spring
5 The Phoenix
6 The Nature Co
7 Martin's
8 The Gap
9 Cignal
10 Hats in the Belfry
11 Old Print Gallery
12 Olsson's Books & Records
13 Britches of G'town
14 Sunny's Surplus
15 Racquet & Jog
16 Abercrombie & Finch
16 Ann Taylor
16 Athlete's Foot
16 Crabtree & Evelyn
16 F.A.O. Schwarz
16 J Crew
16 The Limited
16 Martin Lawrence Galleries
16 Pavo Real
16 Platypus
16 Polo/Ralph Lauren
16 The Sharper Image
16 Victoria's Secret
16 Waldenbooks
16 Williams-Sonoma
17 Banana Republic
18 Pleasure Chest Ltd
19 Urban Outfitters
20 Earl Allen
21 Logic & Literature
22 Antiques Center
23 The American Hand
24 G.K.S. Bush
25 Justine Mehlman
26 Lorenzo
27 Conrans
28 Yes!

Listed Alphabetically

Abercrombie & Finch, 16. 3222 M St NW ☎ 965-6500

The American Hand, 23. 2906 M St NW ☎ 965-3273

Ann Taylor, 16. 3222 M St NW ☎ 338-5290

Antiques Center, 22. 2918 M St NW ☎ 338-3811

Appalachian Spring, 5. 1415 Wisconsin Ave NW ☎ 337-5780

Athlete's Foot, 16. 3222 M St NW ☎ 965-7262

Banana Republic, 17. 3200 M St NW ☎ 333-2554

Benetton, 1. 5300 Wisconsin Ave NW ☎ 362-6970

Britches of Georgetown, 13. 1247 Wisconsin Ave NW ☎ 338-3330

Cignal, 9. 1249 Wisconsin Ave NW ☎ 333-8787

Conrans, 27. 3227 Grace St NW ☎ 298-8300

Crabtree & Evelyn, 16. 3222 M St NW ☎ 342-1934

Earl Allen, 20. 3109 M St NW ☎ 338-1678

F.A.O. Schwarz, 16. 3222 M St NW ☎ 342-2285

The Gap, 9. 1258 Wisconsin Ave NW ☎ 333-2657

G.K.S. Bush, 24. 2828 Pennsylvania Ave NW ☎ 965-0653

Hats in the Belfry, 10. 1237 Wisconsin Ave NW ☎ 342-2006

J Crew, 16. 3222 M St NW ☎ 965-4090

Justine Mehlman, 25. 2824 Pennsylvania Ave NW ☎ 337-0613

The Limited, 16. 3222 M St NW ☎ 342-5150

Little Caledonia, 4. 1419 Wisconsin Ave NW ☎ 333-4700

Logic & Literature, 30. 1222 31st St NW ☎ 625-1668

Lorenzo, 26. 2812 Pennsylvania Ave NW ☎ 965-6149

Martin Lawrence Galleries, 16. 3222 M St NW ☎ 965-4811

Martin's, 7. 1304 Wisconsin Ave NW ☎ 338-6144

Miller & Arney Antiques, 2. 1737 Wisconsin Ave NW ☎ 338-2369

The Nature Co, 6. 1323 Wisconsin Ave NW ☎ 333-4100

Old Print Gallery, 11. 1220 31st St NW ☎ 965-1818

Olsson's Books & Records, 12. 1239 Wisconsin Ave NW ☎ 338-9544

Pavo Real, 16. 3222 M St NW ☎ 338-2405

Platypus, 16. 3222 M St NW ☎ 338-7680

Pleasure Chest Ltd, 18. 1063 Wisconsin Ave NW ☎ 333-8570

The Phoenix, 5. 1514 Wisconsin Ave NW ☎ 338-4404

Polo/Ralph Lauren, 16. 3222 M St NW ☎ 965-0904

Racquet & Jog, 15. 3225 M St NW ☎ 333-8113

Santa Fe Style, 3. 1413 Wisconsin Ave NW ☎ 333-3747

The Sharper Image, 16. 3222 M St NW ☎ 337-9361

Sunny's Surplus, 14. 3342 M St NW ☎ 333-8550

Urban Outfitters, 19. 3111 M St NW ☎ 342-1012

Victoria's Secret, 16. 3222 M St NW ☎ 965-5457

Waldenbooks, 16. 3222 M St NW ☎ 333-8033

Williams-Sonoma, 16. 3222 M St NW ☎ 965-3422

Yes!, 28. 1035 31st St NW ☎ 338-7874

Area Shopping Centers

Listed Alphabetically

Ballston Commons, 16. ☎ 703/243-8088

Chevy Chase Pavilion, 5. ☎ 686-5335

City Place, 4. ☎ 301/589-1091

Dupont Circle Area, 9.

Eastern Market, 14.

Fair Oaks Mall, 20. ☎ 703/359-8300

Fashion Center, 15. ☎ 703/415-2400

Galleria at Tyson's II, 18. ☎ 703/827-7700

Georgetown Park, 10. ☎ 298-5577

Lake Forest Mall, 1. ☎ 301/670-0599

Landmark Center, 21. ☎ 703/354-8405

Landover Mall, 8. ☎ 301/341-3200

Mazza Gallerie, 6. ☎ 966-6114

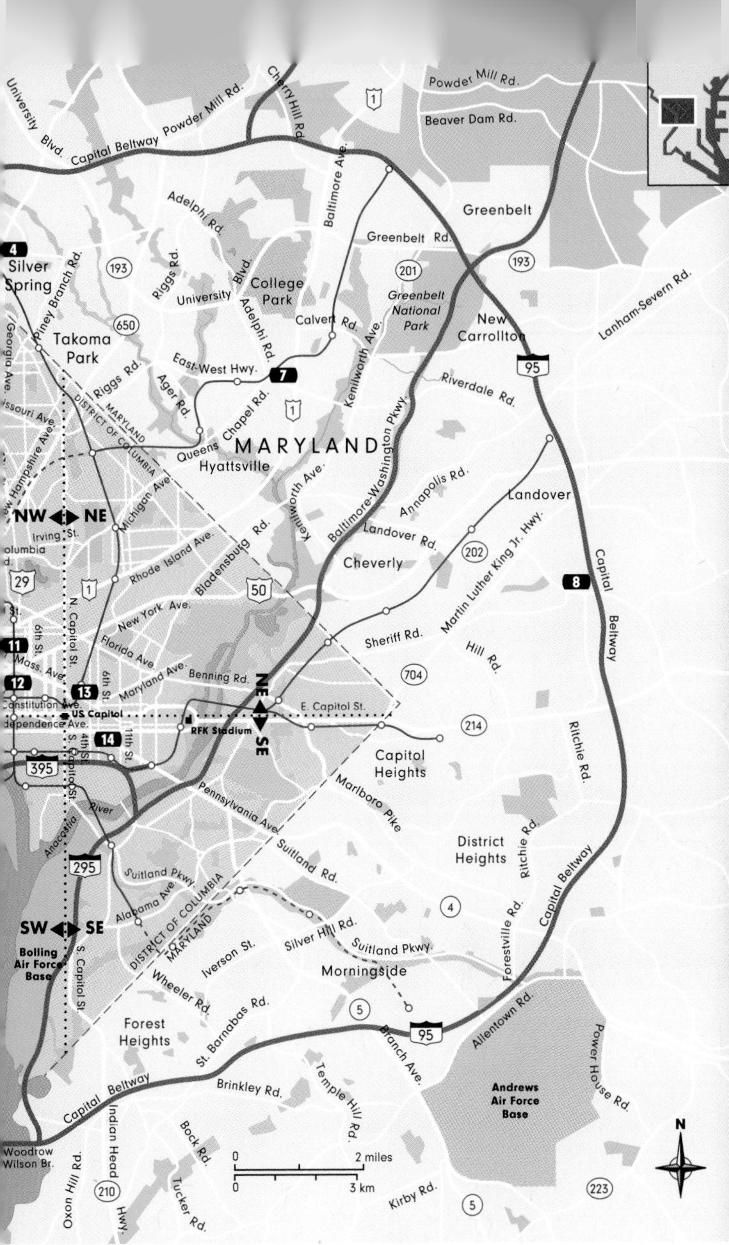

Listed Alphabetically (cont.)

Montgomery Mall, 3. ☎ 301/469–6000

The Pavilion at the Old Post Office, 12. ☎ 289–4224

Potomac Mills Mall, 23. ☎ 703/643–1203

Prince George's Plaza, 7. ☎ 301/559–8844

Seven Corners Center, 17. ☎ 703/385–1677

The Shops at National Place, 11. ☎ 783–9090

Springfield Mall, 22. ☎ 703/971–3600

Tysons Corner Center, 19. ☎ 703/893–9400

Union Station, 13. ☎ 289–1908

White Flint, 2. ☎ 301/468–5777

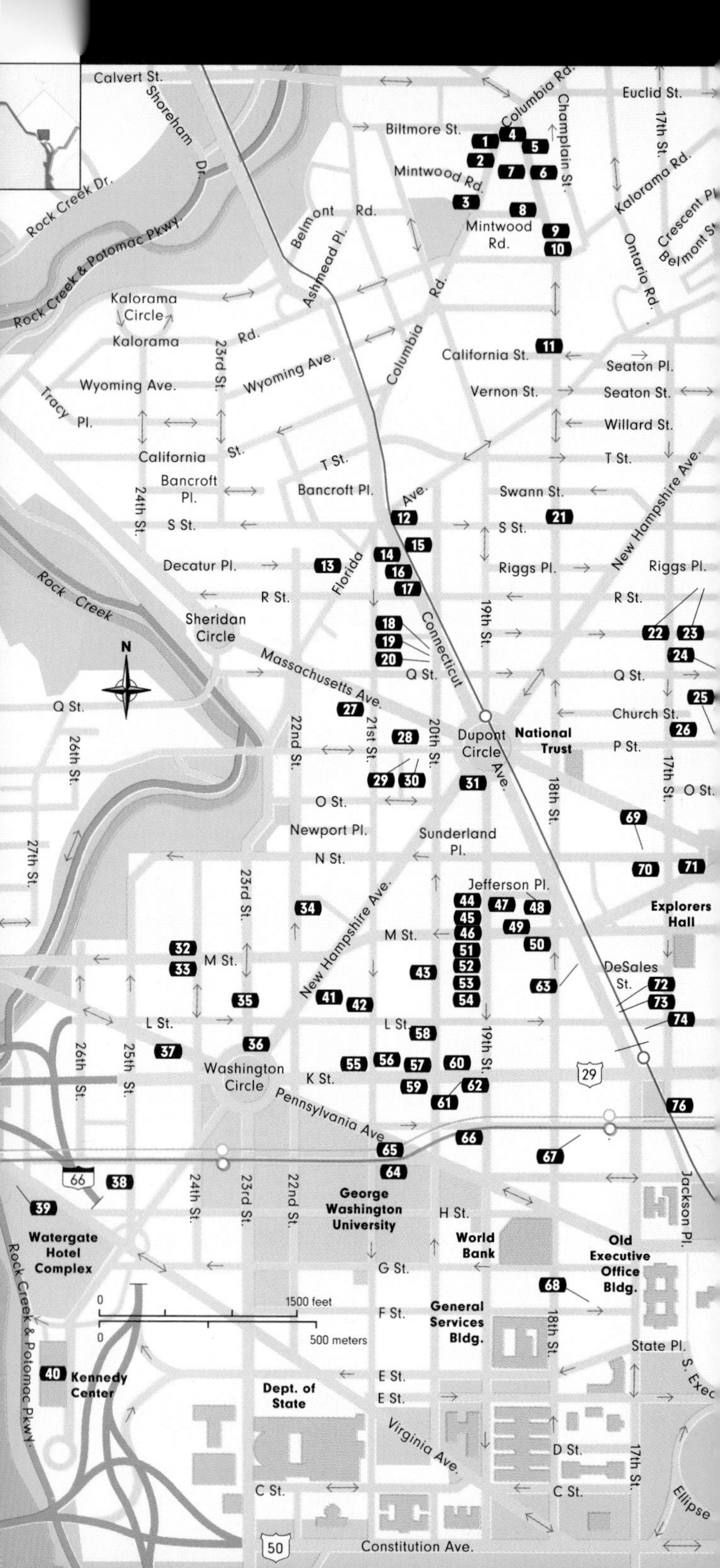

Calvert St.
Shoreham Dr.
Rock Creek Dr.
Rock Creek & Potomac Pkwy.
Biltmore St.
Columbia Rd.
Champlain St.
Euclid St.
17th St.
Kalorama Rd.
Crescent Pl.
Belmont St.
Mintwood Rd.
Belmont Rd.
Ashmead Pl.
Mintwood Rd.
Ontario Rd.
Kalorama Circle
Kalorama Rd.
Columbia Rd.
California St.
Seaton Pl.
23rd St.
Wyoming Ave.
Wyoming Ave.
Vernon St.
Seaton St.
Tracy Pl.
Willard St.
California St.
T St.
T St.
Bancroft Pl.
Bancroft Pl.
Swann St.
24th St.
S St.
Ave.
S St.
New Hampshire Ave.
Decatur Pl.
Florida
Riggs Pl.
Riggs Pl.
Rock Creek
R St.
R St.
Sheridan Circle
Connecticut
19th St.
Massachusetts Ave.
Q St.
Q St.
N
Q St.
Church St.
26th St.
22nd St.
21st St.
20th St.
Dupont Circle
National Trust
P St.
Ave.
18th St.
17th St.
O St.
O St.
Newport Pl.
Sunderland Pl.
27th St.
N St.
23rd St.
Jefferson Pl.
Explorers Hall
New Hampshire Ave.
M St.
M St.
DeSales St.
L St.
L St.
26th St.
25th St.
Washington Circle
K St.
19th St.
29
Pennsylvania Ave.
66
24th St.
23rd St.
22nd St.
George Washington University
H St.
Jackson Pl.
Watergate Hotel Complex
World Bank
Old Executive Office Bldg.
G St.
0
1500 feet
F St.
General Services Bldg.
18th St.
0
500 meters
State Pl.
Rock Creek & Potomac Pkwy.
Kennedy Center
E St.
E St.
S. Exec.
Dept. of State
Virginia Ave.
D St.
17th St.
C St.
C St.
Ellipse
50
Constitution Ave.
1
2
3
4
5
6
7
8
9
10
11
12
13
14
15
16
17
18
19
20
21
22
23
24
25
26
27
28
29
30
31
32
33
34
35
36
37
38
39
40
41
42
43
44
45
46
47
48
49
50
51
52
53
54
55
56
57
58
59
60
61
62
63
64
65
66
67
68
69
70
71
72
73
74
76

Howard University
Clifton St.
Chapin St.
Belmont St.
Florida Ave.
Barry Pl.
Bryant St.
W St.
V St.
U St.
Elm St.
Caroline St.
Wallach St.
T St.
Swann St.
S St.
French St.
Riggs Pl.
R St.
Rhode Island Ave.
Corcoran St.
Vermont Ave.
Warner St.
Q St.
Church St.
Logan Circle
O St.
Neal Pl.
Scott Circle
N St.
Thomas Circle
M St.
Massachusetts Ave.
L St.
Bus Terminal
K St.
Mt. Vernon Square
Washington Convention Center
I St.
H St.
New York Ave.
National Museum of American Art
G St.
F St.
White House
Hamilton
Penn.
Freedom Plaza
E St.
D St.
Pennsylvania Ave.
Indiana Ave.
Market Pl.
C St.
The Ellipse
Commerce Dept.
Constitution Ave.
Madison Pl.
Johnson Ave.
Sherman Ave.
Georgia Ave.
15th St.
14th St.
13th St.
12th St.
11th St.
10th St.
9th St.
8th St.
7th St.
6th St.
5th St.
4th St.

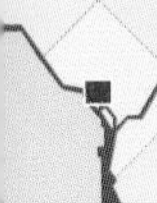

Listed by Site Number

1 Café Atlantico
2 Perry's
3 Grill from Ipanema
4 I Mattti
5 Red Sea
6 La Fourchette
7 Meskerem
8 Belmont Kitchen
9 Peyote Café
10 Saigonnais
11 Addis Ababa
12 Ruth's Chris Steakhouse
13 Nora
14 Food for Thought
15 Anna Maria's
16 Cafe Petitto
17 Odeon
18 Zorba's Cafe
19 Childe Harold
20 Vincenzo's
21 Lauriol Plaza
22 La Fonda
23 El Bodegon
24 Jefferson Restaurant
25 Cafe Luna
25 Skewers
26 Boss Shepherds
27 Jockey Club
28 Obelisk
29 Pan Asian Noodles & Grill
30 Sala Thai
31 Front Page
32 The Colonnade
33 Melrose
34 Blackie's House of Beef
35 Goldoni
36 West End Cafe
37 Bristol Grill
38 Foggy Bottom Café
39 Jean-Louis
40 Roof Terrace
41 Washington Grill
42 Galileo
43 Marrocco's
44 i Ricchi
45 Sam & Harry's
46 Vildalia
47 Palm
48 Bacchus
49 Gusti's
50 Gary's
51 Take-Sushi
52 Star of Siam
53 Cafe Asia
54 Luigi's
55 Mr K's
56 Ginza Japanese
57 Thai Kingdom
58 Oodles Noodles
59 Prime Rib
60 Tiberio
61 Mykonos
62 Tequila Grill
63 Le Lion d'Or
64 Primi Piatti
65 Kinkead's
66 Charlie Chiang's
67 Taberna Del Alabardero
68 Maison Blanche
69 Tabard Inn
70 Iron Gate Inn
71 Herb's Restaurant
72 Cafe Promenade
73 Charlie's Crab
74 Ascot
75 Fran O'Brien's Steak House
76 Bombay Club
77 Allegro
78 Jacques
79 Gerard's Place
80 Health Zone
81 Georgia Brown's
82 Montpelier Room
83 Harvest Veranda
84 Notte Luna
85 BenKay
86 Tuscana West
87 Cafe Mozart
88 Morrison-Clark Inn
89 Cour de Lion
90 Capitol City Brewing Co
90 Haad Thai
90 Luigino
91 Old Ebbitt Grille
92 Two Continents
93 Occidental
94 Willard Room
95 Red Sage
96 American Café
97 Friday's
98 Les Halles
99 Dock Street Brewing Company
100 Blossoms
101 Dixie Grill
102 Marrakesh
103 China Inn
104 Tony Cheng's
105 Ruby
106 Coco Loco
107 Li Ho Food
108 Hunan's Chinatown
109 Thai Shan
110 Golden Palace
111 Hard Rock Cafe
112 Jaleo
113 Peasant
114 701 Pennsylvania
115 Bice

Listed Alphabetically

Addis Ababa, 11. 2106 18th St NW
☎ 232-6092. Ethiopian. $$$

Allegro, 77. 923 16th St NW
☎ 879-6900. Continental. $$$$

American Café, 97.
1331 Pennsylvania Ave NW
☎ 626-0770. American. $

Anna Maria's, 15.
1737 Connecticut Ave NW
☎ 667-1444. Italian. $$

Ascot, 75. 1708 L St NW
☎ 296-7640. Continental. $$

Bacchus, 48. 1827 Jefferson Plaza NW
☎ 785-0734. Middle Eastern. $$

Belmont Kitchen, 8. 2400 18th St NW
☎ 667-1200. American. $$

BenKay, 85. 727 15th St NW
☎ 737-1515. Japanese. $

Bertolinis, 111.
801 Pennsylvania Ave NW
☎ 638-2140. Italian. $$$

Bice, 116. 601 Pennsylvania Ave NW
☎ 638-2423. Italian. $$$$

Blackie's House of Beef, 34.
1217 22nd St NW
☎ 333-1100. American. $$

Blossoms, 100.
Old Post Office Pavilion NW
☎ 371-1838. American. $$

Bombay Club, 76.
815 Connecticut Ave NW
☎ 659-3727. Indian. $$

Bombay Palace, 63. 2020 K St NW
☎ 331-4200. Indian. $

Bristol Grill, 37.
2430 Pennsylvania Ave NW
☎ 955-6400. American. $$$

Cafe Asia, 53. 1134 19th St NW
☎ 659-2696. Asian. $

Café Atlantico, 1.
1819 Columbia Rd NW
☎ 393-0812. Caribbean. $$

Cafe Luna, 25. 1633 P St NW
☎ 387-4005. American. $

Cafe Mozart, 87. 1331 H St NW
☎ 347-5732. German. $

Cafe Petitto, 16.
1724 Connecticut Ave NW
☎ 462-8771. Italian. $

Cafe Promenade, 72.
1127 Connecticut Ave NW
☎ 347-8900. Mediterranean. $$

Capitol City Brewing Co, 90.
1100 New York Ave NW
☎ 628-2222. American. $$

Casa Blanca, 25.
1014 Vermont Ave NW
☎ 393-4430. Peruvian. $

Charlie Chiang's, 66. 1912 I St NW
☎ 293-6000. Chinese. $$

Charlie's Crab, 73.
1101 Connecticut Ave NW
☎ 785-4505. Seafood. $$

Childe Harold, 19. 1610 20th St NW
☎ 483-6702. American. $$

China Inn, 103. 631 H St NW
☎ 842-0909. Chinese. $$

Coco Loco, 106. 810 7th St NW
☎ 289-2626. Brazilian. $$

Cour de Lion, 89.
926 Massachusetts Ave NW
☎ 638-5200. Continental. $$$

The Colonnade, 32. 2401 M St NW
☎ 429-2400. Continental. $$$$

Dixie Grill, 101. 518 10th St NW
☎ 628-4800. Southern. $$

Dock Street Brewing Company, 99.
1299 Pennsylvania Ave NW
☎ 639-0403. American. $$

El Bodegon, 23. 1637 R St NW
☎ 667-1710. Spanish. $$$

Foggy Bottom Café, 38.
924 25th St NW
☎ 338-8707. American. $$

Food for Thought, 14.
1738 Connecticut Ave NW
☎ 797-1095. Vegetarian.

Fran O'Brien's Steak House, 75.
631 16th & L Sts NW
☎ 783-2599. American. $$$

Friday's, 97.
1201 Pennsylvania Ave NW
☎ 628-8443. American. $

Front Page, 31.
1333 New Hampshire Ave NW
☎ 296-6500. American. $$

Galileo, 42. 1110 21st St NW
☎ 293-7191. Italian. $$$

Gary's, 50. 1800 M St NW
☎ 463-6470. American. $$$

$$$$ = ***over $35*** $$$ = ***$25-$35*** $$ = ***$15-$25*** $ = ***under $15***
Based on cost per person, excluding drinks, service, and 9% sales tax.

Listed Alphabetically (cont.)

Georgia Brown's, 81. 950 15th St NW ☎ 393-4499. Southern. $$

Gerard's Place, 79. 915 15th St NW ☎ 737-4445. French. $$$

Ginza Japanese, 56. 1009 21st St NW ☎ 833-1244. Japanese. $$

Golden Palace, 110. 720 7th St NW ☎ 783-1225. Chinese. $$

Goldoni, 35. 1113 23rd St NW ☎ 293-1511. Italian. $$

Grill from Ipanema, 3. 1858 Columbia Rd ☎ 986-0757. Brazilian. $$

Gusti's, 49. 1837 M St NW ☎ 331-9444. Italian. $$

Haad Thai, 90. 1100 New York Ave NW ☎ 682-1111. Thai. $$

Hard Rock Cafe, 111. 999 E St NW ☎ 737-7625. American. $$

Harvest Veranda, 83. 1400 M St NW ☎ 429-1700. American. $$$$

Health Zone, 80. 1445 K St NW ☎ 371-2900. Vegetarian. $

Herb's Restaurant, 71. 1615 Rhode Island Ave NW ☎ 333-4372. American. $$

Hunan Chinatown, 108. 624 H St NW ☎ 783-5858. Chinese. $$

I Matti, 4. 2436 18th St NW ☎ 462-8844. Italian. $$

i Ricchi, 44. 1220 19th St NW ☎ 835-0459. Italian. $$$

Iron Gate Inn, 70. 1734 N St NW ☎ 737-1370. Mediterranean. $$

Jacques, 78. 915 15th NW ☎ 737-4445. French. $$

Jaleo, 112. 480 7th St NW ☎ 628-7949. Spanish. $$

Jean-Louis, 39. 2650 Virginia Ave NW ☎ 298-4488. French. $$$$

Jefferson Restaurant, 24. 1200 16th St NW ☎ 347-2200. Continental. $$$$

Jockey Club, 27. 2100 Massachusetts Ave NW ☎ 659-8000. Continental. $$$$

Kinkead's, 65. 2000 Pennsylvania Ave NW ☎ 296-7700. Seafood. $$$$

La Fonda, 22. 1739 R St NW ☎ 232-6965. Mexican. $$

La Fourchette, 6. 2429 18th St NW ☎ 332-3077. French. $$

Lauriol Plaza, 21. 1801 18th St NW ☎ 387-0035. Southwestern. $$

Legal Sea Foods, 59. 2020 K St NW ☎ 496-1111. Seafood. $$

Le Lion d'Or, 63. 1150 Connecticut Ave NW ☎ 296-7972. French. $$$$

Les Halles, 98. 1201 Pennsylvania Ave NW ☎ 347-6848. French. $$$

Li Ho Food, 107. 501 H St NW ☎ 289-2059. Szechuan. $$

Luigino, 90. 1100 New York Ave NW ☎ 371-0595. Italian. $$

Luigi's, 54. 1132 19th St NW ☎ 331-7574. Italian. $$

Maison Blanche, 68. 1725 F St NW ☎ 842-0070. French. $$$$

Marrakesh, 102. 617 New York Ave NW ☎ 393-9393. Moroccan. $$

Marrocco's, 43. 1120 20th St NW ☎ 331-9664. Italian. $$

Melrose, 33. 2400 M St NW ☎ 955-3899. American. $$$

Meskerem, 7. 2434 18th St NW ☎ 462-4100. Ethiopian. $

Montpelier Room, 82. 15th & M Sts NW ☎ 862-1712. Continental. $$$

Morrison-Clark Inn, 88. 1015 L St NW ☎ 289-8580. American. $$$$

Mr K's, 55. 2121 K St NW ☎ 331-8868. Chinese. $$$$

Mykonos, 61. 1835 K St NW ☎ 331-0370. Greek. $

Nora, 13. 2132 Florida Ave NW ☎ 462-5143. American. $$$

Notte Luna, 84. 809 15th St NW ☎ 408-9500. Italian. $$

Obelisk, 28. 2029 P St NW ☎ 872-1180. Italian. $$$

Occidental, 93. 1475 Pennsylvania Ave NW ☎ 639-8718. American. $$$

Odeon, 17. 1714 Connecticut Ave NW ☎ 328-6228. Italian. $$

Old Ebbitt Grill, 91. 675 15th St NW ☎ 347-4800. American. $$$

Oodles Noodles, 53. 1010 20th St NW ☎ 293-3138. Asian. $

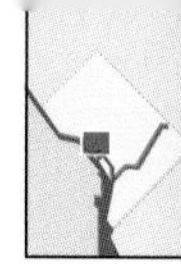

Palm, 47. 1225 19th St NW
☎ 293-9091. American. $$$$

Pan Asian Noodles & Grill, 29. 2020 P St NW ☎ 872-8889. Thai. $

Peppers, 28. 1527 17th St NW
☎ 328-8193. Southwest. $

Perry's, 2. 1811 Columbia Rd NW
☎ 234-6218. Japanese. $$

Peyote Café, 9. 2319 18th St NW
☎ 462-8330. Southwestern. $.

Planet Hollywood, 99. 1101 Pennsylvania Ave NW
☎ 347-1588. American. $

Prime Rib, 59. 2020 K St NW
☎ 466-8811. American. $$$$

Primi Piatti, 64. 2013 I St NW
☎ 223-3600. Italian. $$

Red Sage, 95. 605 14th St NW
☎ 638-4444. Southwestern. $$$

Red Sea, 5. 2463 18th St NW
☎ 483-5000. Ethiopian. $

Roof Terrace, 40. Kennedy Center NW
☎ 416-8555. American. $$$

Ruby, 105. 609 H St NW
☎ 842-0060. Chinese. $

Ruth's Chris Steakhouse, 12. 1801 Connecticut Ave NW
☎ 797-0033. Steakhouse. $$$

Saigonnais, 10. 2307 18th St NW
☎ 232-5300. Vietnamese. $$

Sala Thai, 30. 2016 P St NW
☎ 872-1144. Thai. $$

Sam & Harry's, 45. 1200 19th St NW
☎ 296-4333. American. $$$$

701 Pennsylvania, 114. 701 Pennsylvania Ave NW
☎ 393-0701. American. $$$

Skewers, 25. 1633 P St NW
☎ 387-7400. Middle Eastern. $$

Star of Siam. 52. 1136 19th St NW
☎ 785-2839. Thai. $$

Tabard Inn, 69. 1739 N St NW
☎ 833-2668. American. $$$

Taberna del Alabardero, 67. 1776 I St NW ☎ 429-2200. Spanish. $$$$

Take-Sushi, 51. 1140 19th St NW
☎ 466-3798. Japanese. $$

Tequila Grill, 62. 1990 K St NW
☎ 833-3640. Southwestern. $

Thai Kingdom, 57. 2021 K St NW
☎ 835-1700. Thai. $

Thai Shan, 109. 622 H St NW
☎ 639-0266. Cantonese. $

Tiberio, 60. 1915 K St NW
☎ 452-1915. Italian. $$$$

Tony Cheng's, 104. 619 H St NW
☎ 842-8669. Mongolian. $$

Tuscana West, 86. 1350 I St NW
☎ 289-7300. Italian. $$

Two Continents, 92. 15th & Pennsylvania Ave NW
☎ 347-4499. Continental. $$

Vidalia, 46. 1990 M St NW
☎ 659-1990. American. $$$

Vincenzo's, 20. 1606 20th St NW
☎ 667-0047. Italian. $$$

Washington Grill, 41. 1143 New Hampshire Ave NW
☎ 775-0800. American. $$

West End Cafe, 36. 1 Washington Circle NW
☎ 293-5390. International. $$$

Willard Room, 94. 1401 Pennsylvania Ave NW
☎ 637-7440. American. $$$$

Zorba's Cafe, 18. 1612 20th St NW
☎ 387-8555. Greek. $

$$$$ = ***over $35*** $$$ = ***$25-$35*** $$ = ***$15-$25*** $ = ***under $15***
Based on cost per person, excluding drinks, service, and 9% sales tax.

Listed by Site Number

1 America
1 Pizzeria Uno
2 Dubliner
3 Capitol View Club
4 La Colline
5 Monocle
6 Hunan Capitol Hill
7 American Café
8 La Brasserie
9 Bangkok Orchid
10 Armands Pizzeria
11 Two Quail
12 Café Berlin
13 Vie de France Café
14 HI Ribsters
14 Hogate's
15 Le Rivage
16 Philips Flagship
17 Pier 7
18 GangPlank
19 Tortilla Coast
20 Bullfeathers
21 Chesapeake Bagel Bakery
21 Hunan Dynasty
22 Le Mistral
23 Sherrill's Bakery
24 Young Chow
25 Burrito Brothers
26 Hill Cafe
27 Tune Inn
28 Hawk & Dove
29 Provisions
30 Market Lunch
31 Mister Henry's
32 Bread & Chocolate
33 Caffe Italiano
34 Cool Breeze's Place
35 San Antonio Tex-Mex
36 Trattorio Alberto

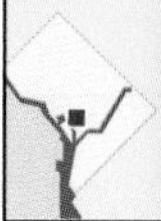

Listed Alphabetically

America, 1. 50 Massachusetts Ave NE ☎ 682-9555. American. $

American Café, 7. 227 Massachusetts Ave NE ☎ 547-8500. American. $

Armands Pizzeria, 10. 226 Massachusetts Ave NE ☎ 547-6600. Italian. $

Bangkok Orchid, 9. 301 Massachusetts Ave NE ☎ 546-5900. Thai. $$

Bread & Chocolate, 32. 666 Pennsylvania Ave SE ☎ 547-2875. French. $

Bullfeathers, 20. 410 1st St SE ☎ 543-5005. American. $

Burrito Brothers, 25. 205 Pennsylvania Ave SE ☎ 543-6835. Mexican. $

Café Berlin, 12. 322 Massachusetts Ave NE ☎ 543-7656. German. $

Caffe Italiano, 33. 1129 Pennsylvania Ave SE ☎ 544-5500. Italian. $

Capitol View Club, 3. 400 New Jersey Ave NW ☎ 639-8439. American. $$

Chesapeake Bagel Bakery, 21. 215 Pennsylvania Ave SE ☎ 546-0994. Bakery. $

Cool Breeze's Place, 34. 507 11th St SE ☎ 543-3184. Chili. $

Dubliner, 2. 520 N Capitol St NW ☎ 737-3773. Irish. $

GangPlank, 18. 600 Water St SW ☎ 554-5000. Seafood. $$

Hawk & Dove, 28. 329 Pennsylvania Ave SE ☎ 543-3300. American. $

HI Ribsters, 14. 800 Water St SW ☎ 479-6857. American. $$

Hill Cafe, 26. 332 Pennsylvania Ave SE ☎ 547-8668. Japanese. $

Hogate's, 14. 800 Water St SW ☎ 484-6301. Seafood. $$$

Hunan Capitol Hill, 6. 201 D St NE ☎ 544-0102. Chinese. $$

Hunan Dynasty, 21. 215 Pennsylvania Ave SE ☎ 546-6161. Chinese. $

La Brasserie, 8. 239 Massachusetts Ave NE ☎ 546-9154. French. $$$

La Colline, 4. 400 N Capitol St NW ☎ 737-0400. French. $$$

Le Mistral, 22. 223 Pennsylvania Ave SE ☎ 543-7747. French. $$

Le Rivage, 15. 1000 Water St SW ☎ 488-8111. French. $$

Market Lunch, 30. 225 7th St SE ☎ 547-8444. Seafood. $

Mister Henry's, 31. 601 Pennsylvania Ave SE ☎ 546-8412. American. $

Monocle, 5. 107 D St NE ☎ 546-4488. American. $$$

Philips Flagship, 16. 900 Water St SW ☎ 488-8515. Seafood. $$$

Pier 7, 17. Maine Ave & 7th St SW ☎ 554-2500. Continental. $$

Pizzeria Uno, 1. 50 Massachusetts Ave NE ☎ 842-0438. American. $$

Provisions, 29. 218 7th St SE ☎ 543-0694. Deli. $

San Antonio Tex-Mex, 35. 500 8th St SE ☎ 543-0002. Mexican. $$

Sherrill's Bakery, 23. 233 Pennsylvania Ave SE ☎ 544-2480. American. $

Tortilla Coast, 19. 400 1st St SE ☎ 546-6768. Mexican. $$

Trattorio Alberto, 36. 506 8th St SE ☎ 544-2007. Italian. $

Tune Inn, 27. 331 1/2 Pennsylvania Ave SE ☎ 543-2725. American. $

Two Quail, 11. 320 Massachusetts Ave NE ☎ 543-8030. American/Seafood. $$

Vie de France Café, 13. 600 Maryland Ave NW ☎ 554-7870. French. $

Young Chow, 24. 312 Pennsylvania Ave SE ☎ 544-3030. Chinese. $

$$$$ = *over $35* $$$ = *$25-$35* $$ = *$15-$25* $ = *under $15*

Based on cost per person, excluding drinks, service, and 9% sales tax.

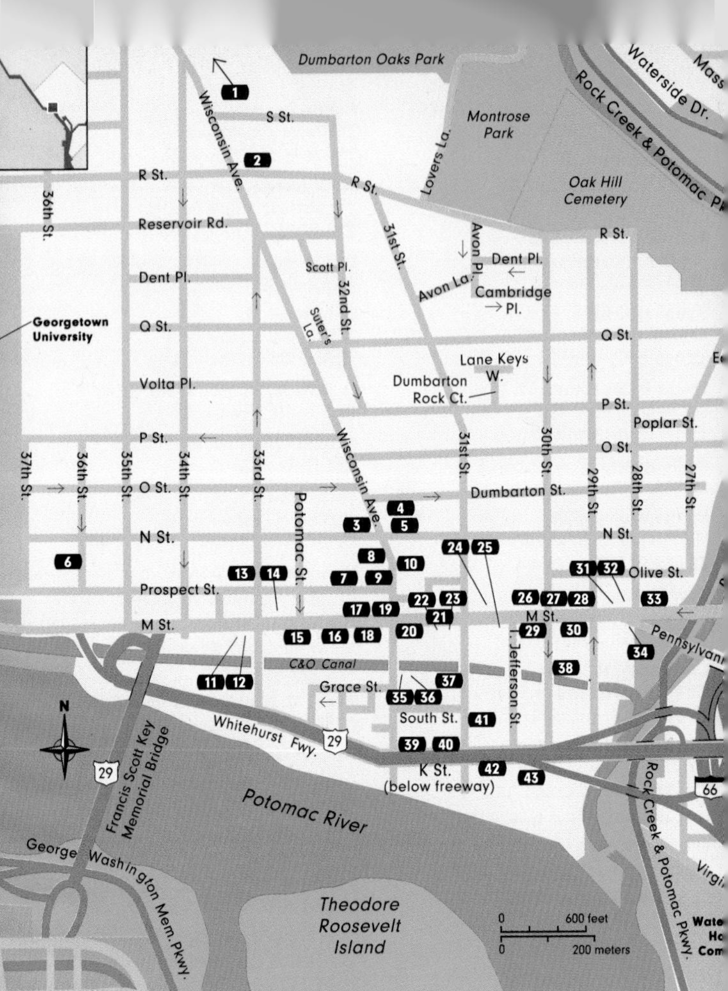

Listed by Site Number

1 Austin Grill
2 Japan Inn
3 Paolo's
4 Au Pied de Cochon
5 Aux Fruits de Mer
6 1789
7 Cafe Milano
7 Morton's of Chicago
8 Martin's Tavern
9 Third Edition
10 Il Radicchio
11 Madurai
11 Zed's Ethiopian
12 Tandoor
13 Aditi
14 Las Pampas
15 El Caribe
16 Clyde's
17 Fettoosh
18 Samauri Japan Steak
19 Pizzeria Uno
20 Nathan's
21 Burrito Brothers
22 Bistro Francais
23 Mr. Smith's
24 Georgetown Seafood
25 Le Steak
26 Charing Cross
27 Garretts Terrace
28 Gepettos
28 The Guards
29 Citronelle
30 Vietnam Georgetown
31 La Chaumière
32 Enriqueta's
33 Hunan Garden
34 Aux Beaux Champs
35 Houston's
36 Filomena's
37 Sea Catch
38 Music City Roadhouse
39 The River Club
40 Chadwick's Georgetown
41 Paper Moon
42 Hisago
43 Sequoia
43 Tony & Joe's

Listed Alphabetically

Aditi, 13. 3299 M St NW ☎ 625-6825. Indian. $$

Au Pied du Cochon, 4. 1335 Wisconsin Ave NW ☎ 333-5440. French. $

Austin Grill, 1. 2404 Wisconsin Ave NW ☎ 337-8080. Tex-Mex. $$

Aux Beaux Champs, 34. 2800 Pennsylvania Ave NW ☎ 342-0810. Continental. $$$$

Bistro Francais, 22. 3128 M St NW ☎ 338-3830. French. $$$

Burrito Brothers, 21. 3273 M St NW ☎ 965-3963. Mexican. $

Cafe Milano, 7. 3251 Prospect St NW ☎ 333-6183. Italian. $$

Chadwick's Georgetown, 40. 3205 K St NW ☎ 333-2565. American. $

Charing Cross, 26. 3027 M St NW ☎ 338-2141. Italian. $

Citronelle, 29. 3000 M St NW (Lathem Hotel) ☎ 625-2150. American. $$$

Clyde's, 16. 3236 M St NW ☎ 333-0294. American. $$

El Caribe, 15. 3288 M St NW ☎ 338-3121. Latin American. $$$

Enriqueta's, 32. 2811 M St NW ☎ 338-7772. Mexican. $$

Fettoosh, 17. 3277 M St NW ☎ 342-1199. Lebanese. $

Filomena's, 36. 1063 Wisconsin Ave NW ☎ 338-8800. Italian. $$

Garretts Terrace, 27. 3003 M St NW ☎ 333-1033. American. $

Georgetown Seafood, 24. 3063 M St NW ☎ 333-7038. Seafood. $$

Gepettos, 28. 2917 M St NW ☎ 333-2602. Italian. $

The Guards, 28. 2915 M St NW ☎ 965-2350. American. $$

Hisago, 42. 3050 K St NW ☎ 944-4282. Japanese. $$$$

Houston's, 35. 1065 Wisconsin Ave NW ☎ 338-7760. American. $$

Hunan Garden, 33. 1201 28th St NW ☎ 965-6800. Szechuan. $

Il Radicchio, 10. 1211 Wisconsin Ave NW ☎ 337-2627. Italian. $$

Japan Inn, 2. 1715 Wisconsin Ave NW ☎ 337-3400. Japanese. $$

La Chaumière, 31. 2813 M St NW ☎ 338-1784. French. $$$

Las Pampas, 14. 3291 M St NW ☎ 333-5151. Argentinian. $$

Le Steak, 25. 3060 M St NW ☎ 965-1627. Steakhouse. $$

Maison de Crepe, 5. 1329 Wisconsin Ave NW ☎ 333-2333. Seafood. $$

Martin's Tavern, 8. 1264 Wisconsin Ave NW ☎ 333-7370. American. $

Morton's of Chicago, 7. 3251 Prospect St NW ☎ 342-6258. Steakhouse. $$$$

Mr. Smith's, 23. 3104 M St NW ☎ 333-3104. American. $$

Music City Roadhouse, 38. 1050 30th St NW ☎ 337-4444. Southern. $

Nathan's, 20. 3150 M St NW ☎ 338-2000. Italian. $$$

Paolo's, 3. 1303 Wisconsin Ave NW ☎ 333-7353. Italian. $$

Paper Moon, 41. 1073 31st St NW ☎ 965-6666. Italian. $$

Pizzeria Uno, 19. 3211 M St NW ☎ 965-6333. American. $

The River Club, 39. 3223 K St NW ☎ 333-8118. American. $$$

Samauri Japan Steak, 18. 3222 M St NW ☎ 333-1001. Japanese. $$

Sea Catch, 37. 1054 31 St NW ☎ 337-8855. Seafood. $$$

Sequoia, 43. 3000 K St NW ☎ 944-4200. American. $$

1789, 6. 1226 36th St NW ☎ 965-1789. American. $$$$

Tandoor, 12. 3316 M St NW ☎ 333-3376. Indian. $

Third Edition, 9. 1218 Wisconsin Ave NW ☎ 333-3700. American. $

Vietnam Georgetown, 30. 2934 M St NW ☎ 337-4536. Vietnamese. $

Zed's Ethiopian Cuisine, 11. 3318 M St NW ☎ 333-4710. Ethiopian. $

$$$$ = ***over $35*** $$$ = ***$25-$35*** $$ = ***$15-$25*** $ = ***under $15***

Based on cost per person, excluding drinks, service, and 9% sales tax.

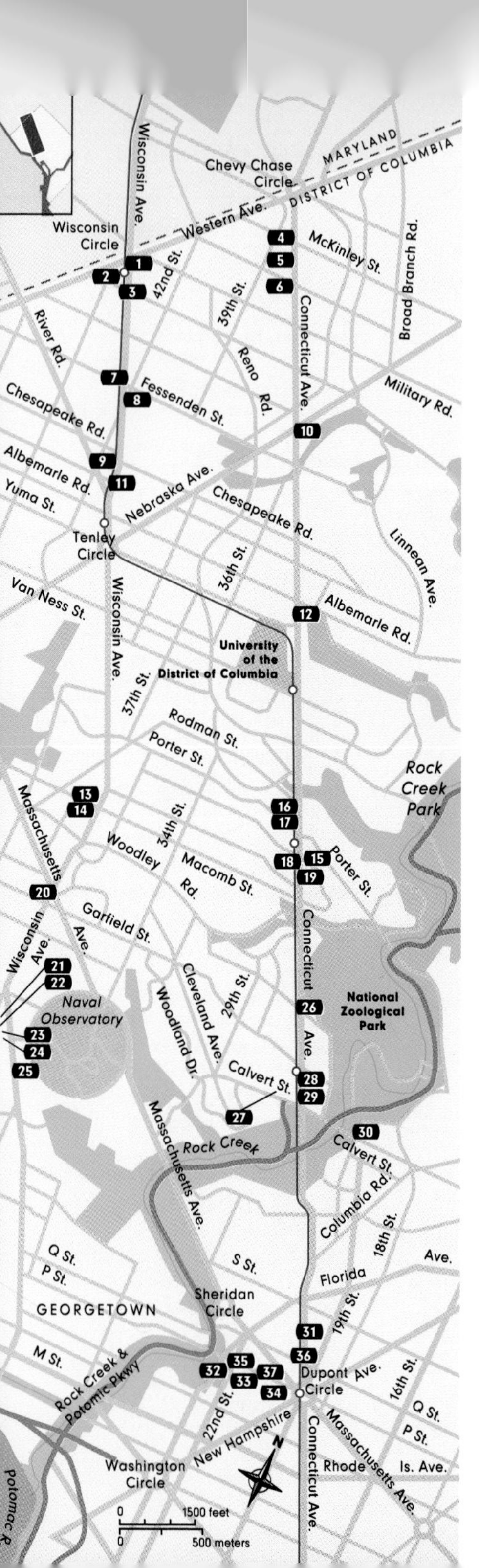

Listed by Site Number

1 Cheesecake Factory
2 Pleasant Peasant
3 Chadwick's
4 Bread & Chocolate
5 American City Diner
6 Parthenon
7 Floriana
8 Round Table
9 Toojays
10 Thai Room
11 Dancing Crab
12 Shanghai Garden
13 Thai Flavor
14 Cactus Cantina
15 Lavandou
16 Ivy's Place
17 Caffe Italiano
18 Ireland's Four Provinces
19 Gallagher's Pub
20 Primavera
21 Old Europe
22 Austin Grill
23 Germaine's
24 Le Caprice
25 Sushi-Ko
26 Mrs. Simpson's
27 New Heights
28 Petitto's Ristorante d'Italia
29 Lebanese Taverna
30 Calvert Restaurant
31 City Lights of China
32 Gabriel
33 Donna Adele
34 Pesce
35 Brickskeller
36 Bistro Twenty Fifteen
37 Obelisk
37 Pizza Paradiso

Listed Alphabetically

American City Diner, 5.
5532 Connecticut Ave NW
☎ 244-1949. American. $

Austin Grill, 22. 2404 Wisconsin Ave NW
☎ 337-8080. Tex-Mex. $

Bistro Twenty Fifteen, 36.
2015 Massachusetts Ave NW
☎ 939-4250. American. $$

Bread & Chocolate, 4.
5542 Connecticut Ave NW
☎ 966-7413. French. $

Brickskeller, 35. 1523 22nd St NW
☎ 293-1885. American. $

Cactus Cantina, 14.
3300 Wisconsin Ave NW
☎ 686-7222. Tex-Mex. $$

Caffe Italiano, 17.
3615 Connecticut Ave NW
☎ 966-2172. Italian. $$

Calvert Restaurant, 30.
1967 Calvert St NW
☎ 232-5431. Middle Eastern. $

Chadwick's, 3. 5247 Wisconsin Ave NW
☎ 362-8040. American. $$

Cheesecake Factory, 1.
5345 Wisconsin Ave NW
☎ 364-0500. American. $$

City Lights of China, 31.
1731 Connecticut Ave NW
☎ 265-6688. Chinese. $

Dancing Crab, 11.
4611 Wisconsin Ave NW
☎ 244-1882. Seafood. $$

Donna Adele, 33. 2100 P St NW
☎ 296-1142. Italian. $$

Floriana, 7. 4934 Wisconsin Ave NW
☎ 362-9009. Italian. $$

Gabriel, 32. 2121 P St NW
☎ 822-8157. Mediterranean. $$$

Germaine's, 23.
2400 Wisconsin Ave NW
☎ 965-1185. Asian. $$

Ireland's Four Provinces, 18.
3412 Connecticut Ave NW
☎ 244-0860. Irish. $$

Ivy's Place, 16.
3520 Connecticut Ave NW
☎ 363-7802. Thai. $

Lavandou, 15.
3321 Connecticut Ave NW
☎ 966-3003. American. $$

Le Caprice, 24.
2348 Wisconsin Ave NW
☎ 337-3394. French. $$$

Lebanese Taverna, 29.
2641 Connecticut Ave NW
☎ 265-8681. Middle Eastern. $$

Mrs. Simpson's, 26.
2915 Connecticut Ave NW
☎ 332-8300. American. $$

Nanny O'Brien's, 19.
3319 Connecticut Ave NW
☎ 686-9189. Irish. $

New Heights, 27. 2317 Calvert St NW
☎ 234-4110. American. $$$

Obelisk, 37. 2029 P St NW
☎ 872-1180. Italian. $$$$

Old Europe, 21.
2434 Wisconsin Ave NW
☎ 333-7600. German. $$

Parthenon, 6.
5510 Connecticut Ave NW
☎ 966-7600. Greek. $$

Pesce, 34. 2016 P St NW ☎ 466-3474.
Seafood. $$$

Petitto's Ristorante d'Italia, 28.
2653 Connecticut Ave NW
☎ 667-5350. Italian. $$

Pizza Paradiso, 37. 2029 P St NW
☎ 223-1245. Italian. $$

Pleasant Peasant, 2.
5300 Wisconsin Ave NW
☎ 364-2500. American. $$$

Primavera, 20.
3700 Massachusetts Ave NW
☎ 342-0224. Italian. $$

Round Table, 8.
4859 Wisconsin Ave NW
☎ 362-1250. Italian/American. $$

Shanghai Garden, 12.
4469 Connecticut Ave NW
☎ 362-3000. Chinese. $

Sushi-Ko. 25. 2309 Wisconsin Ave NW
☎ 333-4187. Japanese. $$

Thai Flavor, 13.
2605 Connecticut Ave NW
☎ 745-2000. Thai. $

Thai Room, 10.
5037 Connecticut Ave NW
☎ 244-5933. Thai. $

Krupins Deli, 9. 4620 Wisconsin Ave
NW ☎ 686-1989. American. $$

$$$$ = over $35 $$$ = $25-$35 $$ = $15-$25 $ = under $15
Based on cost per person, excluding drinks, service, and 9% sales tax.

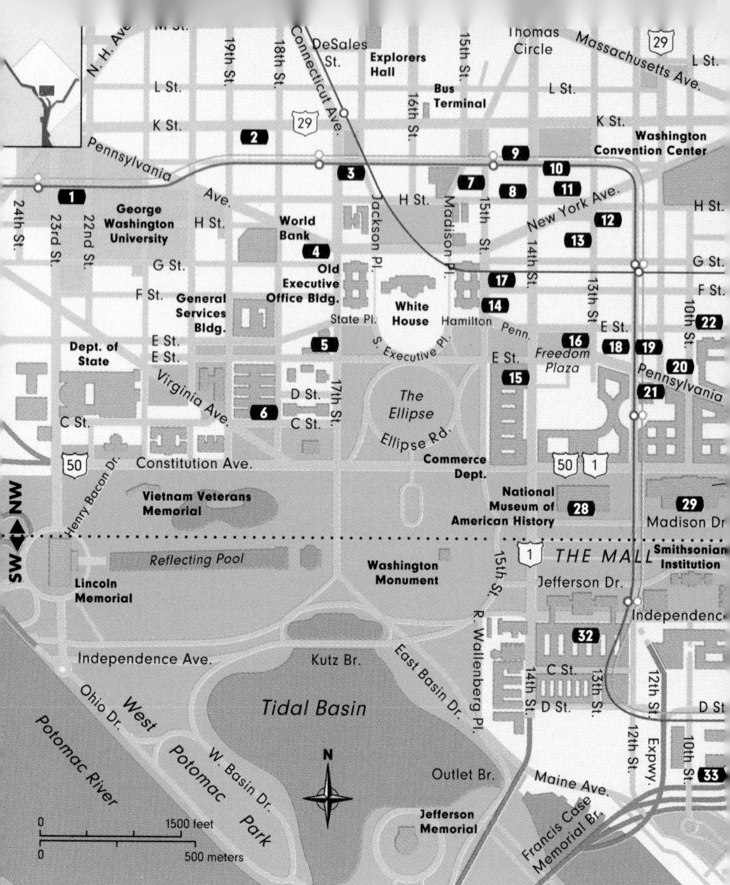

Listed Alphabetically

Air & Space Museum Cafeteria, 31. Independence Ave & 6th St SW

American History Museum Cafeteria, 28. Madison Dr & 13th St NW

Au Bon Pain, 9. 1401 I St NW

Cafe Mozart, 11. 1331 H St NW

Capitol City Brewery, 13. 700 13th St NW

Chesapeake Bagel Bakery, 41. 215 Pennsylvania Ave SE

Corcoran Gallery, 5. 500 17th St NW

Department of Agriculture, 32. Independence Ave & 13th St SW

Department of Health & Human Services, 35. 330 Independence Ave SW

Department of Housing & Urban Development, 34. 451 7th St SW

Department of the Interior, 6. 1800 C St NW

Dirksen Senate Office Cafeteria, 38. Constitution Ave & First St NE

Dutch Mill Deli, 25. 639 Indiana Ave NW

Federal Trade Commission, 26. Pennsylvania Ave & 6th St NW

Friday's, 18. 1201 Pennsylvania Ave NW

Garden of Eatin', 1. George Washington Univ, 2300 H St NW

Gourmet Too, 33. 609 L'Enfant Plaza East SW

Hard Rock Cafe, 22. 999 E St NW

Hirshhorn Outdoor Cafe, 30. Independence Ave & 7th St SW

Hot Shoppes, 4. 1750 Pennsylvania Ave NW

Hotel Washington, 14. 515 15th St NW

International Sq, 2. 1850 K St NW

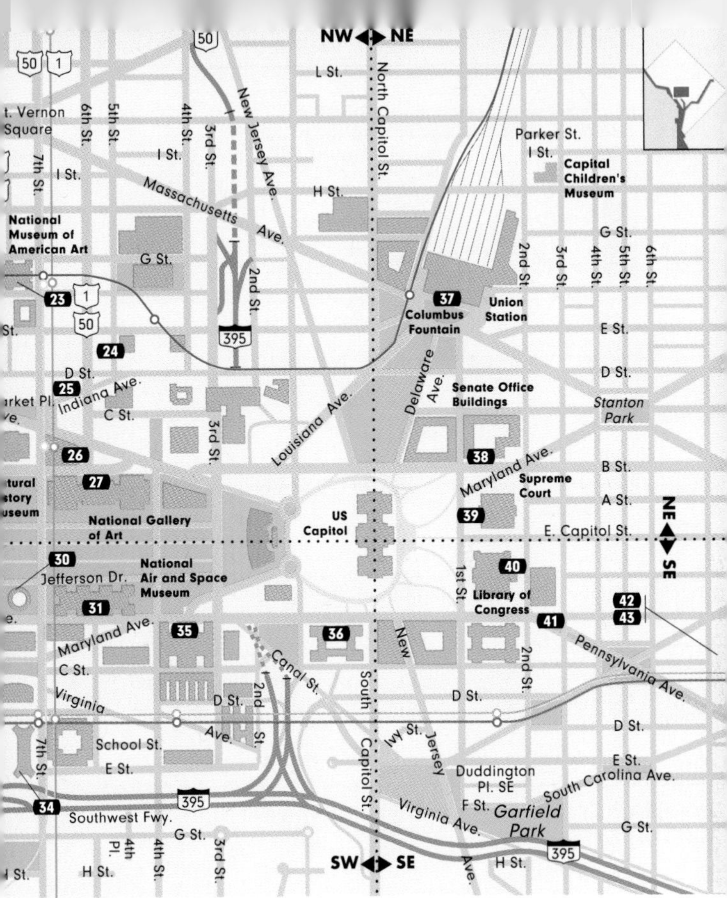

Listed Alphabetically (cont.)

JW Marriott, 16. 1331 Penn Ave NW

Kitcheteria, 19. 436 11th St NW

Lawsons Gourmet Deli, 10. 1350 I St NW

Library of Congress Cafeteria, 40. 101 Independence Ave SE

Loeb's Restaurant, 7. 832 15th St NW

Market Lunch, 43. 225 7th St SE

National Aquarium Cafeteria, 15. Constitution Ave & 14th St NW

National Gallery of Art Cafeteria, 27. Constitution Ave & 6th St NW

National Portrait Gallery Cafeteria, 23. F & 8th Sts NW

Natural History Museum Cafeteria, 29. Madison Dr & 10th St NW

New Executive Office Building Cafeteria, 3. H & 17th Sts NW

Old Ebbit Grill Express, 17. 675 15th St NW

The Pavilion-Old Post Office, 21. 1100 Pennsylvania Ave NW

Provisions, 42. 218 7th St SE

Rayburn House Building Cafeteria, 36. Independence Ave & First St SW

Roy Rogers, 24. 450 5th St NW

Shops at National Place, 16. 1331 Pennsylvania Ave NW

Skyline Cafe, 12. 1250 H St NW

Supreme Court Cafeteria, 39. 1 First St NE

Union Station Pavilion, 37. 50 Massachusetts Ave NE

Via Cucina, 20. 1001 Pennsylvania Ave NW

Wall St Deli, 8. 1401 H St NW

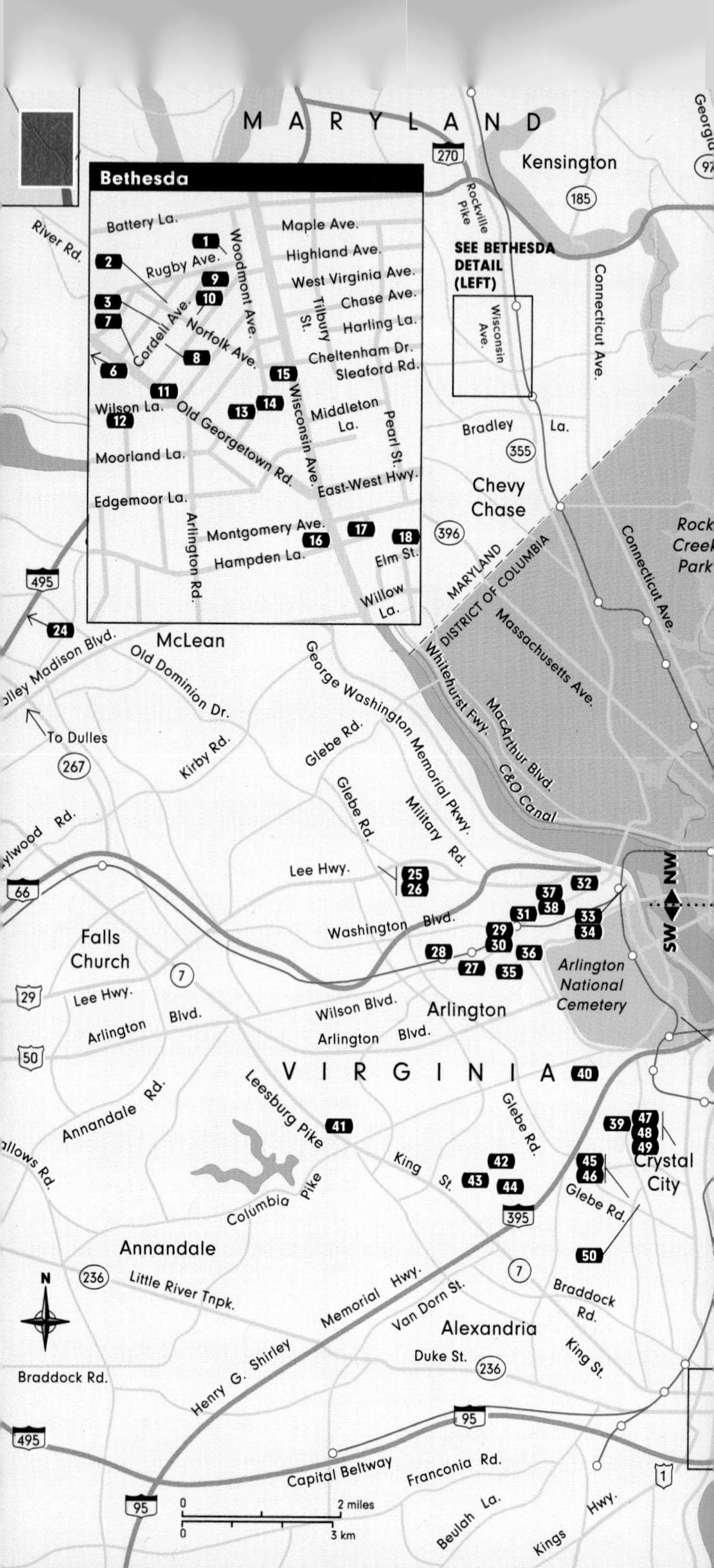

MARYLAND
Kensington
Bethesda
Battery La.
Maple Ave.
Highland Ave.
Rugby Ave.
Woodmont Ave.
West Virginia Ave.
Chase Ave.
Tilbury St.
Harling La.
Cordell Ave.
Norfolk Ave.
Cheltenham Dr.
Sleaford Rd.
Wilson La.
Old Georgetown Rd.
Wisconsin Ave.
Middleton La.
Pearl St.
Moorland La.
East-West Hwy.
Edgemoor La.
Arlington Rd.
Montgomery Ave.
Hampden La.
Elm St.
Willow La.
River Rd.
Rockville Pike
SEE BETHESDA DETAIL (LEFT)
Connecticut Ave.
Bradley La.
Chevy Chase
Rock Creek Park
MARYLAND
DISTRICT OF COLUMBIA
Massachusetts Ave.
Whitehurst Fwy.
MacArthur Blvd.
C&O Canal
McLean
Old Dominion Dr.
Dolley Madison Blvd.
To Dulles
Kirby Rd.
Glebe Rd.
George Washington Memorial Pkwy.
Military Rd.
Lee Hwy.
Washington Blvd.
Falls Church
Arlington National Cemetery
Wilson Blvd.
Arlington Blvd.
Arlington
VIRGINIA
Annandale Rd.
Leesburg Pike
King St.
Columbia Pike
Crystal City
Annandale
Little River Tnpk.
Memorial Hwy.
Van Dorn St.
Alexandria
Braddock Rd.
Duke St.
Henry G. Shirley
Capital Beltway
Franconia Rd.
Beulah La.
Kings Hwy.
2 miles
3 km
NW
SW
N

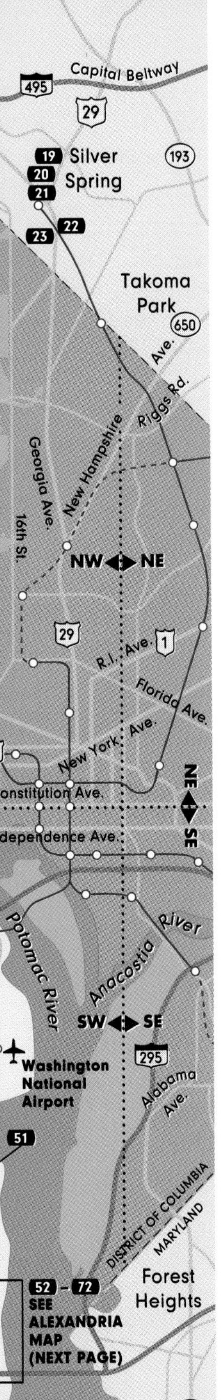

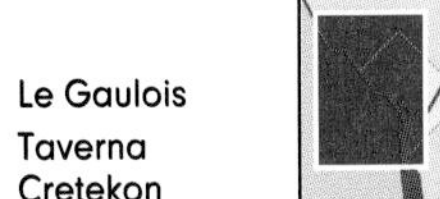

Listed by Site Number

1 Frascati
2 Bacchus-Bethesda
3 La Panetteria
4 Calasia
5 Tragara
6 Jean-Michel
7 North China
8 Matuba-Bethesda
9 Tastee Diner
10 La Miche
11 La Madelaine
12 Cafe Bethesda
13 Rio Grande
14 Haandi
15 Tako Grill
16 Pines of Rome
17 Vagabond
18 Andalucia
19 Fred & Harry's
20 Golden Flame
21 Mrs K's Tollhouse
22 Siddhartha
23 Chrisfields
24 L'Auberge Chez Francois
25 Alpine
26 Shanghai
27 Pizzaria Uno
28 Rio Grande
29 Pines of Capri
30 Queen Bee
31 Red, Hot & Blue
32 The View
33 L'Alouette
34 Orleans House
35 Chesapeake Crab
36 Blue & Gold
37 Faccia Luna
38 Whitlow's
39 Edoya
40 Bob & Edith's
41 Duangrat's
42 Thai in Shirlington
43 Carlyle Grand
44 Bistro Bistro
45 Chez Andre
46 Portofino
47 Bangkok Gourmet
48 Chez Froggy
49 Woo Lae Oak
50 R T's
51 Potowmack Landing
52 Le Gaulois
53 Taverna Cretekon
54 East Wind
55 South Austin Grill
56 Geranio
57 California Pizza Kitchen
58 Le Refuge
59 La Madelaine
60 Santa Fe East
61 Gadsby's Tavern
62 Bilbo
63 La Bergerie
64 219
65 Warehouse B & G
66 Il Porto
67 Chart House
68 The Wharf
69 Fish Market
70 Alamo
71 Union Street Public House
72 Chadwicks

Listed Alphabetically

BETHESDA, MD

Andalucia 18. 4931 Elm St ☎ 301/907-0052. Spanish. $$$

Bacchus-Bethesda, 2. 7945 Norfolk Ave ☎ 301/657-1722. Lebanese. $$

Cafe Bethasda, 12. 5027 Wilson Lane ☎ 301/657-3383. American. $$

Calasia, 4. 7929 Norfolk Ave ☎ 301/654-6444. Asian-American. $$$

Frascati, 1. 4806 Rugby Ave ☎ 301/652-9514. Italian. $$

Haandi, 14. 4904 Fairmont Ave ☎ 301/718-0121. Indian. $

Jean-Michel, 6. 10223 Old Georgetown Rd ☎ 301/564-4910. French. $$

La Madelaine, 11. 7607 Old Georgetown Rd ☎ 301/215-9139. French Bakery/Cafe. $

La Miche, 10. 7905 Norfolk Ave ☎ 301/986-0707. French. $$$

La Panetteria, 3. 4921 Cordell Ave ☎ 301/951-6433. Italian. $$

Matuba-Bethesda, 8. 4918 Cordell Ave ☎ 301/652-7449. Japanese. $$

North China, 7. 7814 Old Georgetown Rd ☎ 301/656-7922. Chinese. $

Pines of Rome, 16. 4709 Hampden La ☎ 301/657-8775. Italian. $

Rio Grande, 13. 4919 Fairmont Ave ☎ 301/656-2981. Tex-Mex. $

Tako Grill, 15. 7756 Wisconsin Ave ☎ 301/652-7030. Japanese. $$

Tastee Diner, 9. 7731 Woodmont Ave ☎ 301/652-3970. American. $

Tragara, 15. 4935 Cordell Ave ☎ 301/951-9935. Italian. $$$

Vagabond, 17. 7315 Wisconsin Ave ☎ 301/654-2575. Romanian. $$

SILVER SPRING, MD

Crisfield, 23. 8012 Georgia Ave ☎ 301/589-1306. Seafood. $$

Fred & Harry's, 19. 10110 Colesville Rd ☎ 301/593-7177. Seafood. $$

Golden Flame, 20. 8630 Fenton St ☎ 301/588-7250. Continental. $$

Mrs K's Tollhouse, 21. 9201 Colesville Rd ☎ 301/589-3500. American. $$

Siddhartha, 22. 8241 Georgia Ave ☎ 301/585-0550. Indian/Vegetarian. $

GREAT FALLS, VA

L'Auberge Chez Francois, 24. 332 Springvale Rd ☎ 703/759-3800. French. $$$$

ARLINGTON, VA

Alpine, 25. 4770 Lee Hwy ☎ 703/528-7600. Italian. $$

Bistro Bistro, 44. 4021 S. 28th St ☎ 703/379-0300. American. $$

Blue & Gold Brewpub, 36. 3100 Clarendon Blvd ☎ 703/908-4995. American. $$

Bob & Edith's, 40. 2310 Columbia Pike ☎ 703/920-6103. Diner. $

Carlyle Grand, 43. 4000 S. 28th St ☎ 703/931-0777. American. $$

Chesapeake Seafood Crab House, 35. 3607 Wilson Blvd ☎ 703/528-8888. Vietnamese. $

Duangrat's, 41. 5878 Leesburg Pike ☎ 703/820-5775. Thai. $$

Faccia Luna, 37. 2909 Wilson Blvd ☎ 703/276-3099. Italian. $$

L'Alouette, 33. 2045 Wilson Blvd ☎ 703/525-1750. French. $$

Orleans House, 34. 1213 Wilson Blvd ☎ 703/524-2929. American. $$

Pines of Capri, 29. 2721 N Washington Blvd ☎ 703/276-8789. Italian. $

Pizzaria Uno, 27. 4201 Wilson Blvd ☎ 703/527-8988. Italian. $

Portofino, 46. 526 S 23rd St ☎ 703/979-8200. Italian. $$

Queen Bee, 30. 3181 Wilson Blvd ☎ 703/527-3444. Vietnamese. $

Red, Hot & Blue, 31. 1600 Wilson Blvd ☎ 703/276-7427. Southern/BBQ. $

Rio Grande, 28. 4301 N Fairfax Dr ☎ 703/528-3131. Tex-Mex. $

Shanghai, 26. 5157 Lee Hwy ☎ 703/536-7446. Chinese. $

Thai in Shirlington, 42. 4029 S. 28th St ☎ 703/931-3203. Thai. $$

The View, 32. 1401 Lee Hwy ☎ 703/243-1745. American. $$$

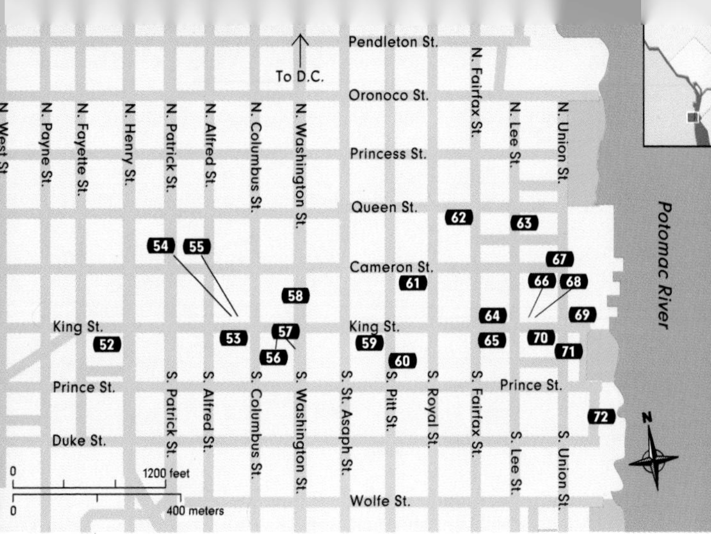

Listed Alphabetically (cont.)

Whitlow's on Wilson, 38. 2854 Wilson Blvd ☎ 703/525-9825. Diner. $

Woo Lae Oak, 49. 1500 S. Joyce St ☎ 703/521-3706. Korean. $

CRYSTAL CITY, VA

Bangkok Gourmet, 47. 523 S 23rd St ☎ 703/521-1305. Thai. $$

Chez Froggy, 48. 509 S 23rd St ☎ 703/979-7676. French. $$$

Endoya, 39. 2301 S. Jefferson Davis Hwy ☎ 703/418-2345. Japanese. $$

ALEXANDRIA, VA

Alamo, 70. 1100 King St ☎ 703/739-0555. Mexican. $$

Bilbo Baggins, 62. 208 Queen St ☎ 703/683-0300. American. $$

California Pizza Kitchen, 57. 700 King St ☎ 703/706-0404. Italian. $

Chadwick's, 72. 203 S. Strand St ☎ 703/836-4442. American. $$

Chart House, 67. 1 Cameron St ☎ 703/684-5080. American. $$$

Chez Andre, 45. 10 E Glebe Rd ☎ 703/836-1404. French. $$

East Wind, 54. 809 King St ☎ 703/836-1515. Vietnamese. $$

Fish Market, 69. 105 King St ☎ 703/836-5676. Seafood. $$

Gadsby's Tavern, 61. 138 N Royal St ☎ 703/548-1288. American. $$$

Geranio, 56. 722 King St ☎ 703/548-0088. Italian. $$

Il Porto, 66. 121 King St ☎ 703/836-8833. Italian. $$

La Bergerie, 63. 218 N Lee St ☎ 703/683-1007. French. $$$

Le Gaulois, 52. 1106 King St ☎ 703/739-9494. French. $$

La Madelaine, 59. 500 King St ☎ 703/739-2853. French Bakery/Cafe. $

Le Refuge, 58. 127 N Washington St ☎ 703/548-4661. French. $$$

Potowmack Landing, 51. Washington Marina ☎ 703/548-0001. Seafood. $$$

R T's, 50. 3804 Mt Vernon St ☎ 703/684-6010. Seafood. $$

Santa Fe East, 60. 110 Pitt St ☎ 703/548-6900. Mexican. $$

South Austin Grill, 55. 801 King St ☎ 703/684-8969. Tex-Mex. $

Taverna Cretekou, 53. 818 King St

$$$$ = over $35 $$$ = $25-$35 $$ = $15-$25 $ = under $15

Based on cost per person, excluding drinks, service, and 9% sales tax in DC, 4.5% in VA, and 5% in MD

Listed by Site Number

1 Holiday Inn-Georgetown
2 Savoy Suites
3 Days Inn-Uptown
4 Kalorama-Woodley
5 Omni Shoreham
6 Sheraton Washington
7 Kalorama-Kalorama Park
8 Adams Inn
9 Hotel Windsor Park
10 Normandy Inn
11 Pullman Highland
12 Washington Courtyard
13 Washington Hilton
14 Carlyle Suites
15 Windsor Inn
16 Embassy Inn
17 Dupont Plaza Hotel
18 Embassy Row
19 Radisson Barcelo
20 Ritz-Carlton
21 Georgetown Inn
22 Georgetown Marbury
23 Four Seasons
24 Doubletree Guest Suites
25 Wyndham Bristol
26 River Inn
27 Inn at Foggy Bottom
28 Watergate
29 Howard Johnson's
30 Doubletree Guest Suites
31 Lombardy
32 One Washington Circle
33 The Westin
34 Park Hyatt
35 ANA Hotel
36 Embassy Suites
37 Marriott
38 Sheraton City Center
39 Lincoln Suites
40 Embassy Square Suites
41 Hampshire
42 Tabard Inn
43 Canterbury

Listed by Site Number (cont.)

44 Governors House
45 Quality Hotel-Downtown
46 Doubletree Park Terrace
47 Holiday Inn-Central
48 Howard Johnson
49 Jefferson
50 Mayflower
51 Madison
52 Washington Vista
53 Holiday Inn-Franklin Square
54 Center City Travelodge
55 Morrison-Clark Inn
56 Days Inn-Convention Center
57 AYH Hostel
58 Henley Park
59 Howard Johnson Inn
60 Capital Hilton
61 Sheraton-Carlton
62 Hay-Adams
63 Hotel Washington
64 Willard Inter-Continental
65 JW Marriott
66 Harrington
67 Marriott Metro Center
68 Grand Hyatt
69 Washington DC Renaissance at Tech World
70 Comfort Inn
71 Super 8
72 Washington Court
73 Phoenix Park
74 Bellevue
75 Hyatt Regency
76 Holiday Inn-Capitol
77 Holiday Inn-Capitol
78 Capitol Hill Hotel
79 Channel Inn
80 Loew's L'Enfant Plaza
81 Best Western Skyline Inn

Listed Alphabetically

Adams Inn, 8. 1744 Lanier Pl NW ☎ 745-3600. $

ANA Hotel, 35. 2401 M St NW ☎ 429-2400. FAX 457-5010. $$$$

AYH Hostel, 57. 1009 11th St NW ☎ 737-2333. $

Bellevue, 74. 15 E St NW ☎ 638-0900. FAX 638-5132. $$

Best Western Skyline Inn, 81. 10 I St SW ☎ 488-7500. FAX 488-0790. $

Canterbury, 43. 1733 N St NW ☎ 393-3000. FAX 785-9581. $$$

Capital Hilton, 60. 1001 16th St NW ☎ 393-1000. FAX 639-5784. $$$$

Capitol Hill Hotel, 78. 200 C St SE ☎ 543-6000. FAX 547-2608. $$$

Carlyle Suites, 14. 1731 New Hampshire Ave NW ☎ 234-3200. FAX 387-0085. $

Center City Travel Lodge, 54. 1201 13th St NW ☎ 682-5300. FAX 371-9624. $

Channel Inn, 79. 650 Water St SW ☎ 554-2400. FAX 863-1164. $$

Comfort Inn, 70. 500 H St NW ☎ 289-5959. FAX 682-9152. $

Days Inn-Convention Center, 56. 1201 K St NW ☎ 842-1020. FAX 289-0336. $

Days Inn-Uptown, 3. 4400 Connecticut Ave NW ☎ 244-5600. FAX 244-6794. $

Doubletree Guest Suites, 24. 2500 Pennsylvania Ave NW ☎ 333-8060. FAX 338-3818. $$$

Doubletree Guest Suites, 30. 801 New Hampshire Ave NW ☎ 785-2000. FAX 785-9485. $$$

Doubletree Park Terrace, 46. 1515 Rhode Island Ave NW ☎ 232-7000. FAX 332-7152. $$$

Dupont Plaza Hotel, 17. 1500 New Hampshire Ave NW ☎ 483-6000. FAX 265-1680. $$$

Embassy Inn, 16. 1627 16th St NW ☎ 234-7800. FAX 234-3309. $

Embassy Row, 18. 2015 Massachusetts Ave NW ☎ 265-1600. FAX 328-7526. $$$

Embassy Square Suites, 40. 2000 N St NW ☎ 659-9000. FAX 429-9546. $$

Embassy Suites, 36. 1250 22nd St NW ☎ 857-3388. FAX 293-3173. $$$

Four Seasons, 23. 2800 Pennsylvania Ave NW ☎ 342-0444. FAX 944-2076. $$$$

Georgetown Inn, 21. 1310 Wisconsin Ave NW ☎ 333-8900. FAX 625-1744. $$$

Georgetown Marbury, 22. 3000 M St NW ☎ 726-5000. FAX 337-4250. $$$

Governors House, 44. 1615 Rhode Island Ave NW ☎ 296-2100. FAX 331-0227. $

Grand Hyatt, 68. 1000 H St NW ☎ 582-1234. FAX 637-4781. $$$$

Hampshire, 41. 1310 New Hampshire Ave NW ☎ 296-7600. FAX 293-2476. $$

Harrington, 66. 436 11th St NW ☎ 628-8140. FAX 393-2311. $

Hay-Adams, 62. 800 16th St NW ☎ 638-6600. FAX 638-2716. $$$$

Henley Park, 58. 926 Massachusetts Ave NW ☎ 638-5200. FAX 638-6740. $$$

Holiday Inn-Capitol, 76. 415 New Jersey Ave NW ☎ 638-1616. FAX 638-0707. $$

Holiday Inn-Capitol, 77. 550 C St SW ☎ 479-4000. FAX 479-4353. $$

Holiday Inn-Central, 47. 1501 Rhode Island Ave NW ☎ 483-2000. FAX 797-1078. $

Holiday Inn-Franklin Square, 53. 1155 14th St NW ☎ 737-1200. FAX 783-5733. $$

Holiday Inn-Georgetown, 1. 2101 Wisconsin Ave NW ☎ 338-4600. FAX 333-6113. $$

Hotel Washington, 63. 515 15th St NW ☎ 638-5900. FAX 638-4275. $$

Hotel Windsor Park, 9. 2116 Kalorama Rd NW ☎ 483-7700. FAX 332-4547. $

Howard Johnson, 48. 1430 Rhode Island Ave NW ☎ 462-7777. FAX 332-3519. $

Howard Johnson Inn, 59. 600 New York Ave NE ☎ 546-9200. FAX 546-6348. $

Howard Johnson's, 29. 2601 Virginia Ave NW ☎ 965-2700. FAX 337-5417. $

Hyatt Regency, 75. 400 New Jersey Ave NW ☎ 737-1234. FAX 393-7927. $$$$

Listed Alphabetically (cont.)

Inn at Foggy Bottom, 27. 824 New Hampshire Ave NW ☎ 337-6620. FAX 298-7499. $$

Jefferson, 49. 1200 16th St NW ☎ 347-2200. FAX 331-7982. $$$$

JW Marriott, 65. 1331 Pennsylvania Ave NW ☎ 393-2000. FAX 626-6991. $$$$

Kalorama Guesthouse at Kalorama Park, 7. 1854 Mintwood Pl NW ☎ 667-6369. $

Kalorama Guesthouse at Woodley Park, 4. 2700 Cathedral Ave NW ☎ 328-0860. $

Lincoln Suites, 39. 1823 L St NW ☎ 223-4320. FAX 223-8546. $$$

Loew's L'Enfant Plaza, 80. 480 L'Enfant Plaza SW ☎ 484-1000. FAX 646-4456. $$$

Lombardy, 31. 2019 Pennsylvania Ave NW ☎ 828-2600. FAX 872-0503. $$

Madison, 51. 1177 15th St NW ☎ 862-1600. FAX 785-1255. $$$$

Marriott, 37. 1221 22nd St NW ☎ 872-1500. FAX 872-1424. $$$$

Marriot Metro Center, 67. 775 12th St NW ☎ 737-2200. FAX 347-5886. $$$

Mayflower, 50. 1127 Connecticut Ave NW ☎ 347-3000. FAX 776-9182. $$$$

Morrison-Clark Inn, 55. 1015 L St NW ☎ 898-1200. FAX 289-8576. $$$

Normandy Inn, 10. 2118 Wyoming Ave NW ☎ 483-1350. FAX 387-8241. $

Omni Shoreham, 5. 2500 Calvert St NW ☎ 234-0700. FAX 232-4140. $$$$

One Washington Circle, 32. 1 Washington Circle NW ☎ 872-1680. FAX 887-4989. $$$

Park Hyatt, 34. 1201 24th St NW ☎ 789-1234. FAX 457-8823. $$$$

Phoenix Park, 73. 520 N Capitol St NW ☎ 638-6900. FAX 393-3236. $$$

Pullman Highland Hotel, 11. 1914 Connecticut Ave NW ☎ 797-2000. FAX 462-0944. $$$

Quality Hotel-Downtown, 45. 1315 16th St NW ☎ 232-8000. FAX 667-9827. $

Radisson Barcelo, 19. 2121 P St NW ☎ 293-3100. FAX 857-0134. $$$

Ritz-Carlton, 20. 2100 Massachusetts Ave NW ☎ 293-2100. FAX 293-0641. $$$$

River Inn, 26. 924 25th St NW ☎ 337-7600. FAX 337-6520. $$$

Savoy Suites, 2. 2505 Wisconsin Ave NW ☎ 337-9700. FAX 337-3644. $$

Sheraton-Carlton, 61. 923 16th St NW ☎ 638-2626. FAX 638-4231. $$$$

Sheraton City Center, 38. 1143 New Hampshire Ave NW ☎ 775-0800. FAX 331-9491. $$$

Sheraton Washington, 6. 2660 Woodley Rd NW ☎ 328-2000. FAX 234-0015. $$$

Super 8 Washington, 71. 501 New York Ave NE ☎ 543-7400. FAX 544-2327. $

Tabard Inn, 42. 1739 N St NW ☎ 785-1277. FAX 785-6173. $$

Washington Court, 72. 525 New Jersey Ave NW ☎ 628-2100. FAX 879-7918. $$$$

Washington Courtyard, 12. 1900 Connecticut Ave NW ☎ 332-9300. FAX 328-7039. $$

Washington DC Renaissance at Tech World, 69. 999 9th St NW ☎ 898-9000. FAX 289-0947. $$$

Washington Hilton, 13. 1919 Connecticut Ave NW ☎ 483-3000. FAX 232-0438. $$$$

Washington Vista, 52. 1400 M St NW ☎ 429-1700. FAX 785-0786. $$$

Watergate, 28. 2650 Virginia Ave NW ☎ 965-2300. FAX 337-7915. $$$$

The Westin Hotel, 33. 2350 M St NW ☎ 429-0100. FAX 429-9759. $$$$

Willard Inter-Continental, 64. 1401 Pennsylvania Ave NW ☎ 628-9100. FAX 637-7326. $$$$

Windsor Inn, 15. 1842 16th St NW ☎ 667-0300. FAX 667-4503. $

Wyndham Bristol, 25. 2430 Pennsylvania Ave NW ☎ 955-6400. FAX 955-5765. $$$

$$$$ = ***over $190*** $$$ = ***$130-$190*** $$ = ***$100-$130*** $ = ***under $100***

All prices are for a standard double room, excluding 10% room tax, and are weekday rates; weekend rates are often reduced.

MARY
Rockville
Potomac
Kensington
Bethesda
Chevy Chase
Glen Echo
Somerset
Langley
McLean
Tysons Corner
Vienna
Falls Church
Arlington
VIRGINIA
Annandale
ALEXANDRIA
NW
Potomac River
MARYLAND
DISTRICT OF COLUMBIA
Muncaster Mill Rd.
Darnestown Rd.
Frederick Rd.
Norbeck Rd.
Bonifant
Bel Pre Rd.
W. Montgomery Ave.
Rockville Pike
Georgia Ave.
Meetinghouse Rd.
Falls Rd.
Seven Locks Rd.
Montrose Rd.
Randolph Rd.
Veirs Mill Rd.
Arcola Ave.
Tuckerman La.
Democracy Blvd.
River Rd.
Bradley Blvd.
Goldsboro Rd.
Bradley La.
Military Rd.
Connecticut Ave.
Wisconsin Ave.
Massachusetts Ave.
Canal Rd.
George Washington Memorial Pkwy.
Old Dominion Dr.
Georgetown Pike
Dolley Madison Blvd.
Leesburg Pike
Dulles Airport Access Rd.
Maple Ave.
Kirby Rd.
Gallows Rd.
Lee Hwy.
Arlington Blvd.
King St.
Main St.
Capital Beltway
Little River Tnpk.
Braddock Rd.
Henry G. Shirley Memorial Hwy.
Van Dorn St.
Edsall Rd.
Duke St.
Washington St.
Old Keene Mill Rd.
New Hampshire
N
0 2 miles
0 3 km

Listed by Site Number

ROCKVILLE, MD

1 Marriott Courtyard
2 Quality Suites
3 Best Western
4 Doubletree Guest Suites

BETHESDA, MD

5 Marriott
6 Ramada Inn
7 Holiday Inn
8 American Inn
9 Hyatt Regency
10 Manor Inn
11 Residence Inn

CHEVY CHASE, MD

12 Holiday Inn

SILVER SPRING, MD

13 Holiday Inn
14 Quality Hotel
15 Courtyard by Marriott

COLLEGE PARK, MD

16 Holiday Inn
17 Quality Inn

DULLES INT'L AIRPORT, VA

18 Holiday Inn Dulles
19 Hyatt Dulles
20 Hilton Washington at Dulles

McLEAN, VA

21 McLean Hilton at Tysons Corner
22 Best Western
23 Ritz-Carlton
24 Holiday Inn-Tysons Corner

VIENNA, VA

25 Sheraton Premiere at Tysons Corner
26 Embassy Suites
27 Marriott

FALLS CHURCH, VA

28 Doubletree Guest Suites
29 Quality Inn-Governor
30 Quality Inn Executive

ARLINGTON, VA

31 Ramada Renaissance Ballston
32 Holiday Inn-Arlington
33 Quality Inn
34 Holiday Inn Westpark
35 Hyatt Arlington
36 Marriott-Key Bridge
37 Econo Lodge-Pentagon
38 Sheraton National
39 DoubleTree Inn
40 Embassy Suites
41 Holiday Inn-Airport
42 Marriott-Crystal Gateway
43 Ritz-Carlton Pentagon City
44 Sheraton Crystal
45 Marriott-Crystal City
46 Stouffers Concourse
47 Hyatt Regency
48 Howard Johnson's

ALEXANDRIA, VA

49 Ramada Inn-Old Town
50 Holiday Inn Suites
51 Morrison House
52 Holiday Inn-Old Town
53 Econo Lodge
54 Radisson Plaza
55 Days Hotel
56 Doubletree Guest Suites

Listed Alphabetically

BETHESDA, MD

American Inn, 8. 8130 Wisconsin Ave ☎ 301/656-9300. FAX 656-2907. $

Holiday Inn, 7. 8120 Wisconsin Ave ☎ 301/652-2000. FAX 652-4525. $$

Hyatt Regency, 9. Bethesda Metro Ctr ☎ 301/657-1234. FAX 657-6453. $$

Manor Inn, 10. 7740 Wisconsin Ave ☎ 301/656-2100. FAX 986-0375. $

Marriott, 5. 5151 Pooks Hill Rd ☎ 301/897-9400. FAX 897-0192. $$$

Ramada Inn, 6. 8400 Wisconsin Ave ☎ 301/654-1000. FAX 654-0751. $$

Residence Inn, 11. 7335 Wisconsin Ave ☎ 301/718-0200. FAX 718-0679. $$$

CHEVY CHASE, MD

Holiday Inn, 12. 5520 Wisconsin Ave ☎ 301/656-1500. FAX 656-5045. $$

COLLEGE PARK, MD

Holiday Inn, 16. 10,000 Baltimore Ave ☎ 301/345-6700. FAX 441-4923. $

Quality Inn, 17. 7200 Baltimore Ave ☎ 301/864-5820. FAX 927-8634. $

ROCKVILLE, MD

Best Western, 3. 1251 W Montgomery Ave ☎ 301/424-4940. FAX 424-1047. $

Doubletree Guest Suites, 4. 1750 Rockville Pike ☎ 301/468-1100. FAX 468-0163. $$

Marriott Courtyard, 1. 2500 Research Blvd ☎ 301/670-6700. FAX 670-9023. $

Quality Suites, 2. 3 Research Court ☎ 301/840-0200. FAX 258-0160. $

SILVER SPRING, MD

Courtyard by Marriott, 15. 12521 Prosperity Dr ☎ 301/680-8500. FAX 680-9232. $

Holiday Inn, 13. 8777 Georgia Ave ☎ 301/589-0800. FAX 587-4791. $

Quality Hotel, 14. 8727 Colesville Rd ☎ 301/589-5200. FAX 588-6681. $

ALEXANDRIA, VA

Days Hotel, 55. 110 S Bragg St ☎ 703/354-4950. FAX 354-4950. $

Doubletree Guest Suites, 56. 100 S Reynolds St ☎ 703/370-9600. FAX 370-0467. $$

Econo Lodge, 53. Rte 1 & Mt Vernon Hwy ☎ 703/780-0300. FAX 780-0842. $

Holiday Inn-Old Town, 52. 480 King St ☎ 703/549-6080. FAX 684-6508. $$

Holiday Inn Suites, 50. 625 First St ☎ 703/548-6300. FAX 548-8032. $

Holiday Inn Westpark, 34. 1900 N Ft Meyer Dr ☎ 703/527-4814. FAX 522-8864. $$

Morrison House, 51. 116 S Alfred Rd ☎ 703/838-8000. FAX 684-6283. $$$$

Radisson Plaza, 54. 5000 Seminary Rd ☎ 703/845-1010. FAX 845-7662. $$

Ramada Plaza Hotel, 49. 901 N Fairfax ☎ 703/683-6000. FAX 683-7597. $

ARLINGTON, VA

DoubleTree Hotel, 39. 300 Army Navy Dr ☎ 703/416-4100. FAX 416-4162. $$

Econo Lodge-Pentagon, 37. 5666 Columbia Pike ☎ 703/820-5600 FAX 379-7482. $

Embassy Suites, 40. 1300 Jefferson Davis Hwy ☎ 703/979-9799. FAX 920-5947. $$

Holiday Inn-Airport, 41. 1489 Jefferson Davis Hwy ☎ 703/416-1600. FAX 416-1615. $$

Holiday Inn-Arlington, 32. 4610 N. Fairfax ☎ 703/243-9800. FAX 527-2677. $$$

Howard Johnson's, 48. 2650 Jefferson Davis Hwy ☎ 703/684-7200. FAX 684-3217. $

Hyatt Arlington, 35. 1325 Wilson Blvd ☎ 703/525-1234. FAX 875-3393. $$$

Hyatt Regency, 47. 2799 Jefferson Davis Hwy ☎ 703/418-1234. FAX 418-1289. $$$

Marriott-Crystal City, 45. 1999 Jefferson Davis Hwy ☎ 703-413-5500. FAX 413-0192. $$$

Marriott-Crystal Gateway, 42. 1700 Jefferson Davis Hwy ☎ 703/920-3230. FAX 271-5212. $$$

Listed Alphabetically (cont.)

Marriott-Key Bridge, 36. 1401 Lee Hwy ☎ 703/524-6400. FAX 524-8964. $$$

Quality Inn, 33. 1200 N Courthouse Rd ☎ 703/524-4000. FAX 522-6814. $

Ramada Renaissance Ballston, 31. 950 N Stafford St ☎ 703/528-6000. FAX 528-4386. $$

Ritz-Carlton Pentagon City, 43. 1250 S Hayes St ☎ 703/415-5000. FAX 415-5061. $$$$

Sheraton Crystal, 44. 1800 Jefferson Davis Hwy ☎ 703/486-1111. FAX 920-5827. $$

Sheraton National, 38. 900 S Orme St ☎ 703/521-1900. FAX 521-0332. $$

Stouffers Concourse, 46. 2399 Jefferson Davis Hwy ☎ 703/418-6800. FAX 418-3763. $$$

DULLES INTERNATIONAL AIRPORT, VA

Hilton Washington Dulles, 20. 13869 Park Center Rd, Herndon ☎ 703/478-2900. FAX 834-1996. $$

Holiday Inn Dulles, 18. 1000 Sully Road, Dulles ☎ 703/471-7411. FAX 471-7411. $

Hyatt Dulles, 19. 2300 Dulles Corner Blvd, Herndon ☎ 703/713-1234. FAX 713-3410. $$

FALLS CHURCH, VA

Doubletree Guest Suites, 28. 7801 Leesburg Pike, Falls Church ☎ 703/893-1340. FAX 847-9520. $

Quality Inn Executive, 30. 6111 Arlington Blvd ☎ 703/534-9100. FAX 534-5589. $

Quality Inn-Governor, 29. 6650 Arlington Blvd ☎ 703/532-8900. FAX 532-7121. $

MCLEAN, VA

Best Western, 22. 8401 Westpark Dr ☎ 703/734-2800. FAX 821-8872. $

Holiday Inn-Tysons Corner, 24. 1960 Chain Bridge Road, McLean ☎ 703/893-2100. FAX 356-8218. $

McLean Hilton at Tysons Corner, 21. 7920 Jones Branch Dr, McLean ☎ 703/847-5000. FAX 761-5100. $$

Ritz-Carlton, 23. 1700 Tysons Blvd, McLean ☎ 703/506-4300. FAX 503-2694. $$$$

VIENNA, VA

Embassy Suites, 26. 8517 Leesburg Pike ☎ 703/883-0707. FAX 883-0694. $$$

Marriott, 27. 8028 Leesburg Pike ☎ 703/734-3200. FAX 734-5763. $$$

Sheraton Premiere at Tysons Corner, 25. 8661 Leesburg Pike, Tysons Corner ☎ 703/448-1234. FAX 893-8193. $$

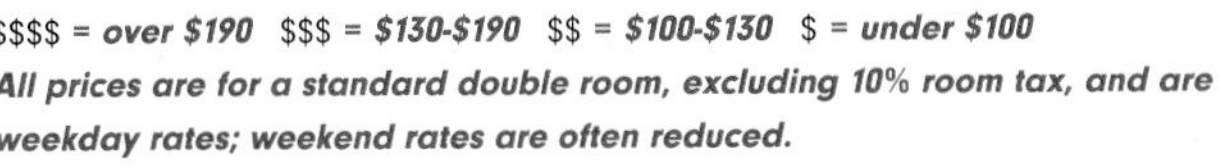

$$$$ = ***over $190*** $$$ = ***$130-$190*** $$ = ***$100-$130*** $ = ***under $100***
All prices are for a standard double room, excluding 10% room tax, and are weekday rates; weekend rates are often reduced.

Listed by Site Number

1 Washington Cathedral
2 Gala Hispanic Theater
3 Carter Barron Amphitheatre
4 Source Theatre Co
5 Lincoln Theater
6 Olney Theatre
7 National Shrine, Immaculate Conception
8 Dance Place
9 Duke Ellington Theatre
10 Phillips Collection
11 Joy of Motion
12 Church St Theatre
13 Woolly Mammoth
14 Studio Theatre
15 Trinity Players
16 Wolf Trap-The Barns
17 Bayou
18 Improv
19 Lisner Auditorium
20 Concert Hall

Listed by Site Number (cont.)

20 Eisenhower Theatre
20 Opera House
20 Terrace Theatre
21 Hammer Auditorium
22 Constitution Hall
23 National Theatre
24 Warner Theatre
25 Ford's Theatre
26 Washington Stage Guild
27 Shakespeare at the Lansburgh
28 Carmichael Auditorium
29 Baird Auditorium
30 National Gallery of Art
31 Sylvan Theatre
32 Discovery Theatre
33 Fort Dupont Summer Theatre
34 Signature
35 Arena Stage
35 Kreeger Theatre
35 Old Vat Room

Performing Arts

Listed Alphabetically (cont.)

Arena Stage, 35. Maine Ave & 6th St SW ☏ 488-3300

Baird Auditorium, 29. National Museum of Natural History, Constitution Ave & 10th St NW ☏ 357-3030

Bayou, 17. 3135 K St NW ☏ 783-7212

Carmichael Auditorium, 28. National Museum of American History, Constitution Ave & 14th St NW ☏ 357-2700

Carter Barron Amphitheatre, 3. Colorado Ave & 16th St NW ☏ 426-6837

Church St Theatre, 10. 1742 Church St NW ☏ 265-3748

Concert Hall, 20. Kennedy Center, 2700 F St NW ☏ 467-4600

Constitution Hall, 22. 18th & D Sts NW ☏ 638-2661

Dance Place, 8. 3225 8th St NE ☏ 269-1600

Discovery Theatre, 32. 900 Jefferson Dr SW ☏ 357-1500

Duke Ellington Theatre, 9. 3500 R St NW ☏ 342-7589

Eisenhower Theatre, 20. Kennedy Center, 2700 F St NW ☏ 467-4600

Ford's Theatre, 25. 511 10th St NW ☏ 347-4833

Fort Dupont Summer Theatre, 33. Minnesota Ave & F St SE ☏ 675-7646

Gala Hispanic Theater, 2. 1624 Park St NW ☏ 234-7174

Hammer Auditorium, 21. Corcoran Gallery, New York Ave & 17th St NW ☏ 638-3211

Improv, 18. 1140 Connecticut Ave NW ☏ 296-7008

Joy of Motion, 11. 1643 Connecticut Ave NW ☏ 387-0911

Kreeger Theatre, 35. Maine Ave & 6th St SW ☏ 488-3300

Lincoln Theater, 5. 1215 U st NW ☏ 328-9177

Lisner Auditorium, 19. 21st & H Sts NW ☏ 994-6800

National Gallery of Art, 30. Constitution Ave & 6th St NW ☏ 737-4215

National Shrine, Immaculate Conception, 7. Michigan Ave & 4th St NE ☏ 526-8300

National Theatre, 23. 1321 Pennsylvania Ave NW ☏ 628-6161

Old Vat Room, 35. Maine Ave & 6th St SW ☏ 488-3300

Olney Theatre, 6. 2001 Route 108, Olney, MD ☏ 301/924-3400

Opera House, 20. Kennedy Center, 2700 F St NW ☏ 467-4600

Phillips Collection, 10. 1600 21st St NW ☏ 387-2151

Shakespeare at the Lansburgh, 27. 450 7th St NW ☏ 393-2700

Signature Theater, 34. 3806 Four Mile Run Arlington, VA ☏ 703/218-6500

Source Theatre Co, 4. 1835 14th St NW ☏ 462-1073

Studio Theatre, 14. 1333 P St NW ☏ 332-3300

Sylvan Theatre, 31. Washington Monument Grounds ☏ 343-1100 (Park Service)

Terrace Theatre, 20. Kennedy Center, 2700 F St NW ☏ 467-4600

Trinity Players, 15. 3514 O St NW ☏ 965-4680

Warner Theatre, 24. 513 13th St NW ☏ 783-4000

Washington Cathedral, 1. Wisconsin & Massachusetts Aves NW ☏ 537-6200

Washington Stage Guild, 26. 924 G St NW ☏ 529-2084

Wolf Trap-The Barns, 16. 1624 Trap Rd, Vienna, VA ☏ 703/938-2404

Woolly Mammoth, 13. 1401 Church St NW ☏ 393-3939

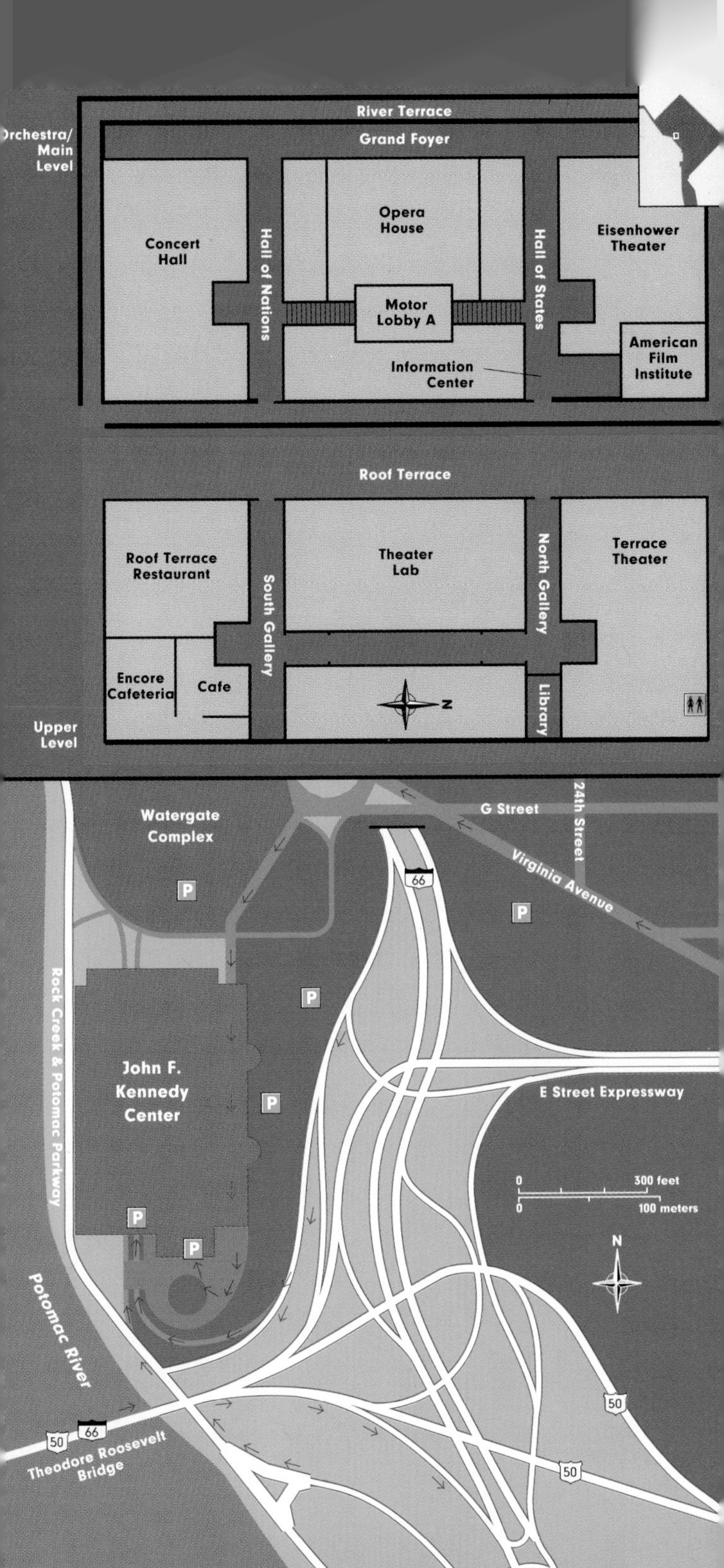

Orchestra/
Main
Level
River Terrace
Grand Foyer
Concert
Hall
Hall of Nations
Opera
House
Motor
Lobby A
Information
Center
Hall of States
Eisenhower
Theater
American
Film
Institute
Roof Terrace
Roof Terrace
Restaurant
South Gallery
Theater
Lab
North Gallery
Terrace
Theater
Encore
Cafeteria
Cafe
N
Library
Upper
Level
Watergate
Complex
G Street
24th Street
Virginia Avenue
66
P
Rock Creek & Potomac Parkway
John F.
Kennedy
Center
E Street Expressway
0
300 feet
0
100 meters
N
Potomac River
50
66
Theodore Roosevelt
Bridge
50
50

Listed by Site Number

1 Avalon
2 Paris
3 United Artists Bethesda
4 Cineplex Odeon Cinema
5 Outer Circle
6 Mazza Galerie
7 Tenley
8 Wisconsin
9 Uptown
10 MacArthur III
11 Janus III
12 Embassy
13 Dupont Circle V
14 Key
15 Foundry
16 American Film Institute
17 Biograph
18 West End 1-4

Listed Alphabetically

AMC Courthouse, 20.
2150 Clarendon Blvd, Arlington
☎ 703/998-4262

American Film Institute, 16.
Kennedy Center, 2700 F St NW
☎ 785-4600

Avalon, 1.
5612 Connecticut Ave NW
☎ 966-2600

Biograph, 17.
2819 M St NW ☎ 333-2696

Cineplex Odeon Cinema, 4.
5100 Wisconsin Ave NW ☎ 966-7248

Cineplex Odeon Dupont Circle V, 13.
1350 19th St NW ☎ 872-9555

Cineplex Odeon Embassy, 12.
1927 Florida Ave NW ☎ 387-1344

Cineplex Odeon Foundry, 15.
1055 Thomas Jefferson St NW
☎ 333-8613

Cineplex Odeon Janus III, 11.
1660 Connecticut Ave NW
☎ 265-9545

Cineplex Odeon MacArthur III, 10.
4859 MacArthur Blvd NW ☎ 337-1700

Cineplex Odeon Mazza Galerie, 6.
4600 Wisconsin Ave NW ☎ 364-8504

Cineplex Odeon Uptown, 9.
3426 Connecticut Ave NW
☎ 842-7773

Cineplex Odeon West End 1-4, 18.
L & 23rd Sts NW
☎ 293-3152

Listed by Site Number (Cont.)

19 West End 5-7
20 AMC Courthouse
21 Union Station IX
22 National Air & Space IMAX Theatre
23 Sony Pentagon City

Listed Alphabetically (Cont.)

Cineplex Odeon West End 5-7, 19. M & 23rd Sts NW ☎ 452–9020

Cineplex Odeon Wisconsin, 8. 4000 Wisconsin Ave NW ☎ 244–7789

Key, 14. 1222 Wisconsin Ave NW ☎ 333–5100

National Air & Space IMAX Theatre, 22. 6th St & Independence Aves SW ☎ 357–1686

Outer Circle, 5. 4849 Wisconsin Ave NW ☎ 244–3116

Paris, 2. 5300 Wisconsin Ave NW ☎ 686–7700

Sony Pentagon City, 23. 1100 S Hayes St, Arlington ☎ 703/415–4333

Tenley, 7. 4200 Wisconsin Ave NW ☎ 363–4340

Union Station IX, 21. 50 Massachusetts Ave ☎ 703/998–4AMC

United Artists Bethesda, 3. 7272 Wisconsin Ave ☎ 301/718–4323

1
Harvard St.
Woodley Rd.
Woodley Pl.
Adams Mill Rd.
Ontario Rd.
Lanier Pl.
Columbia Rd.
Fuller St.
16th St.
15th St.
14th St.
Girard St.
Fairmont St.
2
3
8
Euclid St.
13th St.
Calvert St.
4
Euclid St.
17th St.
Clifton St.
Clifton
28th St.
Woodland Dr.
Normanstone Dr.
Biltmore St.
Ontario Rd.
Kalorama Rd.
Chapin St.
Belmont St.
Mintwood
6
5
Mintwood Rd.
Champlain St.
Crescent Pl.
Belmont St.
Belmont St.
Florida Ave.
Rock Creek Dr.
Benton Pl.
30th St.
Belmont Rd.
Ashmead Pl.
W St.
Rock Creek & Potomac Pkwy.
Kalorama Circle
7
Kalorama Rd.
Columbia Rd.
California St.
V St.
Waterside Dr.
Wyoming Ave.
Wyoming Ave.
10
Vernon St.
Seaton St.
U St.
Tracy Pl.
24th St.
23rd St.
California St.
Willard St.
Caroline St.
Wallach St.
12
T St.
T St.
Massachusetts Ave.
Bancroft Pl.
Bancroft Pl.
Ave.
Swann St.
Swann St.
13
S St.
S St.
New Hampshire Ave.
Johnson Ave.
Rock Creek
Florida
Riggs Pl.
Riggs Pl.
Riggs Pl.
Oak Hill Cemetery
Decatur Pl.
14
R St.
R St.
R St.
Sheridan Circle
17
19th St.
17th St.
Corcoran St.
Massachusetts Ave.
Q St.
Q St.
28th St.
29th St.
Q St.
21
22
Church St.
Church St.
Vermont
30th St.
15
21st St.
Dupont Circle
20th St.
P St.
23
Logan Circle
P St.
26th St.
18th St.
National Trust
O St.
Rhode Island Ave.
O St.
O St.
Newport Pl.
Sunderland Pl.
Connecticut Ave.
24
Scott Circle
N St.
13th St.
16
27th St.
N St.
23rd St.
22nd St.
New Hampshire Ave.
N St.
Jefferson Pl.
Explorers Hall
Thomas Circle
Olive St.
18
19
20
M St.
16th St.
15th St.
Massachusetts
M St.
M St.
25
DeSales St.
C&O Canal
L St.
L St.
19th St.
Bus Terminal
L St.
26th St.
25th St.
Washington Circle
26
K St.
K St.
29
Pennsylvania Ave.
29
28
66
31
27
30
H St.
Ave.
Rock Creek & Potomac Pkwy.
24th St.
23rd St.
22nd St.
George Washington University
H St.
World Bank
Jackson Pl.
Madison Pl.
15th St.
New York
Watergate Hotel Complex
G St.
Old Executive Office
14th St.
Kennedy Center
F St.
General Services Bldg.
18th St.
33
State Pl.
White House
Hamilton Pl.
Penn.
Freedom Plaza
E St.
Dept. of State
E St.
E St.
S. Executive Pl.
E St.
D St.
Virginia Ave.
17th St.
The Ellipse
C St.
C St.
Ellipse Rd.
Theodore Roosevelt Br.
50
66
50
Constitution Ave.
Commerce Dept.
50
1
Henry Bacon Dr.
Vietnam Veterans Memorial
NW
SW
National Museum of American History
Reflecting Pool
Washington Monument
1
Lincoln Memorial
15th St.
Jefferson Dr.
Arlington Memorial Br.
Independence Ave.
Kutz Br.
East Basin Dr.
R. Wallenberg Pl.
C St.
14th St.
15th St.
D St.
Ohio Dr.
West
Tidal Basin
W. Basin Dr.
Potomac
Park
N
Columbia Island
Outlet Br.
Maine Ave.
Jefferson Memorial
Potomac River
George Washington Memorial Parkway
Francis Case Memorial Br.
395
Jefferson Davis Highway
Boundary Dr.
41
42
395
East Potomac Park
Buckeye Dr.
Dr. King Dr.
L.B.J. Memorial
1

Listed by Site Number

1. Nanny O' Briens
2. Ireland's Four Provinces
3. City Blues Cafe
4. Marquee Lounge
5. Cities
6. Cafe Lautrec
7. Heaven
8. Chief Ike's Mambo Room
9. Takoma Station Tavern
10. Kilimanjaro
11. 9:30 Club
12. Madam's Organ
13. Black Cat
14. Food for Thought
15. Brickskeller
16. Grog & Tankard
17. La Tomate
18. Brasil Tropical
19. One Step Down
20. Deja Vu
21. Afterwords
22. Buffalo Billiards
23. New Vegas Lounge
24. Planet Fred
25. Improv
26. 15 Minutes
27. Spy Club
28. Zei Alley
29. Allegro
30. Cafe Mozart
31. Bombay Club
32. Marley's Lounge
33. The Nest
34. Dixie Grill
35. The Ritz
36. Fifth Column
37. Insect Club
38. Irish Times
39. Dubliner
40. Tracks
41. Birchmere
42. Headliners
43. GangPlank

Listed Alphabetically

Afterwords, 21. 1517 Connecticut Ave NW ☏ 387-1462. Rock/Blues

Allegro, 29. 923 16th St NW ☏ 879-6900. Piano

Birchmere, 41. 3901 Mt Vernon Ave ☏ 703/549-5919. Folk

Black Cat, 13. 1831 14th St NW ☏ 667-7960. Rock

Bombay Club, 31. 815 Connecticut Ave NW ☏ 659-3727. Piano

Brasil Tropical, 18. 2519 Pennsylvania Ave NW ☏ 293-1773. Latin

Brickskeller, 15. 1523 22nd St NW ☏ 293-1885. Rock

Buffalo Billiards, 22. 1330 19th St NW ☏ 331-7665. Pool

Cafe Mozart, 30. 1331 H St NW ☏ 347-5732. Piano

Cafe Lautrec, 6. 2431 18th St NW ☏ 265-6436. Jazz

Chief Ike's Mambo Room, 8. 1725 Columbia Rd NW ☏ 332-2211. R&B

Cities, 5. 2424 18th St NW ☏ 328-7194. Dance

City Blues Cafe, 3. 2651 Connecticut Ave NW ☏ 232-2300. Jazz

Club Heaven, 7. 2327 18th St NW ☏ 667-4355. Dance

Deja Vu, 20. 2119 M St NW ☏ 452-1966. Dance

Dixie Grill, 34. 1518 10th St NW ☏ 628-4800. Jazz

Dubliner, 39. 4 F St NW ☏ 737-3773. Folk

15 Minutes, 26. 1030 15th St NW ☏ 408-1855. Rock

Fifth Column, 36. 915 F St NW ☏ 393-3632. Dance

Food for Thought, 14. 1738 Connecticut Ave NW ☏ 797-1095. Folk

GangPlank, 43. 600 Water St SW ☏ 554-5000. Piano

Grog & Tankard, 16. 2408 Wisconsin Ave NW ☏ 333-3114. Rock

Headliners, 42. I-395 & Seminary Rd ☏ 703/379-4242. Comedy

Improv, 25. 1140 Connecticut Ave NW ☏ 296-7008. Comedy

Insect Club, 37. 625 E St NW ☏ 347-8884. Rock

Ireland's Four Provinces, 2. 3412 Connecticut Ave NW ☏ 244-0860. Folk

Irish Times, 38. 14 F St NW ☏ 543-5433. Folk

Kilimanjaro, 10. 1724 California St NW ☏ 328-3838. Dance

La Tomate, 17. 1701 Connecticut Ave NW ☏ 667-5505. Piano

Madam's Organ, 12. 2003 18th St NW ☏ 667-5370. Rock/Blues

Marley's Lounge, 32. 926 Massachusetts Ave NW ☏ 638-5200. Jazz

Marquee Lounge, 4. 2500 Calvert St NW ☏ 745-1023. Comedy

Nanny O'Briens, 1. 3319 Connecticut Ave NW ☏ 686-9189. Folk

New Vegas Lounge, 23. 1415 P St NW ☏ 483-3971. Jazz

The Nest, 33. Willard Hotel 1401 Pennsylvania Ave NW ☏ 637-7440. Jazz

9:30 Club, 11. 815 V St NW ☏ 393-0930. Rock

One Step Down, 19. 2517 Pennsylvania Ave NW ☏ 331-8863. Jazz

Planet Fred, 24. 1221 Connecticut Ave NW ☏ 296-9563. Dance

The Ritz, 35. 919 E St NW ☏ 638-2582. Dance

Spy Club, 27. 805 15th St NW ☏ 289-1779. Dance

Takoma Station Tavern, 9. 6914 4th St NW ☏ 829-1999. Jazz

Tracks, 40. 1111 First St SE ☏ 488-3320. Dance

Zei Alley, 28. 1415 Zei Alley NW ☏ 842-2445. Dance

Listed by Site Number

1 Old Europe
2 Mountain Lodge
3 Winston's
4 Georgetown Billiards
5 Third Edition
6 Paul Mall
7 Cafe Babalu
8 Blues Alley
9 Manhattans
10 Mr Smith's
11 Garden Terrace Lounge (Four Seasons)
12 Chelsea's
13 The Bayou
14 River Club

Listed Alphabetically

The Bayou, 13. 3135 K St NW ☎ 333-2897. Rock/Latin/Comedy

Blues Alley, 8. 1073 Wisconsin Ave NW ☎ 337-4141. Jazz/Blues/R&B

Cafe Babalu, 7. 3235 M St NW ☎ 965-5353. Jazz

Chelsea's, 12. 1055 Thom. Jefferson St NW ☎ 298-8222. Piano/Cabaret/Comedy

Garden Terrace Lounge, 11. 2800 Pennsylvania Ave NW ☎ 342-0444. Piano

Georgetown Billiards, 4. 3251 Prospect St NW ☎ 965-7665. Billiards

Manhattans, 9. 3116 M St NW ☎ 333-4733. Jazz

Mountain Lodge, 2. 3401 M St NW ☎ 338-5556. Country

Mr Smith's, 10. 3104 M St NW ☎ 333-3104. Piano/Cabaret/Comedy

Old Europe, 1. 2434 Wisconsin Ave NW ☎ 333-7600. Piano/Mystery Theater

Paul Mall, 6. 3235 M St NW ☎ 965-5353. Rock/Latin

The River Club, 14. 3223 K St NW ☎ 965-3229. Jazz/Big Band/Dance

Third Edition, 5. 1218 Wisconsin Ave NW ☎ 333-3700. Dance

Winston's, 3. 3295 M St NW ☎ 333-3150. Dance